THE IMPACT OF ISLAM

To Jill,

from

Emmet.

EMMET SCOTT

Published by New English Review Press
a subsidiary of World Encounter Institute
PO Box 158397
Nashville, Tennessee 37215
&
27 Old Gloucester Street
London, England, WC1N 3AX

Cover Art and Design by Kendra Adams

ISBN: 978-0-9884778-7-2

NEW ENGLISH REVIEW PRESS
newenglishreview.org

THE IMPACT OF ISLAM

To all those writers and public figures who are currently striving to keep the flame of truth alive in the face of an encroaching totalitarianism which wishes to silence all freedom of speech.

CONTENTS

INTRODUCTION

The work that follows is a survey and an evaluation of the impact that Islam as a faith and a civilization had upon Europe during the High Middle Ages, from the late tenth through to the fifteenth or sixteenth century. It is also, to some degree, an examination of how that impact has been viewed by Western academics over the past century. These, as we shall see, have tended to present a sanitized and frankly disingenuous view of Islamic civilization and have fostered a series of myths which are currently causing much mischief in academic and government circles throughout the Western world. The source of this "Islamophilic" viewpoint is a frankly anti-Christian mindset which first appeared during the Enlightenment and thereafter spread inexorably throughout Europe and the Americas. This anti-Christian bias has now become the default mode of thought in academic circles in the West: As Christianity was "talked down" so it became, as the twentieth century progressed, more and more the custom to "talk up" Islam. Take for example the following quote from Bernard Lewis, the doyen of Middle Eastern studies at Princeton, whose 2001 book *What Went Wrong? Western Impact and Middle Eastern Response*, looked at the decline of the Islamic world *vis à vis* the Christian, from the Middle Ages onwards:

"It is often said that Islam is an egalitarian religion. There is much truth in this assertion. If we compare Islam at the time of its advent with the societies that surrounded it – the stratified feudalism of Iran and the caste system of India to the east, the privileged aristocracies of both Byzantine and Latin Europe to the West – the Islamic dispensation does indeed bring a message of equality. Not only does Islam not endorse such systems of social differentiation; it explicitly and absolutely rejects them. The actions and utterances of the Prophet, the honored precedents of the early rulers of Islam as preserved by tradition, are overwhelmingly against

9

privilege by descent, by birth, by status, by wealth, or even by race, and insist that rank and honor are determined only by piety and merit in Islam." (p. 82) Furthermore, "… though this pristine egalitarianism was in many ways modified and diluted, it remained strong enough to prevent the emergence of either Brahmans or aristocrats and to preserve a society in which merit and ambition might still hope to find their reward. In later times this egalitarianism was somewhat restricted. … In spite of this, however, it is probably true that even at the beginning of the nineteenth century a poor man of humble origin had a better chance of attaining to wealth, power and dignity in the Islamic lands than in any states of Christian Europe, including post-Revolutionary France." (pp. 83-4)

Sounds enlightened, doesn't it, almost idyllic? How fortunate those free and forward-looking Muslims compared to the Christians and others, hidebound by decrepit systems of privilege and inequality. On the other hand, equality isn't everything. Stalin's Soviet Union was the most egalitarian society ever to exist and yet it ranks among the most oppressive and brutal regimes in history. And Nazi Germany was a truly egalitarian meritocracy. Any young man of German blood, no matter how humble his circumstances or origins, could rise to the very pinnacle of German society during the 1930s and early 1940s if his abilities were up to it. Of course, not everyone was equal under the Nazis; Jews and Gypsies did not share in the great freedoms provided by the National Socialists. But then again it turns out that not everyone was equal in Islam either. Almost regretfully, Lewis notes that,

"The egalitarianism of traditional Islam is not however complete. From the beginning Islam recognized certain social inequalities, which are sanctioned and indeed sanctified by holy writ. But even in the three basic inequalities of master and slave, man and woman, believer and unbeliever, the situation in the classical Islamic civilization was in some respects better than elsewhere." (pp. 82-3) So, some people were less equal than others, but these had a better time of it in Islam than in other societies. Even the slaves, it seems, had a great life. "Islam, in contrast to ancient Rome and the modern colonial systems, accords the slave a certain legal status and assigns obligations as well as rights to the slaveowner. He is enjoined to treat his slave humanely and can be compelled by a *qadi* to sell or even manumit his slave if he fails in this duty. It is not, however, required, and the institution of slavery is not only recognized but is elaborately regulated by Islamic law. Perhaps for this very reason the position of the slave in Muslim society was incomparably better than in either classical antiquity of nineteenth-century North and South America." (p. 85)

The truth or otherwise of the above assertion may be judged by the following simple fact: In the course of four centuries the Ottoman Empire imported between four to six million slaves from black Africa – most of whom were settled in Anatolia. Of these millions there is barely a trace to be found in the genetic inheritance of modern Turks. A similar number of slaves were imported from the seventeenth to mid-nineteenth centuries into North America, where their descendants now number in excess of thirty millions.

The reality is that the three groups identified by Lewis as not sharing in the general beneficence of Islamic egalitarianism and freedom – women, slaves, and non-Muslims – suffered, throughout the centuries, indescribable hardships at the hands of their Muslim masters; and two of these groups, women and non-Muslims, continue to suffer to this day. That there are no more slaves in Islam (or very few, officially, at least), is due entirely to the efforts of Westerners during the nineteenth and twentieth centuries.

The impact of Islam cannot be understood without a knowledge of what it actually teaches, and an outline of those teachings, and how they have been applied, is provided early in the present study.

An oft-heard assertion in our times, especially among members of the political class who have no doubt been influenced by writers such as Lewis, is that "Islam is a religion of peace," or even that "Islam means peace." It is true that these statements are not made with quite the same frequency or conviction as a decade ago, but they still occur, along with the claim – usually in the aftermath of some new atrocity – that this had "nothing to do with Islam." The *jihadis* who carry out these atrocities (which seem to occur with depressing frequency irrespective of how often Western politicians assert that the threat from Al Qaida is "receding"), claim that the Qur'an instructs them to carry out these attacks; and a substantial proportion of the Muslim populations in the Middle East and in Europe seem to agree.

Most students of religion are familiar with the story of Islam's origins as it has been recounted for over a thousand years. We are told how Muhammad, a young man of Mecca, who was much given to prayer, received a vision of the archangel Gabriel in a cave just outside the city; and how the angel recited to him the contents of the book we now call the Qur'an or Koran. The new revelations conveyed by Muhammad were however rejected by the citizens of Mecca, forcing the young visionary to flee for his life to the city of Medina. In Medina he found much support, and presently returned to Mecca in triumph at the head of a victorious army. Following this, Muhammad led his followers in a series of campaigns throughout the Arabian Peninsula, conquering and converting to Islam the entire country before his death in 632. We are told that upon his death the leadership of the movement devolved upon a series of caliphs, who led the armies of the faithful in a series of astonishing conquests which, within thirty years, established Islam as the dominant power from Libya in the west to the borders of India in the east.

The Qur'an, which the Archangel Gabriel is said to have given Muhammad, is of course the fundamental scripture of Islam; yet as a guide to life or anything else it is woefully inadequate. Most of the book makes little sense, and the apparently disconnected and puzzling incidents recounting the life of Muhammad are "filled out" by the Hadith, a collection of the supposed sayings and deeds of Muhammad. Without the Hadith and Ibn Ishaq's biography (the Sira) of Muhammad the Qur'an would be incomprehensible. It is accepted that most – or all – of the hadiths were written many decades after the lifetime of Muhammad, generally between 700 and 750. The hadiths, as well as Ibn Ishaq's biography (written around 720) portray the life of a warlord who denied himself few of life's pleasures.

The essentially aggressive nature of Islam can only be understood if we pay attention to what is told of Muhammad: He is said to have initiated sixty wars and raids and to have participated in at least twenty-seven of these. Many of these engagements involved massacres of unarmed men and boys. The Prophet of Islam is said to have ordered the killing of all the men and post-pubescent boys in the Jewish settlement of Banu Quraiza, and to have led a series of unprovoked attacks against other Jewish communities in Arabia. During his lifetime, almost all the Jews of Arabia were either killed or forced to convert to Islam. The Prophet is said furthermore to have ordered the assassination of political opponents and encouraged his followers to take up the sword in the propagation of the faith, declaring that a night spent in arms in the cause of Islam carried more merit than a lifetime of fasting, prayer and good works. Before he died, he is reported to have enjoined on his followers to "fight with the peoples" until the whole world should confess that there was no god but Allah.

That he was most definitely not a man of peace is therefore fairly clear – and underlines a dramatic difference between Christianity and Islam: Whilst early Christianity was pacifist to the core, the early spread of Islam was due entirely to military conquest. No one denies this, and it is even conceded that Islamic law and custom sanctifies warfare in the cause of the faith. Indeed, the waging of *jihad* or holy war is fundamental to Islamic custom and belief: Since the first flush of victories in the seventh century, conquered infidels have been presented with a simple choice; either convert or pay a poll tax, known as *jizya*. But the important thing has always been to establish political control. This being the case it is clear that Islam is not a religion at all in the ordinary sense of the word, but a totalitarian political ideology with religious pretensions, a fact noted by Rebecca Bynam in her recent work, *Allah is Dead: Why Islam is not a Religion*. And this clearly accounts for the "egalitarianism" noted and praised by Bernard Lewis: All revolutionary political ideologies, no matter how totalitarian and oppressive, promise a large degree of equality to their followers, with the implied promise of a share in the spoils once the established order is removed. This is precisely how Islam has operated since its inception.

In spite of all this, we are continually assured – in modern times at least – that this warfare, or *jihad*, can also be interpreted as an inner spiritual struggle. In addition, we are informed by scholars such as Bernard Lewis that Islam was always a "tolerant" faith: Once a region or country had been conquered the natives – if they were "people of the Book" (*i.e.*, Jews or Christians) – were permitted to continue with their lives as before, subject of course to the payment of the *jizya*. The conquered Jews and Christians were then classed as *dhimmi* "protected," and safe from any further Muslim attack.

The myth of Islamic tolerance is in fact one of the most pernicious to have gained currency in Western belief over the past century. In fact, Jews and Christians were anything but "protected" under the aegis of Islam. The *dhimmi* communities, as Bat Ye'or has shown in great detail in her excellent series of books on the subject, was subject to a whole raft of humiliating and degrading laws which rendered their lives almost intolerable: One of these was the compulsory wearing of distinctive clothing – an endearing feature copied by the Nazis in their persecution of the Jews during the twentieth century. Worst of all however was the fact that *dhimmi* Christians and Jews did not enjoy equality before the law: The word of a Muslim always trumped that of a *dhimmi*. One consequence of this was a petty tyranny exercised in perpetuity by ordinary Muslims over their Christian or Jewish neighbors. Should any dispute arise, the *dhimmi* had to give way immediately. Failure to do so could result in the Muslim accusing his infidel neighbor of blaspheming Muhammad or the Qur'an – a charge which carried the death penalty. Two other Muslim witnesses were needed to substantiate the claim but, at Bat Ye'or remarked, these were always forthcoming and the *dhimmi* condemned to death. No Christian or Jewish communities could possibly prosper under such a pernicious system; and there are very good grounds for believing that it was this very system which turned vast areas of formerly fertile agricultural land in the Middle East and North Africa into semi-desert within a few decades during the late seventh century: Incoming Arab nomads grazed their goats and camels on the cultivated fields of the conquered Christians and Jews, and these dared not complain.

A fundamental precept of Islamic law – again, underlining its political nature – is that Muslims occupy a privileged position and have a right to live off the labor of infidels – whether they be *dhimmis* living under Islam or unconquered infidels living outside the House of Islam's borders. As may be imagined, such a teaching could only breed a parasitical and lawless attitude which positively encouraged robbery and piracy. Furthermore, the idea – sanctified again by the example of Muhammad – that a Muslim was entitled to take female captives as concubines, as well as to possess male slaves, could only further inflame the passion for banditry. And this is what we find throughout Islamic history.

The position of women in particular was (and is) pitiful in Islamic societies. The absolute property of some man, either a father, brother, or husband, they could be used, abused and put to death without any real protection from the law.

The result was the development of a society in which the abuse of some human beings – especially non-Muslims, slaves, and women (and also boys) – by others, namely adult Muslim men, was written into the law and sanctified by holy writ. The abusers, in addition, had a sense of entitlement which prevented them seeking useful employment and tended to encourage the practice of banditry and other forms of violence. This attitude extended itself through the whole of Muslim society, where the great and the powerful would routinely despoil those lesser (whether Muslim or not) than themselves. Private property was never secure, and the Muslim household tended to have a drab or even decrepit exterior facing the street and any wealth or luxury hidden at the back of the house – all the better to avoid notice. Since an attractive women too could be confiscated by any great man who took a fancy to her (if she was already married her husband could easily be compelled to draw up a writ of divorce), it became *de rigeur* to conceal the attractions of the female sex behind an all-encompassing shroud.

Little wonder that the House of Islam sank into grinding poverty and backwardness as the Middle Ages progressed. Yet it was not always thus: In the middle of the tenth century Islam was one of the wealthiest and most technically advanced civilizations on earth. Europe at the time was an underpopulated and backward outpost of late Roman culture:

Most of the continent was under the control of illiterate barbarians and even those regions which had formed part of the Roman Empire – including Italy – had reverted to a mainly rural and barter economy, supporting virtually no towns of more than 30,000 people. The House of Islam by contrast possessed great urban centers, such as Baghdad, Samarra, Damascus and Alexandria, with upward of 500,000 inhabitants, a populousness and prosperity it had inherited from the great civilizations of the Middle East it had absorbed in the seventh century. It is no surprise then that historians and archaeologists have noted a massive Islamic impact upon Europe at this very time; an impact that was economic, political, philosophical, technological, and religious. It was, in addition, both passive and active. Above all, historians speak of a massive wave of new technologies and ideas originating in the Islamic world. These included: paper-making, the compass, the decimal numbers system, algebra, alcohol distillation, clock-making, and a host of other things. New philosophical and theological ideas also arrived. The Arabs, it seems, were in possession of many texts of the Greek philosophers which had been lost in the West.

How to explain this in a society which was later to become a byword for backwardness and obscurantism? In the words of Sidney Painter: "When the Arabs occupied the Asiatic and African provinces of the [Byzantine] empire, they found many works of classical and Hellenistic times. The Arabs copied these works, studied them, and commented on them. The Arab philosophers Avicenna and Averroes, translated Aristotle and wrote commentaries designed to adjust his ideas to Muslim culture. The geometry of Euclid, the astronomy of Ptolemy, and the medicine of Galen were all translated and used by Arab scholars. But the Arabs did more than simply absorb the Hellenistic knowledge they found in the Byzantine storehouse. In several fields they made important additions. The numbers that we call Arabic were apparently first used in India and adopted from there by the Arabs, who added the zero. Algebra was invented by a Moslem scholar. The Arabs also built observatories, studied astronomy, and created astronomical tables. In medicine the Arabs not only studied the established works but supplemented them by careful observation of diseases."[1]

The latter is a very restrained evaluation of the Arab achievement: other writers, both before and after Painter, have been far more effusive. But how accurate is it? Were the Arabs really such enthusiastic students of the philosophers and scientists of Greece? Closer investigation reveals flaws in such claims. Painter partly gives the game away when he notes that the

---

1 Painter, *A History of the Middle Ages: 284-1500* (Macmillan, 1953), pp. 57-8.

great majority of "Arab" learning was actually derived from the Greeks, through Byzantium, and that other parts, such as the "Arab" numeral system, came from the East. In fact, research has shown that almost all the genuinely new ideas arriving in Europe through the Arab world originated much further to the east. Thus paper-making, the compass, etc., came from China, whilst the "Arab" numerals were an Indian innovation. It is true that these arrived in Europe via the Arabs, but they were not Arab or Muslim inventions. They would surely have arrived in Europe whether Islam had existed or not. Indeed, the process of importing new technologies into the West had begun in the sixth century, before the appearance of Islam, with the appearance there of such Oriental technologies as the stirrup and silk-making. The spread of these eastern ideas seems to have been disrupted for three centuries by the arrival of the Arabs, and then resumed in the latter tenth century. And we should note than even those things which did originate in the Middle East, such as alcohol distillation, algebra, the windmill, etc., were rarely, if ever, the work of Arabs or even Muslims. Almost invariably they were ideas deriving from the work of Persians, Syrians, or Egyptians, who were permitted to continue their work for a short time after the Arab conquests. Once again, it is safe to say that these things would have arrived in the West irrespective of whether Islam existed or not.

What Islam did bring to Europe was war and slavery, on a massive scale. The House of Islam in the tenth century had little use for any of the produce and natural resources of Europe, except one; the bodies of the Europeans themselves. Young women and boys were preferred, but during the tenth century Europeans of almost any age or class, and in almost any part of the continent, could find themselves in chains and on a ship bound for North Africa or the Middle East. During this epoch the Arabs dominated the seas and fleets of Saracen pirates regularly scoured the coastal districts of southern France, Italy, Dalmatia and Greece. Larger raiding parties ventured farther inland in search of booty and captives, and there are reports of Saracen attacks as far north as Switzerland. In Spain, Moorish raiders attacked Christian settlements in the north of the Peninsula on an annual or bi-annual basis in search of captives.

All during this time another "theater" of this vast slaving enterprise had its center in the north of Europe, in Scandinavia, in the British Isles, in northern France, in Germany and, above all, in the land we now call Russia. For the whole Viking phenomenon, which saw Scandinavian pirates wreak havoc throughout the north of Europe for several centuries, was a direct result of the Muslim demand for European slaves. The majority of slaves sold by the Scandinavians to the caliphate were Slavs from east of the Elbe, and indeed the word "slav" implies "slave" in most European languages to this day. Michael McCormick speaks of a "vast arc" of slave supply at this time which brought hundreds of thousands, perhaps millions, of Europeans into bondage in the House of Islam. Whilst the majority of this trade was conducted between the Vikings directly with the Arabs, some Christian Europeans did become involved; particularly the cities of Marseilles and Venice – the latter supplying the Arabs with Slavs captured on the eastern shores of the Adriatic. In an earlier age the Christian religion had virtually abolished slavery in Europe, along with the other barbarous practices of ancient Rome, such as gladiatorial contests, crucifixion, and torture of prisoners. The treatment of captives bound for the caliphate can only have been a source of moral corruption to all who participated: Boys and youths were usually castrated, in an operation of the utmost barbarity which left most of its victims dead. Men who were too old to be sold simply had their throats slit or were thrown into the sea. Women were usually destined for the sexual slavery of the harem. These things need to be said, for a number of modern writers, disdaining any moral judgment, have waxed lyrical about the economic "benefits" that the trade in human misery brought to Europe in the tenth century. Yet even these are illusory: The Scandinavians it is true got their hands on fairly large amounts of Arab gold and silver, as well as various luxuries and trinkets from the East; but these things had little impact on the level of civilization in the North. The real engine of civilization was Christianity, which encouraged peaceful husbandry as opposed to war and piracy, which brought literacy, education, and new farming techniques, and which effected a dramatic increase in the population through its prohibition of infanticide – an absolutely normal practice in pagan societies.

Investigation reveals that it was the spread of Christianity and not contact with Islam which brought about the dramatic revival of Europe from the late tenth century onwards. But Islam did communicate certain ideas to the Christians of the West – most of which were anything but humane or civilized.

The majority of Islamic cultural influences reaching Europe in the tenth and eleventh centuries came by way of Spain. Almost all of the country had been captured by Islamic armies during the eighth century, and Muslims remained in control of parts of the Peninsula for many centuries. A local caliphate, which grew steadily in wealth and prosperity (or so we are told), was established at Cordoba in the middle of the eighth century. There is no question that by the second half of the tenth century, under Abd' er Rahman III, Islamic Spain was opulent and powerful. It was also, to a great degree, technically advanced; and indeed the prosperity and learning of the Spanish Muslims was proverbial throughout Europe in the final years of the tenth century. In more recent times the Caliphate of Cordoba has been extolled by Western Islamophiles as a sort of Muslim utopia; a land of fabulous riches, fine manners and civilized values. The problem with these descriptions is that they are complete nonsense. Even at its most prosperous and civilized the Spanish Caliphate was never a tolerant or humane society. The polity established by Abd' er Rahman III was the center of a vast slave-raiding and trading enterprise. Every year and sometimes twice yearly Christian communities in the north and even in France would be attacked and plundered; their inhabitants marched southward in chains and subjected to indescribable ill-treatment. Vast numbers of slaves, many of them eunuchs, oiled the wheels of the Spanish Caliphate. Yet there was wealth and some prosperity, for a privileged few. Jews were, to begin with, reasonably well-treated, perhaps in acknowledgment of the assistance they had provided the Muslims in the initial conquest of the Peninsula. But such beneficence was soon forgotten and by 1011 Muslim mobs in Cordoba had launched the first ever violent pogroms against the Jews on European soil. In years to come things only became worse: With the arrival of the fanatical Almoravids and Almohads from North Africa in the latter eleventh and twelfth centuries the persecution of Jews and Christians was racheted up to a new intensity. The Almoravids deported virtually all the remaining Christians to North Africa in the early twelfth century, where they were forcibly converted to Islam; whilst in the early years of the thirteenth century the remaining Jews under Islam were forcibly converted by the Almohads.

In order to be sure of the sincerity of the Jewish *conversos*, the Almohads established the first ever religious inquisitions on European soil.

The war of reconquest which the Christians waged against the Muslims of Spain during the eleventh century was to become a *cause célèbre* throughout Christendom and rallied soldiers from France, Germany and Britain to the Peninsula. These campaigns, waged throughout the early and middle years of the eleventh century were to form the vanguard of Europe's fightback against Islam, a fightback which we now call the Crusades.

The Crusades, as it happens, occupy a prominent position in the propaganda battle associated with the present "clash of civilizations" debate. No other part of European history, it could be argued, has been so distorted by ideology and preconceived prejudice. Ever since the Enlightenment, when European liberals first turned their faces against the continent's Christian past, the Crusades have been viewed, to some degree or other in most academic circles, as an act of folly or aggression by a barbarous and uncouth Europe against a civilized and enlightened Muslim world. In popular literature and in countless television documentaries and recent Hollywood movies, the Crusaders are invariably the aggressors and their Muslim foes the innocent victims. According to historian Steven Runciman, it was the Crusades which created the ill-feeling between the House of Islam and Christendom where previously none existed. Prior to that, he claimed, Islam had been tolerant and broad-minded. It has even been claimed that it was the Crusaders who destroyed the learning of the Arab world, rendering it backward and impoverished.

The problem with this scenario of course is that it is utterly untrue. Far from being quiescent and peaceful, the House of Islam was aggressive and expansionist in the years prior to the First Crusade in 1096. In the three decades preceding that date Turkish armies had conquered the whole of Asia Minor and now stood at the very gates of Constantinople, whose capture seemed imminent. It was then that the emperor Alexius Comnenus made his famous appeal to Pope Urban II for assistance. This appeal, together with the brutal treatment of Christian pilgrims to the Holy Land by the same Turks, was what finally roused Europe to action. As even Bernard Lewis has now acknowledged, the Crusades were a late, limited and rather ineffective imitation by the Europeans of the Islamic "holy war" idea.

Barbarous acts were on occasion committed by the Crusaders, but, once again, the Muslims got there first, and they merely copied what they witnessed their Islamic foes already doing.

Before setting out on their disastrous "People's Crusade" led by Peter the Hermit and Walter the Penniless, groups of soldiers and civilian volunteers carried out atrocious massacres of Jews in the Rhineland and elsewhere in central Europe — notwithstanding the attempts of bishops and other church officials to stop them. These were the first ever anti-Jewish pogroms in Christian Europe; and they have, like the crusades themselves, given rise to a whole body of mythology about medieval Europe which has only distorted the picture and promoted radical untruth. Almost without exception, modern studies of the period take it for granted that medieval Europe was anti-Semitic whilst medieval Islam was not. The truth, however, is that Islam was violently anti-Semitic before Christendom, and the first pogroms against the Jews launched on European soil were launched by Muslims, not Christians. The nexus of anti-Semitism in Europe in the eleventh century, just before the launch of the First Crusade and the pogroms against the Jews associated with it, was Spain. Some of those who attacked the Jews in central Europe had earlier campaigned in Spain, where they learned, no doubt, of the mass murder of Jews which had occurred in Granada in 1066. They cannot have been uninfluenced by these events.

Close examination of the phenomenon of medieval anti-Semitism reveals it to be intimately connected with the struggle between Christianity and Islam. The mobs who murdered the Jews of the Rhineland and Bohemia claimed that their victims were secret allies of the Muslims. By then they had no reason or excuse to do so: yet in an earlier age individual Jewish groups and communities had indeed assisted the Muslims. This was the case, for example, in Spain, where both Christian and Muslim – as well as Jewish – sources speak of co-operation between the Islamic invaders and native Jews during the eighth century. It is true, of course, that by the time of the First Crusade such friendly relations had long ceased, and the Jews of Spain were persecuted by the country's Islamic rulers every bit as much as Christians. But the suspicion of Jewish intentions and loyalties had by this time spread throughout Europe, with tragic consequences for the continent's Jewish populations.

Incidentally, the co-operation reported in the early eighth century between Spain's Jews and the Islamic invaders is a clear proof that the accepted narrative of Islam's origins and early spread cannot possibly be true: Had the massacres of Jews which Muhammad is said to have carried out in the Arabian Peninsula during the early seventh century actually occurred, Jewish co-operation with Spain's Islamic conquerors would certainly not have occurred. This whole question of Islam's mysterious origins is briefly examined in the Appendix to the present volume.

The perpetrators of the anti-Jewish massacres during the Middle Ages were under the influence of a despotic and obscurantist Catholic Church which imposed a tyrannical control over men's minds and held Europe in medieval ignorance and backwardness for many centuries. That at least is the opinion encountered routinely in the modern media and even in academic publications; and it is an opinion which has been around for a long time, first appearing, in fact, during the Enlightenment. Indeed, the supposed backwardness of Europe during the Middle Ages is often contrasted with the "progressiveness" of Islam during the same epoch – as we saw in the passages quoted from Bernard Lewis above. But how true are these ideas? Was medieval Europe under the thralldom of an oppressive church, and was the House of Islam at the same time really so "progressive"? Examination of the facts reveals the above statement to be almost the precise opposite of the truth.

It is of course true that, from the time of Pope Innocent III (1198 – 1216), the Catholic Church was involved in the violent suppression of religious dissent. Yet the surprising fact is that until that time religious freedom was more or less the order of the day. In the two centuries prior to Innocent's reign the Cathar (or Albigensian) faith had spread freely and quite openly throughout Western Europe. Such a situation could never of course have existed in the House of Islam, at any time in its history. Christianity, it is true, had never been a particularly tolerant faith: the Church Fathers roundly condemned the pagan cults of the Romans and other peoples of the Empire. They also had extremely strong words of abuse for the early "heresies" such as the Gnostics, Montanists and Arians. In addition, they issued ferocious condemnations of other mainstream Christian churches who may have differed from each other on theological points which most moderns would consider of little or no consequence. So, Christianity was never particularly tolerant; but it rarely resorted to bloodshed to enforce its point of view. This was particularly the case in Western Europe, where the religious tumults of the fifth and sixth centuries, which so disturbed the East, never reached.

Yet violence was eventually applied in the West, when Innocent III declared his crusade against the Cathars and launched the Inquisition.

The strange thing, however, and this is a point rarely if ever made, is that this was not the first religious inquisition in Western Europe: As we saw above, another had been founded in Islamic Spain by the Almohads, fifty years earlier. After forcibly converting the remaining Jews of Al-Andalus (Islamic Spain) to Islam, the Almohads tried to ensure the sincerity of the recent converts by subjecting them to trial and torture and by taking their children from them to be raised as Muslims. That the Muslims had priority in this – as in the mass murder of Jews – does not of course exonerate the Christian Church; nor does it prove that the Muslims influenced the Christians by their example. Yet we surely cannot deny that influence was a possibility and we most certainly cannot continue to extol the supposed "tolerance" of Islam whilst condemning the intolerance of Christianity.

The other accusation leveled against the medieval church is that it was inimical to science and the free exploration of nature and her laws. Yet once again this is almost the precise opposite of the truth. Far from inhibiting science and learning the Christian Church encouraged it in almost every way. The rapid spread of literacy for example in the centuries after the tenth was due entirely to the efforts of the church, which established schools, monasteries and universities throughout the continent of

Europe, including in the formerly barbarian regions of Scandinavia, eastern Germany, Poland, Russia, Hungary and the Balkans. A very important function performed by monks was the copying of books – many of them scientific and philosophical texts of the Greeks and Romans. From the late tenth century onwards monasteries throughout Western Europe could boast extensive libraries of the classical Roman and occasionally also Greek authors. Dramatic new discoveries were made by the monks in very many fields. Agriculture, for example, was revolutionized by them. They adopted and developed new systems of crop management as well as technologies such as the water wheel, windmill, moldboard plow and horse collar. They made extremely important contributions to our knowledge of botany, from which flowed new and important developments in medicine and the treatment of diseases. Monks such as Roger Bacon and Albertus Magnus speculated on the nature of the physical universe and helped establish the empirical method – as did William of Ockham. The sheer dynamism of European society during the Middle Ages is however best illustrated by the fact that, from an under-populated and relatively impoverished (and largely barbarian and illiterate) beginning in the mid-tenth century, by the mid-twelfth century the continent was covered with bustling towns and urban centers which supported rapidly increasing populations. Literacy was now common and Europeans had begun the construction of the great monuments of European civilization, the Gothic cathedrals and castles, which elicit the wonder and admiration of visitors to this day. In another two centuries, just before the voyage of Columbus, Europe stood on the verge of world domination.

What a contrast with the House of Islam, where the above process is viewed in reverse. The mid-tenth century saw the Islamic world covered with great cities and crisscrossed with caravans carrying the wealth of the East and the West into the palaces of the caliphs. By the mid-twelfth century however the population had crashed and everywhere there were signs of decline. No great monuments were constructed from then onwards. And by the late fifteenth century, the time of Columbus, the Islamic world was a barbarous backwater, whose only wealth lay in the plunder it seized from other regions. Not a single scientific or philosophical idea of any merit came out of the Islamic world from the middle of the eleventh century, and the House of Islam has been gripped for almost a thousand years by an obscurantist theocracy which positively discourages all scientific inquiry.

Although the last of the Crusader Kingdoms in the Middle East had fallen to the Muslims during the thirteenth century, Europeans at that time did not regard Islam as constituting any serious threat. It looked a spent force. This was made all the more apparent by the destruction wrought early in the same century by the Mongols, who seemed for a while to be actively targeting Islam. Both Genghis Khan and his immediate successors had wrought immense destruction amongst the Islamic states of Central Asia and they had, at one point, come very close to eliminating the last of the Muslim powers, Mameluke Egypt. This did not happen, yet the House of Islam had been dealt some terrible blows. Few could have predicted that during that very century there would arise, in the east of Anatolia, an Islamic dynasty which would in time constitute the greatest threat to Christian Europe's survival since the days of Charles Martel in the eighth century. This was the Ottomans.

The coming of the Ottomans brought five centuries of exploitation, enslavement and massacre to large areas of eastern and south-eastern Europe. For some considerable time the whole continent was in danger, as vast Turkish hosts returned to the offensive year after year, inexorably pushing their dominion deeper and deeper into the center of Christendom. Twice they reached Vienna, capital of the Empire. The last occasion was near the end of the seventeenth century, and it was not until this attack was beaten off – thanks largely to the efforts of Jan Sobieski – that Europeans could begin to believe they would survive. Some of the regions through which the Turkish hosts passed were depopulated for centuries, and some have never really recovered. Those areas which came under direct Turkish rule were exploited so ruthlessly that they remained economic backwaters till the start of the twentieth century – when they finally freed themselves. But those areas on the borders of Turkish territory suffered almost as much. The slave trade was revived and Muslim raiders and pirates devastated southern Russia, all of Hungary as well as the Balkans, and large areas of the Mediterranean coasts of Italy, France and Spain, in their search for white captives to sell in Constantinople, which in 1453 became the new capital of the Sultans.

The rise of the Ottoman threat – after Islam's apparent decline in the later Middle Ages – merely reinforces an observation made by Winston Churchill over a century ago. "Far from being moribund," he said, "Mohammedanism is a militant and proselytizing faith," one whose power to raise up fanatical followers appears to endure from generation to generation.

The evidence, then, leaving aside politically correct wishful thinking, shows that Islam's impact upon Europe has been overwhelmingly destructive. The few benefits which "the Arabs" brought in the tenth and early eleventh centuries turn out, on closer inspection, to be not Arab at all, but pre-Arab Persian or Byzantine; or else from China and India. What Islam did bring that was truly Islamic was war and banditry: For one thing, it breathed new life into the slave trade in Europe both in the tenth century and later between the fourteenth and seventeenth centuries. With Islam came the revival of such inhuman practices as crucifixion and torture – practices which Christianity had succeeded in abolishing between the fourth and sixth centuries. And some of the more noxious habits of the Muslims were picked up by Europeans, especially by those who inhabited territories bordering the House of Islam. Slave-owning, for example, was common amongst Spanish Christians long after it had disappeared elsewhere in Europe.

Finally, the re-emergence in the fourteenth century of a major Islamic power, the Ottoman Empire, closed off once again easy communication between Europe and the Far East, a communication which had briefly flourished during the period of the Mongol Empire. Europeans now turned west, to the Atlantic, in search of a way to China and the Indies which bypassed hostile Muslim territories. Their efforts were first directed towards circumnavigating Africa and crossing the Indian Ocean. During the 1480s however an Italian navigator named Christopher Columbus had the bright idea that the Indies and China could be reached by sailing directly west. The Spanish king and queen, hoping to find allies against Islam in the latter regions, finally agreed in 1492 to finance a small expedition.

When the conquest and colonization of the Americas began in the decades which followed, it was the example of Islam which all too often guided Spanish policy. The idea of taking slaves from equatorial Africa, for example, was taken directly from the Muslims of Algeria, Morocco and southern Spain, who had been doing the same thing for centuries. The campaigns of the conquistadors, too, were seen as "crusades" - a continuation and extension of the wars against the unbelievers of Islam which had raged in the Iberian Peninsula for centuries and which had brutalized all those involved.

It goes without saying that a study such as this cannot pretend to be exhaustive, or ground-breaking in any way. None of the facts outlined the pages to follow are disputed or even controversial, though they tend to be discreetly ignored in modern politically correct publications. These seek to present a sanitized view of Islam and its history by a selective presentation of evidence: uncomfortable features are not denied, they are simply side-stepped. Real academic controversy does however arise in the question of Islam's origins, a topic mentioned briefly in *Mohammed and Charlemagne*

Revisited. The latest research, for example, has thrown a question mark over the very existence of an Arab prophet named Muhammad, as well as the supposed conquests of his immediate successors, the "Rightly Guided" caliphs of the seventh century. Since these questions have relevance for our understanding of Islam as an ideology and its impact upon the world stage, I have thought it advisable to present a brief overview of them in an Appendix.

1
A WAVE OF ISLAMIC INFLUENCE

B y the middle of the tenth century Europe began to awake out of the long sleep – or apparent sleep – of the Dark Ages. Everywhere there are signs of renewal and expansion. Towns, which had shriveled and shrank from the third century onwards, began to grow. New urban centers were established and older ones, established under the Romans, began to revive. London, the Roman Londinium, was alive and bustling under the Anglo-Saxons, as was Paris, Lyon, Toulouse, Cologne, and a host of others. But the new towns looked different to the older Roman ones. Things had now a distinctly "medieval" air. The fashionable villas of the Romans, with their marble columns and bright mosaic floors, were a thing of the past. Only churches and royal residences retained some of the color and opulence of the classical age; these structures frequently employed stones and columns cannibalized from older Roman buildings. Indeed, the churches of the period still looked distinctly Roman; so much so that they are now termed "Romanesque." And the afterglow of classical civilization still to some degree illuminated this somewhat dim and shadowy epoch. Latin, though corrupted in the everyday speech of France, Spain, and even Italy, nonetheless remained, in its pure form, the language of learning and the Church; and the monasteries often retained substantial libraries stocked with the works of the pagan Romans – and even occasionally the pagan Greeks.

In spite of this, the mid-tenth century was a deeply troubled time. The whole western part of Europe was threatened by the inroads of the Hungarians, the latest wave of barbarian nomads from the steppes of Asia. Established in the central Hungarian Plain, Magyar armies wrought havoc throughout Germany and France, and threatened to complete the destruction of Christendom which had earlier seemed likely in the time of Attila's Huns – whom the Magyars proudly claimed as their ancestors.

Whilst the Hungarian threat was effectively neutralized by the victory of Otto I (the Great) at the Battle of Lechfeld in 955, this did not mark the end of Europe's woes. Scandinavian pirates, in search of booty and slaves, scoured the shores of France, Britain, Ireland, and northern Germany. Nor were their inroads confined to the coasts: fleets of the raiders, navigating the great rivers, penetrated to the heart of England, France and Germany, bringing terror and slaughter in their wake. Huge armies of Vikings now appeared in England, and for a while the whole country was threatened with conquest.

Yet in spite of all the destruction and uncertainty, the final decades of the tenth century were a period of remarkable growth in Christian Europe, a fact confirmed both by the written sources and more recently by archaeology. Excavation reports from throughout Europe confirm that towns and settlements began to expand at this time – the first urban expansion since the second century! And the written histories agree; not only was there a renewed prosperity, the boundaries of Christendom began to expand. One by one the pagan princes and monarchs of the east and north began to accept Christianity. Harald Bluetooth the King of Denmark was baptized, along with his court and many of his subjects, in 965, whilst King Mieszeko of Poland was baptized a Christian in 966. The Kingdom of Rus, under its ruler Vladimir I of Kiev, adopted the Orthodox version of Christianity in 988, and on Christmas Day 1000 (or New Year's Day 1001), King Stephen of Hungary brought his nation into the Christian fold.

As the Christian faith and "Christendom" grew, so too did economic prosperity and learning. It was just in the final years of the tenth century that a whole series of new technologies began to appear in Europe that would transform the continent forever. Some of these innovations were European inventions, but the vast majority came from the East, from the lands of the Muslims. Indeed, the sheer number of new ideas and technologies reaching Europe from the Islamic world at this time has prompted some writers to speak of an Islamic "Renaissance" of the tenth century and to credit Islam with preserving and propagating the learning of the classical world. Among new ideas and techniques we might mention: the decimal numbers system, with the zero; algebra, paper-making, the windmill, alcohol distillation, etc. These were followed, in the eleventh and twelfth centuries, by knowledge of the compass and a whole series of new ideas in medicine and knowledge of the natural world.

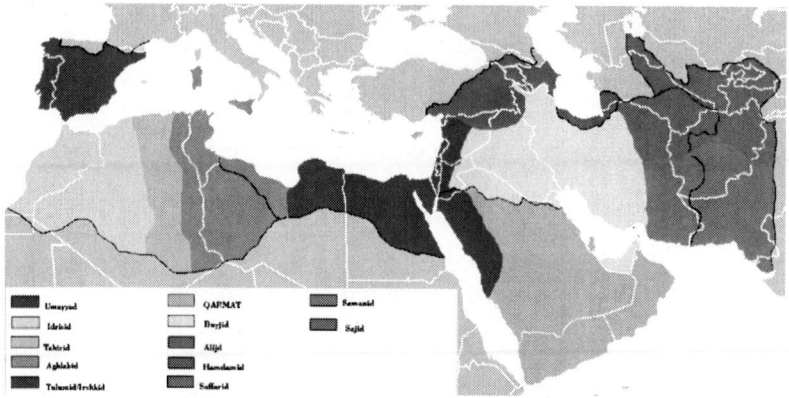

Fig. 1 The Islamic world in tenth century
In the tenth century the Islamic world was vast and took in virtually all the great centers of civilization known to the ancients, with the exception of Italy and Greece.

So far-reaching was the Islamic influence, or the apparent Islamic influence, on Europe at this time that by the late nineteenth century a number of British and French writers began to credit the Arabs with providing the impulse for modern European science and learning. Consider for example the utterances of Anglo-French social historian Robert Briffault in 1919: "It was under the influence of the Arabian and Moorish revival of culture, and not in the fifteenth century, that the real Renaissance took place. Spain, not Italy, was the cradle of the rebirth of Europe. After steadily sinking lower and lower into barbarism, it [Europe] had reached the darkest depths of ignorance and degradation when the cities of the Saracenic world, Baghdad, Cairo, Cordova, Toledo, were growing centres of civilization and intellectual activity."[1] Again, "It is highly probable that but for the Arabs modern European civilization would not have arisen at all; it is absolutely certain that but for them, it would not have assumed the character which has enabled it to transcend all previous phases of evolution."[2]

In support of these statements, Briffault points to a series of Arab inventions, discoveries and innovations. He refers to the astronomers Al-Zarkyal and Al-Farani, who postulated that the orbits of the planets was elliptical rather than circular, as Ptolemy believed.[3] He notes how Ibn Sina (Avicenna) is said to have employed an air thermometer, and Ibn Yunis

---

1 Robert Briffault, *The Making of Humanity* (London, 1919), pp. 188-189.
2 *Ibid*. p. 190.
3 *Ibid*. pp. 190-191.

to have used a pendulum for the measurement of time.[4] He points to the work of Al-Byruny, who travelled forty years to collect mineralogical specimens, and to that of Ibn Baitar, who collected botanical specimens from the whole Muslim world, and who compared the floras of India and Persia with those of Greece and Spain.[5] He lauds the Arab achievement of having introduced the zero into mathematics (though he admits this came originally from India), and points to the Arab invention of algebra, which was to revolutionize mathematics.[6] As if all this were not enough, he asserts that the Arabs invented the empirical method itself, which stands at the foundation of all modern science, and points to the achievements of Arab chemists, or alchemists, whose "organized passion for research ... led them to the invention of distillation, sublimation, filtration, to the discovery of alcohol, or nitric acid and sulphuric acids (the only acid known to the ancients was vinegar), of the alkalis, of the salts of mercury, of antimony and bismuth, and laid the basis of all subsequent chemistry and physical research."[7]

Although the above viewpoint may seem somewhat overstated to the average reader, it is encountered even more widely today than when it was penned. Indeed, it has now become part of received wisdom. Thus the Wikipedia "Islamic Science" page quotes Rosanna Gorini, who notes: "According to the majority of the historians, Al-Haytham was the pioneer of the modern scientific method. With his book he changed the meaning of the term optics and established experiments as the norm of proof in the field. His investigations are based not on abstract theories, but on experimental evidences and his experiments were systematic and repeatable."[8] The same page, which is massive, enumerates the apparently astonishing achievements of the Arab or Muslim scientists. The work of Avicenna (in medicine), Geber (in chemistry), Al-Kindi (Earth sciences), Abu Rayhan al-Biruni or Byruny (in astronomy and medicine), Ibn Zuhr (in surgery), and Ibn al-Haythan, or Alhacen (in optics) are all mentioned. The latter in particular is seen by some as being the inventor of the modern scientific method, whilst the work of the Spaniard Averroes is credited with reviving the entire study of philosophy in the West.

---

4 *Ibid.* p. 191.

5 *Ibid.* p. 198.

6 *Ibid.* p. 194.

7 *Ibid.* p. 197.

8 Rosanna Gorini, "Al-Haytham the Man of Experience. First Steps in the Science of Vision," *International Society for the History of Islamic Medicines* (2003). Institute of Neurosciences, Laboratory and Psychobiology and Psychopharmacology, Rome, Italy.

It is well-known that Muslim scholars, beginning with the Persian Avicenna (Ibn Sina) in the late tenth and early eleventh century, had made extensive commentaries upon the works of Aristotle, which they attempted to integrate, with a very limited degree of success it must be noted, into Islamic thought. In the second half of the twelfth century Avicenna's work was taken up by the Spanish Muslim Averroes (Ibn Rushd), who made his own commentaries and writings on the Greek philosopher. By that time European scholars were very much aware of Arab learning, and men like John of Salisbury even had agents in Spain procuring Arabic manuscripts, which were then translated into Latin. "Soon the commentaries of Averroes were so well known in Europe that he was called 'the Commentator,' as Aristotle was called 'the Philosopher.'"[9] At a slightly earlier stage, Christian Europeans had found their way into Muslim-controlled regions such as Sicily, often in disguise, in order to avail themselves of the scientific and alchemical knowledge they discovered there. No less a person than Gerbert of Aurillac, the genius of the tenth century, on whom the figure of Faust was based, had journeyed into the Muslim regions to acquire knowledge. The profound influence exerted by Islam upon the philosophical and theological thinking of Europeans at this time cannot be stressed too much. Thus, at one stage, Briffault notes how, "The exact parallelism between Muslim and Christian theological controversy is too close to be accounted for by the similarity of situation, and the coincidences are too fundamental and numerous to be accepted as no more than coincidence. ... The same questions, the same issues which occupied the theological schools of Damascus, were after an interval of a century repeated in identical terms in those of Paris."[10] Again, "The whole logomacy [of Arab theological debate] passed bodily into Christendom. The catchwords, disputes, vexed questions, methods, systems, conceptions, heresies, apologetics and irenics, were transferred from the mosques to the Sorbonne"[11]

Even allowing for a certain degree of exaggeration on the part of the above writers, it is clear that during the latter tenth, eleventh and early twelfth centuries the Islamic world was ahead of Christian Europe in terms of science, technology and learning in general, and that Europe was greatly influenced by Islam in this period. However, granting Islam's lead in these centuries, the following question is prompted: If the Islamic world was so ahead of Europe, what went wrong afterward? How is it that by the twelfth or thirteenth century at the latest Europe had taken the lead, a lead which

9 Sidney Painter, *A History of the Middle Ages, 284-1500* (Macmillan, 1953), p. 303.
10 Briffault, *op cit.*, p. 217.
11 *Ibid.* p. 219.

she was never again to relinquish? How is it that it was Europe which made the great scientific breakthroughs from the fourteenth century onwards and that it was Europe which went on to explore and map the earth and give birth to the modern world? And above all, how does this early Islamic respect for learning square with the profound disrespect for learning of almost all kinds displayed by Muslims for centuries, and even to this day?

This latter question has occurred to very many writers over the past few years, including Bernard Lewis, whose 2001 book *What Went Wrong?* poses the question in its title. Lewis could offer no definite answer to the problem, nor have any other writers of a similar view.

But even the suggestion that Islam at one time encouraged science and learning is problematic; and there is much evidence to suggest that the Arabian faith was never, even at the beginning, well-disposed to free thought and the acquisition of knowledge. Most people are aware of the accusation that the Muslim conquerors of Egypt did immense damage to that country's ancient monuments, and a tradition exists that it was the Caliph Umar who ordered the destruction of the great library at Alexandria, shortly after the conquest of Egypt. And were not the numerous Roman cities of Anatolia, Syria and North Africa despoiled by the Arabs; do not their stark remains litter the landscape of these regions to this day? How are these things to be reconciled with the view that Islam was, at one time, tolerant, enlightened and relatively peace-loving? One answer is to suggest that the achievements proudly attributed to medieval Islam were largely illusory; the science of the Arabs, it can be argued, was not theirs at all, it belonged primarily to the peoples they had conquered, the Persians, Syrians, and Egyptians. The philosophers, geographers, mathematicians, and physicians of these peoples were permitted, for a short time, to continue their studies, before they were closed down under the weight of Arab theocracy. But even this solution is problematic: If the philosophers and scientists of Persia, Syria and Egypt were permitted for a brief period to continue their studies, how is it that some of them seem to have been still active three hundred years later, in the tenth century? And how is this initial Arab liberalism to be squared with the evidence of initial fanaticism, such as the destroyed Roman cities of Syria and North Africa?

Finding an answer to these questions seems akin to squaring the proverbial circle. Is it possible to arrive at a solution?

To begin with, there is no question that the early Islamic world was fabulously wealthy, prosperous, and advanced. It could scarcely have been otherwise, when it conquered and, within a very short time, controlled virtually all of the ancient centers of culture and population of the Near East.

By circa 650 Islamic armies had subdued everything from Egypt and Libya in the west, to Persia and Afghanistan in the east. The wealth, and learning, of those regions, including the enormous population centers, with their libraries and universities, were all now at the disposal of Muslim rulers. As well as the actual plunder accrued in successful wars of conquest, the Arabs imposed heavy taxes upon the natives who refused to convert to Islam, whilst the treasures of ancient and venerable churches and temples were more often than not simply looted. This was usually disguised as an act of religious piety, since church treasures were frequently in the form of statues or gold-covered images – idols, which it was the sacred duty of Muslims to destroy. In Egypt, even the tombs of pharaohnic times were plundered.[12] In addition, new sources of gold and silver were discovered around this time. In Khorasan, to the east of Persia, and in Transoxiana beyond it, between Kashmir and the Aral Sea, "vast mines of silver" were discovered, whilst the Arab conquest of Nubia, to the south of Egypt, opened the gold mines of that region to their use.[13] And these new sources of wealth were of such richness that they could scarcely have done else than produce an epoch of prosperity.

For a while, it seems that some Muslim rulers did patronize universities and other seats of learning. Scientific and philosophic treatises were indeed composed, and there is no doubt that Arab, or at least Arabic-speaking scholars were in possession of many classical Greek texts not generally available in Europe. These men, it is evident, made important contributions, in various areas of scientific and scholarly endeavor. In addition, the Arabs, or rather the Arab rulers of the Near East (for the great majority of the population remained non-Arab in language and non-Muslim in religion for several centuries after the conquest), learned the secrets of paper-making, the compass, and various other crucial technologies from the Chinese between the eighth and eleventh centuries, which technologies they utilized and eventually (inadvertently) spread to Europe: But what of the argument that Islam encouraged the arts and sciences? Here, the Islamophiles are on much shakier ground. The Arabs who emerged from Arabia with Caliph Umar were mostly illiterate nomads, whose knowledge of what we call science was non-existent. Like all barbarians, they would of course have been deeply impressed, to begin with at any rate, by the advanced and civilized cultures which they overran. Egypt, Babylonia, and Persia were ancient civilizations with unique attributes. Each had long-established universities, libraries and traditions of learning. When the Arabs

---

12 Hugh Trevor-Roper, *The Rise of Christian Europe* (2nd. ed., London, 1966), p. 90.
13 *Ibid.*

conquered these regions there is evidence that they permitted these institutions, for a time at least, to continue their activities. Furthermore, these nations, and Persia in particular, were conduits through which flowed new ideas and techniques from the great civilizations of the Far East, from India and China. Much, indeed most, of the new technologies and methods that medieval Europeans learned from the Arabs, were not Arab or even Near Eastern at all, but Chinese and Indian. Europeans used the Arabic names for these things (such as "zero," from the Arabic *zirr*), because it was from Arab sources that they learned them. But they were neither Arab nor Middle Eastern.

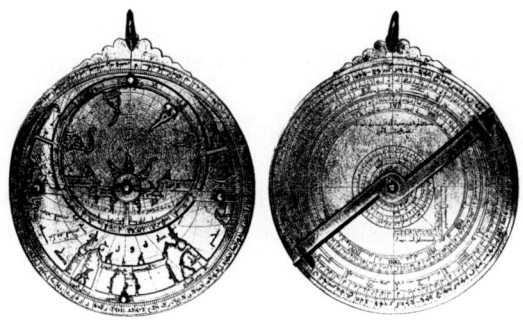

Fig. 2. Astrolabe from Islamic Spain, eleventh century
Such astrolabes, common in the Islamic world at this time, were exact copies of similar machines used in the Byzantine world during the sixth and early seventh centuries.

This is in fact the case with the great majority of the "Arab" learning outlined by such enthusiasts as Briffault. The claim, for example, that the Arabs discovered the distillation of alcohol, which Briffault makes, is quite simply false. Alcohol had been distilled in Babylonia prior to the Arab conquest.[14] Under the Arabs, distillation techniques were improved; but they did not invent distillation. Again, the claim that the Persian Al-Khwarizmi invented algebra is untrue; and it is now widely admitted that the Greek mathematician Diophantes, building on the knowledge of the Babylonians, was the first to outline the principles (in his *Arithmetica*) of what we now call algebra.[15] Al-Khwarizmi did make a number of important innovations, such as the quadratic equation and the introduction of the

14 Charles Simmonds, *Alcohol: With Chapters on Methyl Alcohol, Fusel Oil, and Spirituous Beverages* (Macmillan, 1919), pp. 6ff.

15 See *e.g.* Carl B. Boyer, *A History of Mathematics*, Second Edition (Wiley, 1991), p. 228.

decimal number system from India, but in many other respects his work was not as advanced as that of Diophantes. Furthermore, he clearly owed much to the fifth century Indian mathematician and astronomer Aryabhata, whose 121-verse *Aryabhatiya* expostulated on astronomy, arithmetic, geometry, algebra, trigonometry, methods of determining the movements of the planets and descriptions of their movements, as well as methods of calculating the movements of the sun and moon and predicting their eclipses. And we note too that Aryabhata was manifestly the source of the astronomical ideas attributed to Al-Zarkyal and Al-Farani, which Briffault places such store in.

There is another important consideration to remember: Whilst "Arab" scientists and philosophers of this time used Arab names and wrote in Arabic, the great majority of them were not Arabs or Muslims at all, but Christians and Jews who worked under Arab regimes. The Saracen armies which conquered the Near East in the seventh century imposed their faith and their language in the corridors of power; and the subdued peoples were forced to learn it. At no time, however, not even at the beginning, did genuine Arabs and Muslims show much interest in science and scholarship. Aristotle's work was preserved in Arabic not initially by Muslims at all, but by Christians such as the fifth century priest Probus of Antioch, who introduced Aristotle to the Arabic-speaking world. In fact, during the eighth and ninth centuries, "the whole corpus of Greek scientific and philosophical learning was translated into Arabic, mainly by Nestorian Christians."[16] We know that "Schools, often headed by Christians, were ... established in connection with mosques."[17] The leading figure in the Baghdad school was the Christian Huneyn ibn Ishaq (809-873), who translated many works by Aristotle, Galen, Plato and Hippocrates into Syriac. His son then translated them into Arabic. The Syrian Christian Yahya ibn 'Adi (893-974) also translated works of philosophy into Arabic, and wrote one of his own, *The Reformation of Morals*. Throughout the Muslim world it was Christians and Jews (especially the latter), who did almost all the scientific research and enquiry at this time. And there is much evidence to suggest that the efforts of these scholars were often viewed by their Muslim masters with the deepest suspicion. Certainly there was not the encouragement to learning, much less to new research, that is so frequently boasted.

Even the limited number of "Arab" scholars who were not Jews and Christians were rarely Arabs. We are told that Al-Kindi was "one of the few

---

16 James W. Thompson and Edgar N. Johnson, *An Introduction to Medieval Europe, 300-1500* (New York, 1937), p. 175.

17 *Ibid.*, p. 176.

pure Arabs to achieve intellectual distinction."[18] More often than not they were actually Persians. This was the case, as we saw, with the mathematician Al-Khwarizmi, and also with the great philosopher Avicenna, among many others. The Persian origin of so much "Arab" learning reminds us again that a great deal of what has been attributed to the Arabs was in reality Persian, and that, prior to the Islamicization of Persia in the seventh century, the country had, under the Sassanids, been a cultural and intellectual crossroads, bringing together the latest mathematics from India, the latest technology from China, and the latest philosophy from Byzantium; and making important contributions to all of these herself. This leads to the suspicion that "Al-Khwarizmi" and "Avicenna" (Ibn-Sina), may have been scholars of the Sassanid period, whose works were translated into Arabic and their names "Arabized" during the Abbasid period – perhaps in the early eighth century.

Rodney Stark explains how Islam does not have "a conception of God appropriate to underwrite the rise of science. ... Allah is not presented as a lawful creator but is conceived of as an extremely active God who intrudes in the world as he deems it appropriate. This prompted the formation of a major theological bloc within Islam that condemns all efforts to formulate natural laws as blasphemy in that they deny Allah's freedom to act."[19]

Allah's freedom to act is seen all too clearly in the outlandish events of Muhammad's life, where sacred moral laws are broken by the Prophet and his followers, only to be vindicated – afterward – by new "revelations" from Allah.

Allah's total freedom to act resulted in fatalism and the death of reason; a universe dominated by forces that are utterly incomprehensible. If my house is destroyed by lightning, it is the will of Allah; it has nothing to do with my failure to install a good lightning-rod. This was the very essence of what we now call "Medievalism." Islamic cosmology was explained thus by Maimonides:

> Human intellect does not perceive any reason why a body should be in a certain place instead of being in another. In the same manner they say that reason admits the possibility that an existing being should be larger or smaller than it really is, or that it should be different in form and position from what it really is; *e.g.*, a man might have the height of a mountain, might

---

18 *Ibid.*, p. 178.

19 Rodney Stark, *The Rise of Christianity: A Sociologist Reconsiders History* (Harper Collins, 1996), pp. 20-1.

have several heads, and fly in the air; or an insect might be as small as an insect, or an insect as huge as an elephant.

This method of admitting possibilities is applied to the whole Universe. Whenever they affirm that a thing belongs to this class of admitted possibilities, they say that it can have this form and that it is also possible that it be found differently, and that the one form is not more possible than the other; but they do not ask whether the reality confirms their assumption ...

[They say] fire causes heat, water causes cold, in accordance with a certain habit; but it is logically not impossible that a deviation from this habit should occur, namely, that fire should cause cold, move downward, and still be fire; that the water should cause heat, move upward, and still be water. On this foundation their whole [intellectual] fabric is constructed.[20]

The rejection by Islam and the Islamic world of science and reason is illustrated by a number of significant events, such as the burning by Al Mansur (Caliph of Cordoba, late tenth/early eleventh century) with his own hand, of the "materialist and philosophical works of the library associated with Hakam II,"[21] as well as by the major and obvious facts, such as that by the thirteenth century Europe had overtaken the Islamic world in virtually every field of science and technology – though Islam had, just a few centuries earlier, inherited all the great centers of Greek and Babylonian learning, when Europe had to start from scratch. And if the learning of Islam during the tenth and eleventh centuries has been exaggerated, so has the ignorance of Europe in the same centuries. A commonly-held belief is that Europe of this period was devoid of towns and that building is stone was virtually unknown. We are presented with a picture of rustic hamlets and thatched hovels. Historians speak of a primitive barter economy, universal illiteracy, and all-pervading instability.

It is of course true that during the tenth century the great majority of Europe's population lived in the countryside, and that life was, by modern standards, primitive. Yet high culture was not lacking, and revolutionary developments were transforming the environment. This was the century which saw the widespread adoption of the moldboard plow and the horse-

---

20 Moses Maimonides, *The Guide for the Perplexed*, M. Friedländer, trans. (Barnes and Noble, New York, 2004).

21 Bertrand, *op cit.*, p. 58.

collar, two innovations which permitted the utilization of the heavier soils of northern Europe and were symptomatic of an increasing population. During the same century building in stone, which had fallen into abeyance since the seventh century, was resumed on a large scale, as the still-standing magnificent Romanesque churches testify. Although domestic architecture is scarcer, we know from illustrations on tapestries and manuscripts that the princes and prelates of the time inhabited Roman-style palaces and villas, complete with tiled roofs and pillared porticoes. The Roman system of roads was maintained, as is proved by the frequent travels undertaken by rulers, merchants and churchmen.[22] Evidently too the taverns and hostelries of the Roman epoch were still in operation. And the arts and the sciences were not, contrary to popular opinion, moribund. Some of the artwork that survives from the period can stand comparison with the best achievements of Rome. Indeed, the British Isles experienced something of a golden age in this respect. The distinctive Hiberno-Saxon art of the ninth and tenth centuries has bequeathed to us with some of the finest and most technically advanced miniature art ever produced, both in metal and on parchment.

A major part of Europe's revival during the tenth century was spearheaded by the monks of the Benedictine Order. The Benedictines may not have intended to make their communities into centers of learning, technology and economic progress; yet, as time went on, this is exactly what they became. Indeed, one can scarcely find a single endeavor in the advancement of civilization during Late Antiquity and the Early Middle Ages in which the monks did not play a central role. It is well-known, of course, that they preserved the literary inheritance of the ancient world (much more completely, in fact, than was previously realized), yet they did much more. According to one scholar, they gave "the whole of Europe ... a network of model factories, centers for breeding livestock, centers of scholarship, spiritual fervor, the art of living ... readiness for social action – in a word ... advanced civilization that emerged from the chaotic waves of surrounding barbarity. Without any doubt, Saint Benedict was the Father of Europe. The Benedictines, his children, were the Fathers of European civilization."[23]

We could fill volumes enumerating the achievements of the Benedictines. That they single handedly preserved much of ancient literature

---

22 We know, for example, that Alfred the Great visited Rome, as did numerous other princes of the British Isles, France and Germany.

23 Réginald Grégoire, Léo Moulin, and Raymond Oursel, *The Monastic Realm* (New York, Rizzoli, 1985), p. 277.

is well-known. Not so widely known is the enormous quantity of that literature that they saved. We are accustomed to think that, following the collapse of the Western Empire, most of the literary heritage of Greece and Rome was lost in the west and was only recovered after contact with the Arabs in Spain and Italy during the eleventh century and after the fall of Constantinople during the fifteenth. Yet this notion is quite simply untrue. The great majority of the literature of Greece and Rome that has survived into modern times was preserved by the monks of the sixth and seventh centuries and was never in fact forgotten. Thus for example Alcuin, the polyglot theologian of Charlemagne's court, mentioned that his library in York contained works by Aristotle, Cicero, Lucan, Pliny, Statius, Trogus Pompeius, and Virgil. In his correspondences he quotes still other classical authors, including Ovid, Horace, and Terence. Abbo of Fleury (latter tenth century), who served as abbot of the monastery of Fleury, demonstrates familiarity with Horace, Sallust, Terence, and Virgil. Desiderius, described as the greatest of the abbots of Monte Cassino after Benedict himself, and who became Pope Victor III in 1086, oversaw the transcription of Horace and Seneca, as well as Cicero's *De Natura Deorum* and Ovid's *Fasti*.[24] His friend Archbishop Alfano, who had also been a monk of Monte Cassino, possessed a deep knowledge of the ancient writers, frequently quoting from Apuleius, Aristotle, Cicero, Plato, Varro, and Virgil, and imitating Ovid and Horace in his verse.

By the end of the tenth century we find that monasteries all over Europe were in possession of enormous libraries stacked with the works of the classical authors, and that knowledge of Greek and even Hebrew was widespread. This is important, because it illustrates the continuity between this period and the world of Late Antiquity, and calls into serious question the entire concept of the Dark Age. It shows too that Christian Europe did not need to depend upon other societies and cultures (such as the Islamic) to reacquaint it with letters. Thus we find for example that Gerbert of Aurillac, later Pope Sylvester II, taught Aristotle and logic, and brought to his students an appreciation of Horace, Juvenal, Lucan, Persius, Terence, Statius, and Virgil. We hear of lectures delivered on the classical authors in places like Saint Alban's and Paderborn. A school exercise composed by Saint Hildebert survives in which he had pieced together excerpts from

---

24 Cited from Charles Montalembert, *The Monks of the West: From St. Benedict to St. Bernard*. 5 Vols. (Vol. 5) (London, 1896), p. 146. It is true that Alciun is a man of the ninth century, an epoch from which surviving documents must be treated with the utmost caution. Yet tenth century characters, whose historical reality is not to be doubted, were also well acquainted with the Classical authors.

Cicero, Horace, Juvenal, Persius, Seneca, Terence, and others. It has been suggested that Hildebert knew Horace almost by heart.[25]

If the monks were classical scholars, they were equally natural philosophers, engineers and agriculturalists. Certain monasteries might be known for their skill in particular branches of knowledge. Thus, for example, lectures in medicine were delivered by the monks of Saint Benignus at Dijon, whilst the monastery of Saint Gall had a school of painting and engraving, and lectures in Greek and Hebrew could be heard at certain German monasteries.[26] Monks often supplemented their education by attending one or more of the monastic schools established throughout Europe. Abbo of Fleury, having mastered the disciplines taught in his own house, went to study philosophy and astronomy at Paris and Rheims. We hear similar stories about Archbishop Raban of Mainz, Saint Wolfgang, and Gerbert of Aurillac.[27]

The monks, from the time of Benedict onwards, established schools all over Europe. Indeed, our word "school" is related to the word "Scholastic," a term used to broadly define the system of thought and philosophy developed by the monks of this period. Scholastic thinking was based largely on Aristotle, and represented real continuity with the classical traditions of philosophy and rationality.

As well as teachers and educators, the monks established the first hospitals. These were the first institutions ever to exist providing free medical care to all, irrespective of financial circumstances. In the words of one writer: "Following the fall of the [Western] Roman Empire, monasteries gradually became the providers of organized medical care not available elsewhere in Europe for several centuries. Given their organization and location, these institutions were virtual oases of order, piety, and stability in which healing could flourish. To provide these caregiving practices, monasteries also became sites of medical learning between the fifth and tenth centuries, the classic period of so-called monastic medicine. During the Carolingian revival of the 800s, monasteries also emerged as the principal centers for the study and transmission of ancient medical texts."[28]

As noted by the above writer, their interest in healing led the monks naturally into medical research, and in course of time they accumulated a

---

25 John Henry Newman, in Charles Frederick Harrold, (ed.) *Essays and Sketches*, Vol. 3 (New York, 1948), pp. 316-7.

26 *Ibid.*, p. 319.

27 *Ibid.*, pp. 317-9.

28 Günter B. Risse, *Mending Bodies, Saving Souls: A History of Hospitals* (Oxford University Press, 1999), p. 95.

vast knowledge of physiology, pathology, and medication. Their studies of herbs and natural remedies led them into the investigation of plants, and they laid the foundations of the sciences of botany and biology.

As part of the Rule of Benedict, the monks were committed to a life of work, study and prayer, and the work part often involved manual labor in the fields. This led to a renewed respect for this type of activity amongst the aristocracy who, by the late Roman period, had come to regard manual work with contempt. Their labors in the fields produced a deep interest in agriculture and agricultural techniques. New technologies were developed by the monks, including, almost certainly, the windmill. Everywhere, they introduced new crops, industries, or production methods. Here they would introduce the rearing of cattle and horses, there the brewing of beer or the raising of bees or fruit. In Sweden, the corn trade owed its existence to the monks.

When Benedict established his Rule, much of Europe was still an uncultivated wilderness. This was true primarily of those areas which had never been part of the Roman Empire, such as Germany, but even of parts of Gaul and Spain, as well as Britain and Ireland remained in this condition into the sixth and seventh centuries. These areas the monks brought under cultivation, often deliberately choosing the wildest and most inhospitable tracts of country to set up their houses. Many of the virgin forests and marshes of Germany and Poland were brought into cultivation for the first time by the monks. "We owe," says one writer, "the agricultural restoration of a great part of Europe to the monks." According to another, "Wherever they came, they converted the wilderness into a cultivated country; they pursued the breeding of cattle and agriculture, labored with their own hands, drained morasses, and cleared away forests. By them Germany was rendered a fruitful country." Another historian records that "every Benedictine monastery was an agricultural college for the whole region in which it was located."[29] Even nineteenth century French historian Francois Guizot, a man not especially sympathetic to Catholicism, observed: "The Benedictine monks were the agriculturalists of Europe; they cleared it on a large scale, associating agriculture with preaching."[30]

It would be possible to fill many volumes outlining the contribution made by the monks, particularly those of the Early Middle Ages, to the civilization and prosperity of Europe. Their role cannot be emphasized strongly enough; yet it is one that has been curiously overlooked by many historians. In the 1860s and 1870s, when Comte de Montalembert wrote

29 Alexander Clarence Flick, *The Rise of the Medieval Church* (New York, 1909), p. 223.
30 See John Henry Cardinal Newman, *loc cit.* pp. 264-5.

a six-volume history of the monks of the West, he complained at times of his inability to provide anything more than a cursory overview of great figures and deeds, so enormous was the topic at hand. He was compelled, he said, to refer his readers to the references in his footnotes, in order that they might follow them up for themselves.

2
ISLAM'S TEACHING AND ATTITUDES

As I have shown in some detail in *Mohammed and Charlemagne Revisited*, the arrival of Islam upon the stage of history was marked by a torrent of violence and destruction throughout the Mediterranean world. The great Roman and Byzantine cities, whose ruins still dot the landscapes of North Africa and the Middle East, were brought to a rapid end in the seventh century. Everywhere archeologists have found evidence of massive destruction; and this corresponds precisely with what we know of Islam as an ideology.

Unlike Christianity, early Islam was spread entirely by the sword. Later Muslims believed implicitly that the example was here set by Muhammad. Whether this is correct, or whether anyone named Muhammad ever existed, is another question, one that is briefly examined in the Appendix to the present volume. From the point of view of Islam's impact upon the outside world and Europe in particular, however, the fact is that Muslims have never, since the late seventh century at least, doubted Muhammad's existence and have since then viewed him as the perfect model for human behavior and moral action. In their basic religious texts, the Qur'an, the Hadith (sayings and deeds of Muhammad) and the Sira (Muhammad's biography, written by Ibn Ishaq around 720), a comprehensive picture of the life and teachings of their Prophet emerges: What we find is the story of a desert warlord who was also an extremely sensual man, a man who freely indulged in the more carnal pleasures. Muhammad, we find, used violence to spread his teachings, and advocated that others do the same. During the military campaigns in which he was involved he took slaves for his own gratification and permitted others to follow suit.

This is not, of course, the image of a prophet or holy man most westerners expect. Nor is it in accordance with what most other cultures expect of a man of God. Muhammad is said to have ordered at least sixty raids and wars, and to have personally participated in twenty-seven of these, some of which involved massacres. Gibbon, as unbiased an authority as may be found, attributed the spectacular success of Muhammad's faith to the promise of plunder and comely captives. "From all sides the roving Arabs were allured to the standard of religion and plunder; and the apostle sanctified the licence of embracing female captives as their wives and concubines; and the enjoyment of wealth and beauty was a feeble type of the joys of paradise prepared for the valiant martyrs of the faith. 'The sword,' says Mahomet, 'is the key of heaven and of hell: a drop of blood shed in the cause of God, a night spent in arms, is of more avail than two months of fasting or prayer: whosoever falls in battle, his sins are forgiven ...'"[1] All of the early spread of Islam involved the sword. Contrast this with the growth of Christianity, or Buddhism, for that matter. Islam is virtually unique among world religions in that its primary scriptures advocate the use of military force and its early expansion – indeed its expansion during the first six or seven centuries of its existence – invariably involved military conquest and the use of force.

In 1993 Samuel P. Huntington famously noted that "Islam has bloody borders."[2] He might have added that Islam has always had bloody borders. Before he died, Muhammad is said to have told his followers that he had been ordered to "fight with the people till they say, none has the right to be worshiped but Allah." (Hadith, Vol. 4:196) In this spirit, Islamic theology divides the world into two parts: the Dar al-Islam, "House of Islam" and the Dar al-Harb, "House of War." In short, a state of perpetual conflict exists between Islam and the rest of the world. There can thus never be a real and genuine peace between Islam and the Dar al-Harb. At best, there can be a temporary truce, to allow Muslims to recuperate and regroup. In the words of Bat Ye'or, "the jihad is a state of permanent war [which] excludes the possibility of true peace." All that is allowed are "provisional truces in accordance with the requirements of the political situation."[3] In the words of medieval historian Robert Irwin, "Since the jihad [was] ... a state of permanent war, it [excluded] ... the possibility of true peace, but it [did] ... allow for provisional truces in accordance with

---

1 Gibbon, *Decline and Fall*, Ch. 50.

2 Samuel P. Huntington, "The Clash of Civilizations?" *Foreign Affairs*, (Summer, 1993).

3 Bat Ye'or, *The Dhimmi: Jews and Christians under Islam* (London, 1985), p. 46.

the requirements of the political situation."[4] Also, "Muslim religious law could not countenance the formal conclusion of any sort of permanent peace with the infidel."[5] And this is precisely what we find: In the long stretch of time since the life of Muhammad, it is doubtful if there has been a single year in which Muslims, in some part of the world, have not been fighting against infidels. In the history of relations between Europe and the House of Islam alone, there was continual and almost uninterrupted war between Muslims and Christians since the first attack on Sicily in 652 and on Constantinople in 674. In the great majority of these wars, the Muslims were the aggressors. And even the short periods of official peace were disturbed by the "unofficial" activities of corsairs and slave-traders. For centuries, Muslim pirates based in North Africa made large parts of the Mediterranean shore-line uninhabitable for Christians, and it is estimated that between the sixteenth and nineteenth centuries alone they captured and enslaved something in excess of a million Europeans.

More shall be said of Muslim piracy in the Mediterranean as we proceed.

At the opposite end of the Islamic sphere, in India and the Far East, war was equally endemic, and the horrors committed by successive Muslim invaders of India would need a volume in themselves to enumerate. Suffice to say that, lacking the limited protection extended to followers of religions "of the Book" (Christianity and Judaism), the Hindus and Buddhists of the Subcontinent suffered merciless slaughter and enslavement. This was violence on a completely unprecedented scale. Nothing like it had been seen before. One estimate holds that around fifty million Hindus and Buddhists died in the early centuries of Islamic conquest and rule – a slaughter wholly unprecedented in history and scarcely without parallel even in modern times. It is true that by the sixteenth century Islamic rule was somewhat ameliorated under the wise and tolerant Mughals; but for centuries earlier this was not the case.

The seventeen incursions of Mahmud of Ghazni, who led the original Islamic conquest in 1010,[6] were particularly devastating. In the words of one historian; "Though the court chronicler Utbi clearly exaggerated his sultan's prowess when he claimed that ten thousand Hindu temples

---

4 Robert Irwin, "Islam and the Crusades: 1096-1699," in Jonathan Riley-Smith (ed.) *The Oxford History of the Crusades* (Oxford, 1995), pp. 237.

5 *Ibid.*

6 If we exclude the inroads of Muhammad bin Qasim, three centuries earlier, around 710-720. However, as we shall see in the Appendix, there are grounds for believing that Mahmud of Ghazni and the latter were one and the same person.

were destroyed in Kanauj [district of northern India] alone by Mahmud's sword, it is not difficult to appreciate the legacy of bitter Hindu-Muslim antipathy left by raids that may have taken even 1 percent of that toll."[7] In one of his most notorious attacks, Mahmud assaulted Somnath, whose inhabitants "stood calmly watching the advance of Mahmud's fierce army … confident that Shiva, whose 'miraculous' iron lingam hung suspended within a magnetic field inside Somnath's 'womb-house,' would surely protect his worshippers from harm. Here, too, the chronicler probably exaggerated, for he wrote that fifty thousand Hindus were slain that day and that over two million dinars' worth of gold and jewels were taken from the hollow lingam shattered by Mahmud's sword. Yet the bitter shock of such attacks, whatever the factual sum of their deadly impact, was even more painfully amplified in the memories of those who had watched helplessly as friends and family were slain or enslaved by invaders who came to kill, rape, and rob in the name of God."[8]

One long-term consequence of these invasions was the virtual disappearance from India of the hitherto prevalent and pacifist Buddhism and its replacement by a form of Hinduism whose militancy is summed-up in the fact that its central scripture, the Bhagavad Gita, is an account of how the avatara Krishna urges his devotee (Arjuna) to take part in a bloody battle – in spite of the pacifist arguments advanced by the latter. The impact of Islam also saw the rise, in Northern India, of the even more militantly-inclined Sikh movement.

The disappearance of Buddhism in India, under the impact of Islam, is of great importance in that it shows how Islam tended to produce a more warlike mindset in the regions subject to its aggressive attentions. To this day Hindus point the finger of blame at Buddhism for the ease with which the Muslims conquered the Subcontinent. The very same process seems to have been operational in the West, where the more peaceful regions of the Byzantine world were overthrown with considerable ease by the Muslim invaders, whilst their own doctrine of "holy war" was later adopted by the Christians of Europe.

The centrality of war in Islamic theology is expressed succinctly by Ibn Abi Zayd al Qayrawani, who died in 966:

> Jihad is a precept of Divine institution. Its performance by certain individuals may dispense others from it. We Malikis [one of the four schools of Muslim jurisprudence] maintain that it

---

7 Stanley Wolpert, *A New History of India* (Oxford University Press, 1982), p. 107.
8 *Ibid.*

is preferable not to begin hostilities with the enemy before having invited the latter to embrace the religion of Allah except where the enemy attacks first. They have the alternative of either converting to Islam or paying the poll tax (jizya), short of which war will be declared against them. The jizya can only be accepted from them if they occupy a territory where our laws can be enforced. If they are out of our reach, the jizya cannot be accepted from them unless they come within our territory. Otherwise we will make war against them ...

It is incumbent upon us to fight the enemy without inquiring as to whether we shall be under the command of a pious or depraved leader.

It is not prohibited to kill white non-Arabs who have been taken prisoner. But no one can be executed after having been granted the aman (protection). The promises made to them must not be broken. Women and children must not be executed and the killing of monks and rabbis must be avoided unless they have taken part in battle. Women also may be executed if they have participated in the fighting. The aman granted by the humblest Muslim must be recognized by other [Muslims]. Women and young children can also grant the aman when they are aware of its significance. However, according to another opinion, it is only valid if confirmed by the imam (spiritual leader). The imam will retain a fifth of the booty captured by the Muslims in the course of warfare and he will share the remaining four fifths among the soldiers of the army. Preferably, the apportioning will take place on enemy ground.[9]

Because the present study focuses primarily on Islam's impact upon Europe and European thinking, it behoves us to look at Islam's record in that part of Europe that came under Islamic domination: Spain. A native of that country, Ibn Khaldun, gave, several centuries later, a very similar account to the one quoted above of Islam's attitude to war:

In the Muslim community, the holy war is a religious duty,

---

9 Ibn Khaldun, *The Muqaddimah: An Introduction to History* Vol. 1, Trans. Franz Rosenthal, Bollingen Series 43 (Princeton University Press, 1958) p. 163. Cited from Bat Ye'or, *op cit.*, p. 161.

because of the universalism of the [Muslim] mission and [the obligation to] convert everybody to Islam either by persuasion or by force. Therefore, caliphate and royal authority are united [in Islam], so that the person in charge can devote the available strength to both of them [religion and politics] at the same time.

The other groups did not have a universal mission, and the holy war was not a religious duty to them, save only for purposes of defense. It has thus come about that the person in charge of religious affairs [in other religious groups] is not concerned with power politics at all. [Among them] royal authority comes to those who have it, by accident and in some way that has nothing to do with religion. It comes to them as a necessary result of group feeling, which by its very nature seeks to obtain royal authority, as we have mentioned before, and not because they are under obligation to gain power over other nations, as is the case with Islam. They are merely required to establish their religion among their own [people].

This is why the Israelites after Moses and Joshua remained unconcerned with royal authority for about four hundred years. Their only concern was to establish their religion (1: 473)

Thereafter, there was dissensions among the Christians with regard to their religion and to Christology. They split into groups and sects, which secured the support of various Christian rulers against each other. At different times there appeared different sects. Finally, these sects crystallized into three groups, which constitute the [Christian] sects. Others have no significance. These are the Melchites, the Jacobites, and the Nestorians. We do not think that we should blacken the pages of this book with discussion of their dogmas of unbelief. In general, they are well known. All of them are unbelief. This is clearly stated in the noble Qur'an. [To] discuss or argue those things with them is not up to us. It is [for them to choose between] conversion to Islam, payment of the poll tax, or death.[10]

We need not repeat the assertion that the Caliphate of Cordoba was

10 *Ibid. The Dhimmi*, p. 162.

a haven of peace and tolerance in a Europe benighted by ignorance and violence. It is doubtful if there exists, in any other area of world history, such a radical untruth which has achieved such wide currency. In reality, from the very start, Islamic rule in Spain was marked by the appearance of a barbarism and savagery such as Europe had perhaps not experienced since pre-Christian times. Louis Bertrand mentions an incident early in the conquest of a type that was to become all-too characteristic: "After the capture of Seville and Toledo, when Mousa met his lieutenant Tarik, whom he accused of peculation, he received him with blows of a whip and ordered his head to be shaved. ... Later, when booty was being divided, he wanted to deprive another of his lieutenants of an important prisoner, the Christian governor of Cordova. 'It was I who made this man prisoner,' cried the officer, who was called Moghit, flying into a passion; 'they want to deprive me of him; very well, I will have his head cut off!' And he did so on the spot."[11] "Never," says Bertrand, "were these brutal habits to disappear completely from Musulman Spain. From one end to the other, the history of the Spanish Caliphate is strewn with severed heads and crucified corpses."

Bertrand describes some of the savage and inveterate feuding that characterized the first two or three years of Muslim rule. In his words, "the first part of this period, that of the Emirs dependent upon the Caliphate of Damascus ... is nothing but a long series of intestinal struggles, slaughterings, massacres, and assassinations.

"It was anarchy in all its horror, fed by family hatreds and the rivalry of tribe against tribe – Arabs of the North against Arabs of the South, Yemenites against Kaishites, Syrians against Medinites. All these Asiatics had a common enemy in the nomad African, the Berber, the eternal spoiler of cities and the auxiliary of all invaders."[12]

Executions, normally following torture, were most often by crucifixion. This was the fate even of the ninety year-old Abd el-Malik, who was beaten, slashed with swords and then crucified between a pig and a dog. "After that, Bertrand continues, "Yemenites and Kaishites ... came to blows among themselves. The Kaishites, under the leadership of their chief, Somail, routed their adversaries in the plain of Secunda, the Roman town on the other side of the Guadalquiver opposite Cordova. The victorious Somail had the Yemenite chiefs beheaded in the square in front of the Cathedral of Saint Vincent, which as yet was only half turned into a mosque.

---

11 Bertrand, *op cit.*, p. 35.
12 *Ibid.*, p. 36.

"Seventy heads had already fallen when one of the chiefs in alliance with Somail protested against this horrible butchery, not in the name of humanity, but in the name of Musulman solidarity. Somail, nevertheless, went on with his executions until his ally, indignant at his excessive cruelty, threatened to turn against him."[13]

Again, "Nothing emerges from this perpetual killing but the savagery, the brutality, and the cruelty of the new-comers. Under their domination ... Spain got used to being ridden over and devastated periodically, in a way that soon became as regular as the alteration of the seasons."[14] This pattern, set at the beginning, continued throughout the Muslim period. The savagery inflicted upon fellow Muslims was but a pale reflection of the atrocities committed against the Christian unbelievers in the North, whose territory was raided twice a year by every Muslim ruler.[15] And to top all of this, Islamic Spain became the hub of a vast new slave-trade. Hundreds of thousands of European slaves, both from Christian territories and from the lands of the pagan Slavs, were imported into the Caliphate, there to be used (if female) as concubines or to be castrated (if male) and made into harem guards or the personal body-guards of the caliph. According to Bertrand, "This army of Slavs [eunuchs] ... was the main instrument of the Caliph's authority. His power was a military dictatorship. He maintained himself only thanks to these foreigners."[16]

In such circumstances, the historian can surely be permitted a wry smile at the popular politically-correct definition of Islam as a "religion of peace." Indeed, insofar as the primary injunction of Islam is not to covert unbelievers but to establish political control through force or the threat of force (followed by the application of Shariah Law), it is evident that Islam is not even a religion in the normal sense of the word. It displays in fact all the characteristics of a totalitarian political ideology. There are, it is true, religious features, such as the promise of Paradise to believers; but then again the great totalitarian ideologies of Europe in the nineteenth and twentieth centuries – anarchism, socialism and fascism – also displayed decided religious features. And the fact that it is a political ideology rather than a religion explains the "egalitarianism" which some moderns have noted and praised in Islam.[17] Almost all totalitarian ideologies are egalitar-

---

13 *Ibid.*, pp. 37-8.

14 *Ibid.*, p. 37.

15 *Ibid.*, p. 45.

16 *Ibid.*

17 See *e.g.* Bernard Lewis, *What Went Wrong? Western Impact and Middle Eastern Response* (Oxford University Press, 2002), pp. 82ff.

ian to a greater or lesser degree. That does not however make them progressive or humanitarian. Stalin's Soviet Union, one of the most brutal regimes ever to appear in history, was also one of the most egalitarian: In the Soviet Union a young man or woman of peasant or proletarian background could easily reach the highest offices in the land by merit – or by doing what the regime required. And the "egalitarianism" of Islam, like that of many other extremist ideologies, was not extended to everyone. Three groups were excluded: women, slaves, and non-believers.

It should be noted too that, like anarchism, socialism and fascism, Islam seeks, through political means, to return the world to an imagined age of primeval innocence and pristine morality. Islam, it is claimed, was the way of Adam and Eve before the fall of mankind and its corruption. (Compare with anarchist/socialist ideas of human alienation caused by the development of private property, etc.) Thus Muslims insist that one does not "convert" to Islam, one "reverts" to it.

As regards those groups outside the egalitarian fold, the treatment of one of these, non-believers, has given rise to a whole mythology in recent years. It is said, for example, that after the Arab conquests of the seventh century the Christians and Jews of the Middle East and North Africa were permitted to live unmolested and to worship freely. And this life, enjoyed by Christians and Jews under the mantle of the Islamic polity, was superior to that of Christians and Jews in Europe at the time. In short, Islam's boundaries may have been bloody, but her innards were peaceful and enlightened.

Is this correct?

Although Islam or Islamic power was spread by the sword, it is true that followers of two other religions, specifically "Religions of the Book" (*i.e.*, those of a biblical origin, namely Judaism and Christianity), were permitted to continue the practice of their faiths. Other faiths, such as Buddhism and Hinduism, which had no biblical roots, fared much less well. Nonetheless, in all of the lands conquered by the Muslims it was possible, for centuries afterward, to find sizable Jewish and Christian communities, and these groups were accorded what was known as *dhimmi*, or "protected" status. Jews and Christians must pay a poll tax, named a *jizya*, from which Muslims were exempt. Aside from this, Jews and Christians were almost equal to Muslims before the law.

That at least is the story told in publication after publication. Along with it we find, in the thinking of many modern historians and even theologians, the idea that Islam was a kindred faith; one of the three "Arbahamic" traditions. Such writers are wont to remind their readers that Islam has biblical roots and that the prophets of the Old Testament are honored in the Qur'an. We are reminded too that Islam regarded Jesus as a prophet.

There is no question that Islam does have biblical roots: Characters and events of the Bible – almost exclusively the Old Testament – are found throughout the Qur'an. And it is equally true that Judaism, to begin with at least, was regarded by Muslims in a fraternal light; though this changed radically in the first half of the eighth century – a fact to be examined briefly in the Appendix to the present volume. After that time the Jews were viewed as treacherous apostates who murdered and rejected the prophets of God. As such, they were periodically persecuted and subject to violent attack.

Islam's relationship with Christianity is and always has been fraught. Contrary to popular belief, it is not true that Muslims honored Christ, for they did not believe that Jesus was the Christ, or the Son of God. They did and do however honor Jesus (Isha); but the Jesus of Islamic tradition has nothing in common with the figure encountered in the New Testament. According to Islam, Jesus taught pure Islam – including all that Islam espouses, such as polygamy, the death penalty for adultery and apostasy, spreading the faith by violent struggle, etc – and the Jesus of the Gospels, they say, is a fabrication invented by Christian propagandists in the late first century, or thereabouts. Furthermore, Jesus did not die on the cross – a lookalike took his place – and he did not rise from the dead.[18]

It is evident from this alone that, whatever politically-correct historians and theologians might say, Islam has almost nothing in common with Christianity. It is equally clear that, given the profound doctrinal and theological differences, its relationship with the followers of the latter faith must always have been strained, to say the least. And, as we shall see, the notion that the "Peoples of the Book," the Jews and Christians, enjoyed some kind of favored status in Islamic societies is little more than a cruel fiction. As Bat Ye'or has explained at length in a series of works devoted to the subject, the *dhimmi* Jews and Christians under Sharia Law were subject to a whole series of degrading and oppressive laws which made life all but intolerable. Aside from paying the *jizya* tax, the *dhimmis* were also forbidden to build new churches, to ring church bells, display the cross, ride a horse, build a house larger than that of Muslim neighbors and were compelled to wear a special type of clothing for easy identification – a

---

18 There is much evidence to suggest that the Jesus of the Qur'an is actually based upon Joshua of the Old Testament, who led the Israelites in their conquest of Canaan after the Exodus from Egypt. Joshua and Jesus are one and the same name in Hebrew. This question is considered in the Appendix.

custom copied by the Nazis with regard to the Jews in the 1930s and '40s. Furthermore, a Christian or Jew was not in law the equal of a Muslim: A Muslim's word always took precedence over that of a *dhimmi*. This in effect meant that the Christian or Jew lived in perpetual fear of the predatory attentions of Muslim neighbors. Any dispute whatsoever, be it over a goat or a chicken, could rapidly escalate into a life or death issue for the *dhimmi*. The Muslim had only to claim that the *dhimmi* had insulted Islam to have the latter put on trial for his life. As Bat Ye'or pointed out, the accuser needed two other Muslim witnesses to substantiate the charge of blasphemy, but these were invariably forthcoming, and the *dhimmi* found himself sentenced to death.

The result of such a pernicious system was inevitable: Christians and Jews learned quickly not to enter into dispute with Muslim neighbors, allowing the latter to exercise a petty tyranny over them.

Such humiliations, we are told, provoked many revolts in Spain during the eighth and ninth centuries, and these were punished by massacres. Insurrections erupted in Saragossa in 781 and 881, Cordoba (805, 818), Merida (805-813, 828 and the following year, and in 868), and again in Toledo (811-819). Many of the insurgents were said to have been crucified, as prescribed in the Qur'an (5:33):

"The revolt in Cordova of 818 was crushed by three days of massacres and pillage, with 300 notables crucified and 20,000 families expelled. Feuding was endemic in the Andalusian cities between the different sectors of the population: Arab and Berber colonizers, Iberian Muslim converts (*Muwalladun*) and Christian *dhimmis* (*Mozarabs*). There were rarely periods of peace in the Amirate of Cordova (756-912), nor later. Al-Andalus represented the land of *jihad* par excellence. Every year, sometimes twice a year, raiding expeditions were sent to ravage the Christian Spanish kingdoms to the north, the Basque regions, or France and the Rhone valley, bringing back booty and slaves. Andalusian corsairs attacked and invaded along the Sicilian and Italian coasts, even as far as the Aegean Islands, looting and burning as they went. Thousands of people were deported to slavery in Andalusia, where the caliph kept a militia of tens of thousands of Christian slaves brought from all parts of Christian Europe (the Saqaliba), and a harem filled with captured Christian women."[19]

---

19 Bat Ye'or and Andrew Bostom, "Andalusian Myth, Eurabian Reality," retrieved from www.jihadwatch.org/dhimmiwatch/archives/001665.php (The above-quoted authors are well-known critics of Islam; yet the facts they highlight are not controversial and are denied by no one. The only difference is that while Bat Ye'or and Andrew Bostom state the facts, politically correct writers tend to gloss over them or not mention them

It is of course true, as we shall see, that we should be very cautious about all reports emanating from the Dark Age centuries (roughly mid-seventh to mid-tenth). There are very good grounds for believing that almost all the documentary material relating to this epoch is the product of forgery perpetrated later in the Middle Ages. The likelihood is that much of what passes for eighth and ninth century "history" is simply the history of the tenth century backdated by a couple of hundred years. Nonetheless, there are very good grounds for believing that conditions in Spain during and immediately after the initial Muslim invasion of Spain were indeed savage. Furthermore, during the tenth and eleventh centuries, which are certainly within the period from which we have accurate and truthful documentation, the evidence of Islamic brutality is not difficult to find. Between 1011 and 1013 hundreds of Jews were massacred by Muslim mobs in Cordoba, whilst in Granada, up to five thousand Jews perished in a pogrom in 1066. The Berber Almohads in Spain and North Africa wreaked enormous destruction on the Jewish and Christian populations of both regions in the twelfth and thirteenth centuries. Suspicious of the sincerity of Jewish converts to Islam, the Almohads empowered Muslim "inquisitors" (antedating their Christian Spanish counterparts by three centuries) to remove children from such families and place them in the care of Muslims. A prominent Andalusian jurist, Ibn Hazm of Cordoba (d. 1064), wrote that Allah has established the infidels' ownership of their property merely to provide booty for Muslims.[20]

None of this sounds like the attitude or behavior of a tolerant or enlightened faith. If the Muslims tolerated the existence of Christians within their territories, it was only as an exploitable resource, much in the same way humans tolerate the existence of large numbers of farm animals throughout the countryside. So appalling were conditions for Christians and Jews under Islam that, in the course of centuries, they shrank to vanishing-point throughout the Near East and North Africa. It is also worth remembering that a victor is more inclined to be, and can afford to be, magnanimous. We need not repeat here the calamities suffered by Christians at the hands of Muslims during the century and a half after Muhammad's death, and how a caliphate was founded on the ruins of Christian kingdoms from Syria and Egypt to Spain and the Pyrenees. It is not too difficult to imagine the overwhelming sense of gloom felt by Christians as they observed these events unfold, and the growing sense of terror that the faith of Christ was about to be extinguished even in the heart of Europe.

---

at all.)

20 *Ibid.*

And whilst it is true that most of the conquered Christians were permitted to retain their faith and its practice, the massacre and enslavement of the conquered populations, very often on the slightest pretext, was common.

To describe the treatment of the *dhimmi* communities of Jews and Christians as one of benevolent tolerance is thus to do violence to the meaning of words: The *dhimmi*, by definition, had virtually no rights before the law.

But even the grudging acceptance of the existence of *dhimmi* communities has to be viewed in the context of how Islam came to power: the conquering Muslims of the seventh, eighth and ninth centuries could scarcely enslave or forcefully convert the entire populations of the subdued territories. Such a policy would perchance have involved them in dangerous revolts, revolts which may easily have extinguished the numerically small numbers of conquering Arabs. Far better to appease the conquered peoples with a semblance of toleration and recognition, whilst at the same time imposing punishing financial burdens and closing to them the most important and prestigious positions in society. This has been explained most lucidly by Bat Ye'or:

"The conditions of minorities in Christian countries has often been compared with the fate of the *dhimmis* under Islam, although such generalizations concerning vast territories and periods of time are inappropriate. Rather than looking for similarities between the two, one should acknowledge an essential difference. During the first two centuries of their conquest – and certainly at the outset – the Arabs were themselves a minority. In order to impose their laws, their language, and their foreign culture on ancient civilizations, they had to proceed with caution. A general uprising of the subject populations would have compromised the success of their conquest."[21]

The financial question too is one that cannot be ignored. Christians and Jews, we have noted, were compelled to pay a "poll tax" or *jizya*, an annual tribute which, considering the great numbers of conquered Christians, amounted to a fabulous sum for the government of the caliphate. In such circumstances, it will be obvious that it was financially advantageous to have Christians and Jews as subjects, and to keep them as Christians and Jews. Muslims were exempt from this kind of taxation. So lucrative was the *jizya* system that Muslim rulers did not, in most cases, actually want Christians to convert. Christian conversions meant loss of revenue. In the words of Louis Bertrand, "In general the Caliphal government did not want to see the Christians turn Musulman. The treasury lost too much if they did,

---

21 *Ibid.*, 67-8.

inasmuch as it was they who paid the major part of the taxes."[22] Bat Ye'or comments: "Baladhuri related that when Iraq fell to the Arab conquerors, the soldiers wanted to 'share out' the region of Sawad between themselves. The caliph Umar b. al-Khattab permitted them to divide the booty, but decreed that the land and the camels should be left to the local farmers so as to provide for the Muslims: 'If you divide them among those present, there will be nothing left for those who come after them.' And Ali, the Prophet's son-in-law said of the non-Muslim peasants of Sawad, 'Leave them to be a source of revenue and aid for the Muslims.'"[23] Bertrand rightly concludes; "It is difficult to find, as most of our historians do, an attitude of tolerance and broad-mindedness in this entirely self-interested line of conduct."[24]

Thus, as we noted earlier, Islam's acceptance of the continued existence of Jews and Christians was that they should form the basis of a servile population upon which the Muslims, the ruling elite, could enjoy what can only be described as a parasitical existence in perpetuity.

This then was Arab policy: heavy taxation coupled with periodic violent persecutions of the subject Christians. Egypt, for example, remained predominantly Christian until the thirteenth century, when a ferocious campaign of massacre and repression initiated by the Mameluk rulers compelled the majority to convert to Islam. The end result of such policies, enacted throughout the Muslim-controlled territories, was a progressive diminishing of Christian numbers – eventually in many places to vanishing point – and a commensurate augmentation of Muslim numbers.

We should note too that whilst the Muslims had a doctrinal reason for honoring the founder of Christianity, Christians had no such reason for revering the founder of Islam. Christian prophecy did not look forward to the coming of a prophet who would wage violent war against their faith, and who would both practice and sanction several of the most obnoxious things condemned by Christ: aggressive violence, polygamy, the death sentence for adultery, strict rituals surrounding clean and unclean food, easy divorce, etc. Indeed, if Muhammad were to find a place in the predictions and imaginings of the early Christian writers, it was as the Antichrist – a figure with whom he was, by very many Christian authorities, identified.

And just how tolerant can we really consider a faith that considers it not only legitimate but a duty to spread its message by force of arms; and which, at the same time, prescribes the death penalty for those abandoning it? How tolerant is a faith which reduces to second class citizenship even

22 Bertrand, *op cit.*, p. 33.

23 Bat Ye'or, *op cit.*, p. 68.

24 Bertrand, *op cit.*, p. 33.

the followers of those other few religions which it actually permits to exist? And how tolerant is a faith which considers it legitimate to plunder and destroy the temples and shrines of those religions it considers idolatrous or polytheistic; and which regards the adherents of such faiths as fair game, to be killed or enslaved, or forcibly converted, at the whim of the Muslim conquerors?

All things considered, we can only conclude that those who describe Islam as tolerant and peace-loving do not understand it.

The long-term result of Muslim policies towards non-Muslims was baleful in the extreme. In *Mohammed and Charlemagne Revisited*, I have shown how it was the application of Sharia Law which within a very short time indeed during the seventh century reduced the previously fertile and populous North African and Near Eastern provinces of the Byzantine Empire to a virtual desert. Sharia principles insisted that Muslims had the right to subsist off the labor of the infidel communities which were now subject to the caliph. And the Arab armies were followed closely by Bedouin nomads with their herds of goats and camels. These they allowed to graze freely in the cultivated fields and vineyards of the conquered Christians. Any of the latter who complained were liable to be accused of blasphemy against the Prophet and since, as we saw, the word of a Muslim always trumped that of an infidel, the complainant normally found himself put to death. Under such circumstances, Christian and Jewish farmers learned quickly to say nothing, whilst they watched the goats and camels of their conquerors destroy their livelihoods. Within a short time, huge stretches of previously fertile land was reduced to semi-desert, and the great cities of the region abandoned.

The latter can be seen to this day throughout the whole of North Africa and the Middle East.

Aside from the injunction to "fight with the unbelievers" until the whole world would recognize that "there is no God but Allah," another inducement to aggressive warfare provided by Islam (and mentioned by Gibbon) is its acceptance of slave- and concubine-taking. Indeed, it is possible that the hunt for comely captives was even more important as a spur to war than the desire to spread the faith or even acquire material plunder. Once again, it is Muhammad himself who is said by Muslims to have shown the way and provided the example. In at least two of the Jewish settlements his followers captured he took the most beautiful women as his wives, very shortly after the killing of their husbands. And in the Qur'an he sanctions the taking of women into sexual slavery where he enjoins his followers to abstain from sexual relations with women other than their wives and that which "your right hand possesses" (4:24), in other words, captives or slaves.

It is a fact that to its followers, or its male followers at least, Islam confers almost unlimited sexual license. Even the Islamic Paradise is a carnal one, where faithful Muslims enjoy the favors of 72 dark eyed virgins in perpetuity. This may come as a surprise, given the popular perception in the West of Islam as a morally conservative faith, one which abhors the moral laxity of the modern world. Are not Muslim women encouraged and even forced to dress modestly; and do not the most severe sanctions against sexual immorality apply in the more conservative Muslim lands? This of course is true; yet, it is equally true that the Muslim world is immersed in hypocrisy and denial. This is a civilization, we must not forget, whose supposed founder married at least thirteen wives, the youngest of whom, Ayesha, was a mere nine years of age. This is a society where traditionally a man was permitted four wives and any number of sex slaves (euphemistically described in all mainstream histories as concubines), and where a man could divorce his wife by telling her three times she was dismissed. No man was therefore under any moral requirement to faithfully stand by his aging wife and could quite happily be rid of her (or them) and wed a younger model; and Muslim men have in fact availed themselves of this "right" throughout the ages. This is a civilization in which the rights of men over this property are absolute – including the right to life itself. It is no coincidence that so-called "honor killing" of Muslim women by their male relatives is a widespread scourge throughout the Islamic world to this day.

The contrast between Christendom and the Islamic world in regard to sexual morality could not be greater. Amongst Christians strict monogamy has always been enforced and divorce never permitted; the sexual or physical abuse of women was from the beginning regarded as gravely sinful, and women always enjoyed rights and privileges unheard of in the Islamic world. Arab and other Muslim travelers to Europe throughout the Middle Ages were astonished and generally horrified at the freedoms accorded to Christian women; a phenomenon examined at some length by Bernard Lewis. A well-known example of this, that of the Turkish writer Evliya Celebi, who visited Vienna in 1665 as part of an Ottoman diplomatic mission. In the course of a detailed account of the imperial capital, Evilya describes a "most extraordinary spectacle" that he saw:

> In this country I saw an extraordinary spectacle. Whenever the emperor meets a woman in the street, if he is riding, he brings

his horse to a standstill and lets her pass. If the Emperor is on foot and meets a woman, he stands in a posture of politeness. The woman greets the emperor, who then takes his hat off his head to show respect for the woman. After the woman has passed, the emperor continues on his way. It is indeed an extraordinary spectacle. In this country and in general in the lands of the unbelievers, women have the main say. They are honored and respected out of love for Mother Mary.[25]

Bernard Lewis notes that, "The difference in the position of women was indeed one of the most striking contrasts between Christian and Muslim practice, and is mentioned by almost all travelers in both directions. Christianity, of all churches and denominations, prohibits polygamy and concubinage. Islam … permits both. European visitors to the Islamic lands were intrigued by what they knew or, more accurately, what they heard concerning the harem system, and some of them speak with ill-concealed and ill-informed envy of what they imagine to be the rights and privileges of a Muslim husband and master of the home. Muslim visitors to Europe speak of astonishment, often with horror, of the immodesty and forwardness of Western women, of the incredible freedom and absurd deference accorded to them, and of the lack of manly jealously of European males confronted with the immorality and promiscuity in which their womenfolk indulge. We find this observation even in the most unlikely places. Thus, for example, a Moroccan ambassador who was in Spain in 1766 speaks of the free and easy ways of Spanish ladies, and the absence of a virile sense of honor among their husbands. If this was his impression of the Court of Spain, one shudders to think of what he would have written had he continued his journey into Europe to, for example, the Court of Versailles."[26]

A fact ignored by Lewis and by modern commentators in general is that Islam's attitude to and treatment of women has no parallel elsewhere. The women of ancient Egypt, for example, and Babylonia, had much more freedom than their descendants living under Islam.[27] In Egypt, polygamy was normally confined to the royal family, whilst women could not be summarily dismissed by their husbands. Ancient Egyptian women went

---

25 Taken from Lewis, *op cit.*, p. 65.

26 *Ibid.*, p. 66.

27 The Pharaoh Ramses III proudly boasted that in his time a woman might travel unescorted and perfectly safe through any part of his realm. Such an idea would have been anathema to any Islamic ruler.

abroad unveiled and often achieved important positions in society. Aside from the prominent royal women who at times virtually ruled the country (and actually did rule it on several occasions), women could fill important roles as priestesses, whilst skilled females, such as musicians, took part in great royal and religious events. Several of Egypt's most popular and best-loved deities were female. Women were valued in Egypt and a flourishing literature celebrating the love of men and women existed.

Winston Churchill's view of Islam is reasonably well known, and deserves to be more so. In his opinion, "no stronger retrograde force exists in the world" than Islam. His critique takes in the full gamut of Islamic ideology, yet the Islamic attitude to women is identified for specific criticism:

"How dreadful are the curses which Mohammedanism lays on its votaries! Besides the fanatical frenzy, which is as dangerous in a man as hydrophobia in a dog, there is this fearful fatalistic apathy. The effects are apparent in many countries. Improvident habits, slovenly systems of agriculture, sluggish methods of commerce, and insecurity of property exist wherever the followers of the Prophet rule or live. A degraded sensualism deprives this life of its grace and refinement; the next of its dignity and sanctity. ...The fact that in Mohammedan law every woman must belong to some man as his absolute property, either as a child, a wife, or a concubine, must delay the final extinction of slavery until the faith of Islam has ceased to be a great power among men. Individual Moslems may show splendid qualities - but the influence of the religion paralyses the social development of those who follow it. No stronger retrograde force exists in the world. Far from being moribund, Mohammedanism is a militant and proselytizing faith. It has already spread throughout Central Africa, raising fearless warriors at every step; and were it not that Christianity is sheltered in the strong arms of science, the science against which it had vainly struggled, the civilisation of modern Europe might fall, as fell the civilisation of ancient Rome."[28]

How refreshingly honest and straightforward is Churchill's language; what contrast with the evasiveness, euphemism and downright dishonesty of the intellectual and moral little men who now control the organs of state and public opinion.

There can be no question that the desire to acquire nubile females (as well as pre-pubescent males) as sex-slaves was an important factor in spurring Muslim princes and potentates throughout the centuries to war against the infidel. Just how important a factor it was shall become obvious

28 Winston Churchill, *The River War*, Vol. 2 (Longmans, Green and Company, London, 1899), pp. 248-50.

in the next chapter and thereafter throughout the remainder of the present volume.

3
PIRACY AND SLAVE-RAIDING

A religious ideology such as Islam, as we have delineated it above, could not but come into conflict with other cultures and faiths. The tendency towards violence and the belief, enshrined in Sharia Law, that the Muslim community was entitled to subsist off the labor of unbelievers, was bound to lead to a parasitical attitude, which can only have encouraged disrespect for the rights and property of subdued infidel communities; which in turn would have fostered a predatory and lawless culture. When we combine this with the Islamic attitude to women, whose "rights" within the Islamic ummah were tenuous to say the least, we have all the ingredients for the appearance of a slave-keeping and slave-taking culture. And this is precisely what we find in Islam from the very beginning.

Islam's outlook with regard to slavery is in striking contrast to that of Christianity, which, from the start, worked to alleviate the conditions of slaves and to eventually abolish the institution. Unlike Islam, Christianity taught that the mistreatment of any human being, whether slave or free, was gravely sinful. In the words of one writer, "The effect of the Church upon the [Roman] Empire may be summed up in the word 'freedom'."[1] And, "Close upon the Church's victory [in the Empire] follows legislation more favorable to the slave than any that had gone before."[2] Whilst it is true that "Constantine did not attempt sudden or wholesale emancipation, which would have been unwise and impossible," he nevertheless immediately "sought to lessen his [the slave's] hardships by measures which with all their inequalities are unique in the statute-book of Rome. ... he forbade cruelty towards slaves in terms which are themselves an indict-

---

1 H. F. Stewart, "Thoughts and Ideas of the Period," in *The Cambridge Medieval History: The Christian Empire*, Vol. 1 (2nd ed. 1936), p. 592.
2 *Ibid.*

ment of existing practice."[3] The Gospel passages of relevance here are too numerous to mention, but we should note in particular the story of the Final Judgment as told in Mark 25: 31-46, where the King (God) tells His servants: "So long as you did it to these, the least of my brethren, you did it to me." It should be remarked also, at this point, that the whole concept of human rights, attributed by many contemporary westerners to the thinkers of the Enlightenment, is rooted in this Gospel concept – a fact admitted by the Enlightenment philosophers themselves. Human rights are a moral as well as a judicial concept. If God will hold each of us accountable for our behavior towards the lowliest members of society, this places the latter on a par, in moral terms, with the highest members of society.

Thus from the start, the lives of slaves improved. This was especially the case with female and younger male slaves, whose function, in the past, was very often to provide sexual pleasure for their owners. This type of transgression was especially frowned upon by Christians. And so, whilst the owning of slaves was not, to begin with, illegal, mistreatment – especially of a sexual nature – was. This view led, inexorably, to the abandonment and abolition of the entire slave system. We find therefore, from the earliest times, many Christian leaders, such as Gregory of Nyssa and John Chrysostom, condemning slavery itself and calling for better treatment for slaves. In fact, tradition describes Pope Clement I (92 - 99), Pope Pius I (roughly 158 - 167) and Pope Callixtus I (217 - 222) as former slaves.

As a friend of the outcast and the poor, Jesus himself had given the lead in this issue, and from the beginning the Church made no account of the social condition of the faithful. Bond and free received the same sacraments. Clerics of servile origin were numerous (St. Jerome, Ep. lxxxii). As the Catholic Encyclopedia states, "So complete—one might almost say, so leveling—was this Christian equality that St. Paul (1 Timothy 6:2), and, later, St. Ignatius (Polyc., iv), are obliged to admonish the slave and the handmaid not to condemn their masters, 'believers like them and sharing in the same benefits.' In giving them a place in religious society, the Church restored to slaves the family and marriage. In Roman, law, neither legitimate marriage, nor regular paternity, nor even impediment to the most unnatural unions had existed for the slave (Digest, XXXVIII, viii, i, (sect) 2; X, 10, (sect) 5)."[4]

The above writer continues:

"Primitive Christianity did not attack slavery directly; but it acted as though slavery did not exist. By inspiring the best of its children with

---

3 *Ibid.*, p. 593.

4 www.newadvent.org/cathen/14036a.htm

this heroic charity, examples of which have been given above, it remotely prepared the way for the abolition of slavery. To reproach the Church of the first ages with not having condemned slavery in principle, and with having tolerated it in fact, is to blame it for not having let loose a frightful revolution, in which, perhaps, all civilization would have perished with Roman society. But to say, with Ciccotti (*Il tramonto della schiavitù* (French trans., 1910) pp. 18, 20), that primitive Christianity had not even 'an embryonic vision' of a society in which there should be no slavery, to say that the Fathers of the Church did not feel 'the horror of slavery,' is to display either strange ignorance or singular unfairness. In St. Gregory of Nyssa (In Ecclesiastem, hom. iv) the most energetic and absolute reprobation of slavery may be found; and again in numerous passages of St. John Chrysostom's discourse we have the picture of a society without slaves - a society composed only of free workers, an ideal portrait of which he traces with the most eloquent insistence (see the texts cited in Allard, *Les esclaves chrétiens,* p. 416-23).

"Under the Christian emperors this tendency [to ameliorate the conditions of slaves], in spite of relapses at certain points, became daily more marked ..."[5]

One by one the Christian emperors abolished the more noxious manifestations of slavery, such as gladiatorial contests; and finally, with the Corpus of laws promulgated by Justinian, in the sixth century, we find a formal condemnation of the institution. The rationale was explained in the *Institutiones*, (Title III, Book 1, paragraph 2) where we read the following: "Slavery is an institution of the law of nations, against nature, subjecting one man to the dominion of another." Again, in Title II, Book 1, paragraph 2, it states "... the law of nations is common to the whole human race; for nations have settled certain things for themselves as occasion and the necessities of human life required. For instance, wars arose and then followed captivity and slavery, which are contrary to the law of nature; for by the law of nature all men from the beginning were born free."

The Justinianic code was introduced into Italy (in 554), from where it was to pass to Western Europe in the twelfth century and become the basis of much European law. It passed also to Eastern Europe where it appeared in Slavic editions, and became the cornerstone of Russian law.

The end result of all this was that by the tenth or even ninth century the Church had effectively ended slavery in Europe. And this is a fact well-known. In the words of Rodney Stark, "... slavery ended in medieval Eu-

---

5 *Ibid.*

rope only because the church extended its sacraments to all slaves and then managed to impose a ban on the enslavement of Christians (and Jews). Within the context of medieval Europe, that prohibition was effectively a rule of universal abolition."[6]

The above statement is conservative. In fact, by the eighth century slavery was well on the way to disappearing throughout Europe; but then, at that point, new life was breathed into it, and the slave-trade experienced a massive revival. The revival was a direct result of the arrival of Islam.

Islamic custom and practice with regard to slavery was always diametrically opposed to that of Christianity: For whereas Christianity acted to emphasize the equality of all before God and to alleviate the conditions of slaves, whose bodies were certainly not open to the sexual exploitation which was frequently the fate of the slave in classical antiquity, Islam had no problem whatsoever with slavery. Indeed, the taking of comely captives seems to have been seen as a legitimate bonus owed to the warriors fighting to spread the faith. Thus for example after the slaughter of the male members of the Jewish tribe of Banu Quraiza Muhammad is said to have taken one of the most beautiful female captives as a concubine; whilst other successful military exploits of the Prophet invariably involved his procuring of slaves. And this behavior is fully sanctioned, for later generations, by the authority of the Qur'an. Thus, we read, in Sura 23: 5-6: "...abstain from sex, except with those joined to them in the marriage bond, or (the captives) whom their right hands possess - for (in their case) they are free from blame." See also Sura 4:24.

Slaves are normally procured through banditry and piracy, a circumstance which would lead us to expect widespread Muslim piracy in the seventh century; and there is in fact much circumstantial evidence to suggest that this was the case. However, according to mainstream scholarship the only convincing documentary evidence for large scale Muslim piracy in the Mediterranean comes in the tenth century – precisely three hundred years afterward.[7]

The evidence for widespread Muslim piracy in the seventh century shall be examined presently. The claim that it only began in the tenth century is based on one factor alone: the lack of frequent reference to it in documentary sources before that time. The latter is cited by Michael McCormick in his voluminous study of trade during the Dark Ages. McCormick looked at reports of 239 travelers between Europe and the Near

---

6 Stark, *op cit.*, p. 28.

7 See *e.g.* Richard Hodges and David Whitehouse, *Mohammed, Charlemagne and the Origins of Europe* (Cornell University Press, New York, 1983), p. 167.

East during the seventh to ninth centuries. As he says; "... the single most remarkable thing about these 239 travelers runs counter to the conventional wisdom. For all the dangers modern medievalists have posited along early medieval shipping routes, very few of our travelers had their voyage interrupted by violence. The dangers of overseas travel were real, but they came as much from shipwreck and, I believe, illness, as predatory violence. Attacks did happen ... Yet there is actually only one incident when pirates seized three western envoys, and they returned home, minus their effects, by the end of the year. ... The relative rarity of such experiences, at least for diplomats and, so far as we can tell, pilgrims, is confirmed by the fact that the ambassadors' capture provoked vociferous protest, and was reckoned without parallel. There were even intimations that it was all a Byzantine plot."[8]

McCormick, and many like-minded historians, has been deceived by too trusting a reliance on documents purporting to come from the three Dark Age centuries. In fact, the latest research, which McCormick seems quite unaware of, suggests that the majority, and perhaps even the great majority, of Dark Age written texts are forgeries.[9] It has now emerged that virtually all of the texts claiming to derive from the mid-seventh to mid-tenth centuries were composed for political or propaganda purposes during the High Middle Ages, usually between the twelfth and fourteenth centuries. Thus it is likely that most, or indeed all, of McCormick's 239 travelers were fictitious characters who were conjured into existence in order to set some form of legal precedent, and as such, their journeys cannot be used as evidence for conditions in Europe and the Mediterranean in the seventh, eighth or ninth centuries.

The actual archaeological evidence, which is of various types, suggests a tidal wave of violence engulfing the Mediterranean world from the early to middle seventh century onwards. And the evidence points overwhelmingly to Islam as the source of this violence.

First and foremost, there is the fact highlighted by Henri Pirenne of the rapid disappearance in the West of luxury imports from the East roughly between the 630s and 660s. These included such things as papyrus

---

8 Michael McCormick, *Origins of the European Economy: Communications and Commerce, AD 300-900* (Cambridge University Press, 2001), pp. 170-1.

9 Matthias Schulz, "Schwindel im Skriptorium. Reliquienkult, erfundene Märtyrer, gefälschte Kaiserurkunden - phantasievolle Kleriker haben im Mittelalter ein gigantisches Betrugswerk in Szene gesetzt. Neuester Forschungsstand: Über 60 Prozent aller Königsdokumente aus der Merowingerzeit wurden von Mönchen getürkt," *Der Spiegel*, 29 (1998).

from Egypt, wine from Gaza and spices from further east. Archaeology has confirmed the disappearance of these things and many others at precisely this time. The termination of trade in such products suggests dangerous conditions along the Mediterranean routes.

Secondly, excavation has noted the rapid abandonment during the early to middle decades of the seventh century of the scattered and undefended farms and villas characteristic of the Roman period and their replacement by new settlements on heavily fortified hilltops – the first medieval castles.[10] This process is particularly characteristic of the Mediterranean shore lands of Europe. The retreat to defended hilltops suggests the threat of sudden attack.

Thirdly, archaeologists have noted the appearance throughout the Mediterranean littoral of a layer of subsoil which formed over the late Roman towns and settlements and which blocked harbors. This stratum, known as the Younger Fill, has caused a great deal of comment and has been explained in a number of ways. The best evidence however suggests that it was caused by the abandonment of the Roman system of land use during the seventh century.[11] Dykes, ditches and drainage channels fell into ruin or not repaired and the soil was washed into the valley floors. This again suggests massive disruption at the time.

Finally, evidence has emerged to show that the trade in slaves between the Arab world and Scandinavia – long believed to have commenced only in the ninth century – actually began in the middle of the seventh. This has been suggested by the discovery of a seventh century Scandinavian settlement at Staraja Ladoga in Russia[12] and by the occurrence of hoards of seventh century Islamic coins throughout Scandinavia and Russia.[13] Since it is well understood that the Viking raids were elicited by the Muslim demand for white-skinned European slaves, this would suggest that the Viking raids, and Muslim slave-trading, actually began in the seventh century rather than the ninth.[14] We shall have more to say about the Vikings

---

10 Hodges and Whitehouse, *op cit.*, pp. 45-6.

11 Claudio Vita-Finzi, *The Mediterranean Valleys* (Cambridge University Press, 1969).

12 See H. Clarke and B. Ambrosiani, *Towns in the Viking Age* (St. Martin's Press, New York, 1995).

13 See Henri Pirenne, *Mohammed and Charlemagne* (London, 1939), pp. 239-40. More recently, in 1999 a hoard found at Gotland in Sweden included "Arabic coins from the Sassanidian dynasty from the mid-7th century ..." Ola Korpås, Per Wideström and Jonas Ström, "The recently found hoards from Spillings farm on Gotland, Sweden," Viking Heritage Magazine, 4 (2000).

14 Trevor-Roper, *op cit.*, pp. 90-2.

and their role in the slave trade presently.

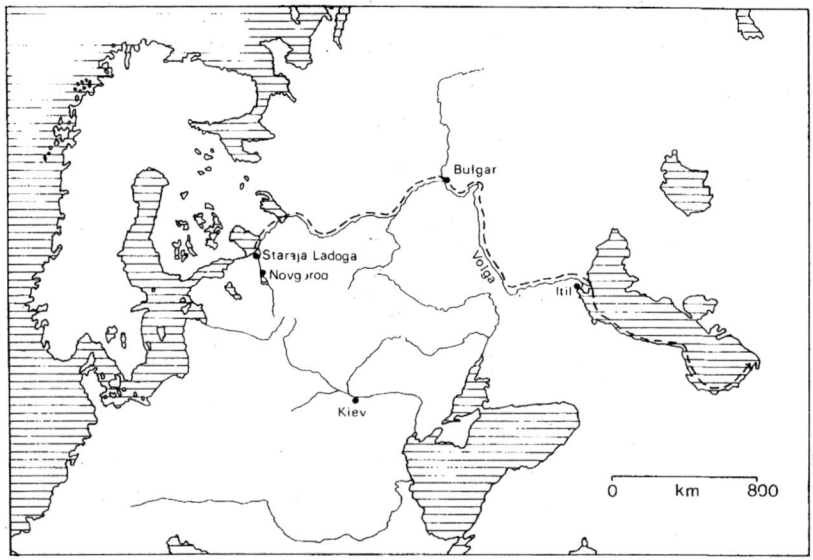

Fig. 3. Viking trade-routes in Russia.
Along the great rivers of Russia the Vikings conveyed thousands of Slavic captives
into the Caliphate during the tenth century.

If all that is not enough, there are in fact many early accounts which seem to hint at widespread violence upon the Mediterranean during the seventh century. These reports usually do not refer specifically to piracy or slave-raiding, but the latter must be strongly suspected, even assumed. The whole of the Levant was scoured by Arab fleets from the 640s onwards, and the very center of the Eastern Empire, Constantinople, was not immune from attack. An Arab army, led by Muawiyah I, laid siege to the city between 674-678. Unable to breach the Theodosian Walls, the Muslims blockaded the metropolis along the Bosporus, but their fleet was eventually destroyed by the famous "Greek Fire" of Kallinikos (Callinicus) the Syrian. Although this was a decisive defeat, within just over half a century the Arabs were back. In 718 an 80,000-strong army led by Maslama, the brother of Caliph Suleiman, crossed the Bosporus from Anatolia to besiege the capital of the Eastern Empire by land, while a massive fleet of Arab war galleys commanded by another Suleiman, estimated to initially number 1,800 ships, sailed into the Sea of Marmara to the south of the city. After some desperate fighting, and the use once again by the defenders of "Greek Fire," this onslaught was also repulsed. Further west, a similar picture emerges. A series of assaults on Sicily in 652, 667 and 720 are recorded; whilst Syracuse was conquered for the first time temporarily in 708. Sardinia was Islamicized in several stages beginning in 711, the very year of the Islamic conquest of Spain. The Italian island of Pantelleria was conquered by the Arabs in 700, and was attacked again a century later, when the Arabs sold the monks they captured into slavery in Spain.[15] In view of these and numerous other reports, we can surely agree with Pirenne's assessment of the situation: "In the Occident ... the coast of the Gulf of Lyons and the Riviera to the mouth of the Tiber, ravaged by war and the [Muslim] pirates, whom the Christians, having no fleet, were powerless to resist, was now merely a solitude and a prey to piracy. The ports and the cities were deserted. The link with the Orient was severed, and there was no communication with the Saracen coasts. There was nothing but death."[16]

Irrespective of the argument about when massive Arab piracy and slave-raiding began, there is no doubt about its reality, in the tenth century at least. By that time the impact of the Arab slave-raiding and trading was felt throughout Europe. Slaves were acquired by the caliphate both from direct raids along the European shores of the Mediterranean and by importing others from northern and eastern Europe. Crete, which was occupied by the Arabs in early tenth century became a major center of this activity. In 904 an Arab pirate force captured the city of Thessalonika – second city of the Byzantine Empire – and carried off 20,000 captives. In the west, fleets of Arab and Moorish pirates brought mayhem to the coasts of France and Italy. Sicily, Corsica and Sardinia, as well as the Balearic Islands, were important bases for the holding and selling of captives, large numbers of whom ended up in Spain, as well as in North Africa and the Middle East. But Arab raiders did not confine themselves to the coastal regions; large raiding parties penetrated far inland – on one occasion at least even as far as Switzerland.

In addition to the Mediterranean theater, the Arabs acquired vast numbers of slaves from northern and eastern Europe, purchased from Viking raiders and their intermediaries. In the words of Michael McCormick:

"The geographic breadth and diversity of networks transporting Europeans into the House of Islam [in the tenth century] is arresting. Beyond Frankish Europe, one famous stream of slaves tramped toward the southeast along the northern arc. They certainly were doing so in the early tenth century, and they may have started arriving earlier, along with the furs and

15 Pirenne, *op cit.*, p. 159.
16 *Ibid.*, p. 184.

Frankish swords, if that is how some of the Slavs of Iraq got there. Many of these slaves are believed to have been collected along the way as tribute or plunder from the Slav tribes whose territories the Rus [eastern Scandinavians] traversed. But at Birka [in Sweden], on the doorstep of the river routes toward Byzantium and the Caliphate, we have already met a troop of Christian slaves from the west. There is no reason to assume that their shipment stopped in the Swedish lakes zone.

"The Black Sea would be notorious for its late medieval slave trade. The large numbers of Byzantine slaves held by the Khazars and freed by Constantine-Cyril and Methodius show that the trade goes back to the ninth century. It was another stream that fed the river of human labor flowing into the Caliphate, for we know that the Khazars exported slaves there. ... Constantinople certainly possessed a slave market, though the details are unknown. Whether or not it played any role in supplying the Caliphate has never been asked.

"In fact, in general terms, we may suspect that, from the southern Mediterranean, the northern shore and its hinterland appeared in the ninth [and tenth] century as a vast arc of slave supply. European slaves certainly reached the Caliphate from Spain, from the Tyrrhenian coast of Italy, and from the Veneto. By 900 they were coming from the northern arc as well. Greece had hitherto been more or less a blank in the map of slave supply. This has occasioned little notice, the more so that slavery is not thought to have been very important inside the Byzantine empire (aside from the salve of captives). Yet Byzantine slaves were not uncommon in the Caliphate: we need look no further than the story of Photius' creature, Leontius, the former Arab slave and would-be ambassador to the west of the patriarch of Alexandria: 'I was born a Byzantine,' as he explained to the 869 Council of Constantinople. We also encounter at Louis the Pious' court the curious case of a eunuch bearing the Slavic name of Drogus, whom Einhard calls a 'Greek.'"[17]

The role of the Vikings in this trade has been well understood for some time, and it has become increasingly evident that the freebooting Scandinavians of the ninth and tenth centuries were first and foremost slave-traders and raiders. Indeed it was the caliphate's demand for European slaves that called forth the Viking phenomenon in the first place. Historian Hugh Trevor-Roper explains how the enormous wealth accumulated by the caliphate in its expansion across Asia and Africa enabled it to purchase what it wanted from Europe. What the Muslims wanted, above all, was "eunuchs and slaves." He continues: "It was one of the functions

---

17 McCormick, *op cit.*, pp. 760-1.

of the Vikings to supply these goods. Half traders, half pirates, they ranged over all northern Europe, and in their ranging, or through the method of piracy, they collected furs and kidnapped human beings. For preference they dealt in heathen Slavs, since Christian States had less compunction in handling a slave-trade in heathen bodies – they could always quote that useful text, Leviticus xxv, 44. So the Vikings fed both Byzantium and the rich new civilization of Islam with the goods which they demanded and for which they could pay. In doing so they penetrated all the coasts and rivers of Europe."[18] In the above quotation Trevor-Roper repeats the erroneous notion, prevalent until the last decades of the twentieth century, that Byzantium somehow escaped the ravages of the Saracens and that in her territory there continued to flourish an intact and prosperous branch of ancient Rome. Constantinople, he imagines, like Damascus, was a wealthy recipient of Russian slaves. Yet by the end of the seventh century, as I have shown in great detail in *Mohammed and Charlemagne Revisited,* the formerly great power of Eastern Rome was little more than an impoverished rump, cut off, just as surely as the West, from the wealth and learning of Asia. If there was a slave trade in Byzantium, it was only as a link in the chain that brought eunuchs and concubines from Russia and eastern Europe in general to Damascus and Baghdad. What little gold Byzantium possessed in the tenth and eleventh centuries was from the taxes levied on Muslim merchants of human flesh, who apparently frequented the Viking-supplied markets of the ancient capital. The gold derived from this infamous trade was known as *aurum arabicum,* Arab gold, or, as humane men preferred to call it, *aurum infelix,* unhappy gold. By the late tenth century large quantities of this Arab gold and silver had found its way to Scandinavia. Viking longboats may even have visited Islamic ports in Iberia, and the occasional Arab traveler returned the compliment by visiting Scandinavia.

Whilst, as Trevor-Roper says, the majority of European slaves delivered to the Arabs were Slavs, by no means all of them were. Indeed, the Vikings plundered all of western Europe to supply the markets of the Caliphate. Dublin, for example, established by the Vikings in Ireland, was a major slave market, with most of the captives bought and sold coming from Ireland and Britain. Nonetheless, there is no doubt that the majority of slaves sold to the Muslims were heathen Slavs, and there is no doubt also that some of the Christian rulers of western Europe were complicit in the trade. Venice, for example, acted as a depot for the collection and sale of Slavic captives from Dalmatia. Marseilles too, it seems, also was active.

---

18 Trevor-Roper, *op cit.,* pp. 90-1.

In the words of Trevor-Roper: "For if the Vikings were the pioneers, the princes of Europe, or some of them, were the middlemen in the new slave-trade. They licensed it and they profited by it, though they left the direct traffic in it to the Jews, who could move most easily across the frontiers of the two societies. We have plenty of evidence of this trade and its routes … Liutprand of Cremona, the ambassador of the West who, in the tenth century, stood agog before the kaleidoscope pageantry of the Byzantine court, tells us that it was the merchants of Verdun who, for the immense profit of the trade, made boys into eunuchs and sold them through Moorish Spain to the rich Moslem world … The trade has left its mark in the languages of both Christendom and Islam. Sclavi, 'Slavs', has formed, in every European language, the word for slaves; and the same word, Sakaliba, has provided the Arabic word for eunuchs."[19]

The coming of Islam, it would appear, signaled a wave of banditry and piracy in the Mediterranean such as had not been seen since before the second century BC, when such activities were severely curtailed by Roman naval power. Indeed, it seems that this new Islamic piracy surpassed in scope and destructiveness anything that had come before.

The fate of captives taken to the caliphate, often passed over without comment in modern studies – which seem to be concerned with little more than economics and wealth creation – was horrific. Generally speaking females were destined for the sex slavery of the harem. Men and young boys, as often as not, were castrated; and in addition were very frequently (if not usually) also the subject of sexual abuse. Several modern authors, to their shame, have spoken approvingly of the "benefits" Europe accrued from this trade. Thus Thomas F. Glick, refuting Pirenne's argument that Muslim piracy on the Mediterranean had isolated Europe culturally, informs us that, "By the tenth century, when the Muslims had taken control of strategically important islands (Crete, Sicily, the Balearics) Islam effectively controlled the Mediterranean, which did not constitute a barrier to trade, but rather a medium whereby all bordering states could participate in a world economy, fertilized by healthy injections of Sudanese gold."[20] One wonders if Glick would extol in similar terms the benefits to Africa of the transatlantic slave trade conducted by the Europeans between the sixteenth and nineteenth centuries. Perhaps the Scandinavians were aesthetically uplifted by the gold and eastern trinkets arriving in their homeland in payment for the human misery they exported to the caliphate, but to

---

19 *Ibid.*, p. 92.

20 Thomas F. Glick, *Islamic and Christian Spain in the Early Middle Ages* (Brill Publishers, New York, 2005), pp. 20-1.

see this as the mechanism by which Europe revived in the eleventh century is of course utter nonsense. Eastern Europe and Scandinavia were civilized in the late tenth century not by Islam but by Christianity. The latter faith discouraged warfare and encouraged agriculture; it brought literacy and schools, and, by forbidding infanticide, produced a great increase in population and expansion of towns.

Fig. 4. A statue of the Buddha from Kashmir, found at Helgö in Sweden.
Such artifacts show the vast extent of Islamic trade and influence during the tenth century.

Muslim freebooting, which almost certainly commenced with the arrival of Islam in the seventh century, was to become a perennial problem. Never again would travel in the Mediterranean be entirely safe. And we should not imagine, as some authors do, that the revival of Europe during the eleventh century and the advance through the Mediterranean of fleets of Crusaders brought Muslim piracy – at least temporarily – to an end. This was emphatically not the case. Large, heavily armed fleets might move safely through the Mediterranean, but it was very different for merchant vessels. These, traveling alone, or in small and lightly-defended groups, were never safe. The Middle Sea in fact remained a very dangerous place for all merchant shipping until the early nineteenth century. And all during these centuries pirates based in North Africa and Egypt, as well as occasionally in Syria, continued to scour the coasts of Christendom for victims. So serious had the problem become by the fourteenth century that the French, at the behest of the Genoese, launched a crusade against the North African pirates based in Mahdia, to the south of Tunis.[21] The campaign was unsuccessful, and the French knights raised the siege after only a few months. Piracy continued unabated.

The long-term effect of this incessant predation, which was the equivalent of the Viking raids in the north lasting a thousand years, was that the Christian populations of southern Europe, especially of Spain and southern Italy, began to take on many of the habits and customs of their Muslim tormentors. These included the keeping and marketing of slaves. It is little surprise then, that the great revival of slave-trading, which marked the European colonization of the Americas, would be driven by freebooters from the Iberian Peninsula, a region whose Christian inhabitants were long familiarized with the customs and practices of Islam. Nor should we forget that, to begin with, the Atlantic slave trade with the Americas was entirely a Spanish and Portuguese enterprise. The nations of northern Europe did not participate. Famously, Queen Elizabeth I of England initially refused to become involved, declaring the trade an outrage against God and humanity. Later however, corrupted no doubt by the example of the Spaniards and Portuguese, she changed tack and began Britain's involvement in the noxious commerce.

The long-term impact of Christian-Islamic coexistence in Spain is a topic I shall return to at a later stage. Suffice for the moment to note that it was immense; and one of the consequences was the continued existence of a substantial slave trade in Christian Spain right throughout the Middle Ages. In the words of Louis Bertrand:

"... it was not without contagion that the Spaniards lived for centuries in contact with a race of men who crucified their enemies and gloried in piling up thousands of severed heads by way of trophies. The cruelty of the Arabs and the Berbers also founded a school in the Peninsula. The ferocity of the emirs and the caliphs who killed their brothers or their sons

---

21 Barbara W. Tuchman, *A Distant Mirror: The Calamitous 14th Century* (Penguin Books, 1978), pp. 458-477.

with their own hands was to be handed on to Pedro the Cruel and Henry of Trastamare, those stranglers under canvas, no better than common assassins."

"For several centuries slavery maintained itself in Christian Spain, as in the Islamic lands. Very certainly, also, it was to the Arabs that the Spaniards owed the intransigence of their fanaticism, the pretension to be, if not the chosen of God, at least the most Catholic nation of Christendom. Philip II, like Abd er Rahman or Al-Mansour, was Defender of the Faith."[22]

---

22 Bertrand *op cit.*, p. 160.

4
ISLAMIC SPAIN

W e have traditionally been told that the first two centuries of the Spanish Emirate, supposedly founded in 756 by Abd' er Rahman I, constituted a veritable Golden Age of Spanish history. And indeed the opulence and prosperity of Spain during these years is contrasted very favorably with the poverty and ignorance of Christian Europe in the same period. The following description of eighth-tenth century Cordoba, written by English historian H. St. L. B. Moss in 1935, may be regarded as fairly typical of the genre: "In Spain ... the foundation of Umayyad power [in 756] ushers in an era of unequalled splendour, which reaches its height in the early part of the tenth century. The great university of Cordova is thronged with students ... while the city itself excites the wonder of visitors from Germany and France. The banks of the Guadalquivir are covered with luxurious villas, and born of the ruler's caprice rises the famous Palace of the Flower, a fantastic city of delights."[1]

The picture Moss paints was derived from medieval Arab chroniclers, who spoke of a city of half a million inhabitants, of three thousand mosques, of one hundred and thirteen thousand houses, and of three hundred public baths - this not even counting the twenty-eight suburbs said to have surrounded the metropolis.

Over the past sixty years intensive efforts have been made to discover this astonishing civilization - to no avail. Try as they might, archaeologists have found hardly anything, hardly a brick or inscription, for the first two centuries of Arab rule in Spain. Between 711 and 911 there is almost nothing, with substantial remains only beginning to appear around 925 or 930. According to the prestigious *Oxford Archaeological Guide*, the first two cen-

1 H. St. L. B. Moss, *The Birth of the Middle Ages; 395-814* (Oxford University Press, 1935), p. 172.

turies of Arab control at Cordoba has revealed, after exhaustive excavations: (a) The south-western portion of the city wall, which is presumed to date from the ninth century; (b) A small bath-complex, of the 9th/10th century; and (c) A part of the Umayyad (8th/9th century) mosque. This is all that can be discovered from two centuries of the history of a city of supposedly half a million people. By way of contrast, consider the fact that Roman London, a city not one-tenth the size that eighth and ninth century Cordoba is said to have been, has yielded dozens of first-class archaeological sites. And even the three locations mentioned in the *Guide* are open to question. The city wall portion is only "presumably" of the ninth century, whilst the part of the mosque attributed to the eighth century is said to have been modeled by Abd' er Rahman I. However, the latter character sounds suspiciously like his namesake and supposed descendant Abd' er Rahman III, of the mid-tenth century, who indisputably made alterations to the mosque (which was originally the Cathedral of Saint Vincent).

Even when real archaeology does appear at Cordoba, from the second quarter of the tenth century onwards, the settlement is absolutely nothing like the conurbation described by the Arab writers. Indeed, at its most opulent, from the late tenth to the late eleventh centuries, the 'metropolis' had, it would seem, no more than about forty thousand inhabitants; and this settlement was built directly upon the Roman and Visigothic city, which had a comparable population.[2] We know that Roman and Visigothic villas, palaces and baths were simply reoccupied by the Muslims, often with very little alteration to the original plan. And when they did build new edifices, the cut-stones, columns and decorative features were more often than not simply plundered from earlier Roman/Visigoth remains. A text of the medieval writer Aben Pascual tells us that there were, in his time, to be seen in Cordoba surviving buildings, "Greek and Roman. ... Statues of silver and gilded bronze within them poured water into receptacles, whence it flowed into ponds and into marble basins excellently carved."

So much for the "vast metropolis" of eighth to tenth century Cordoba. The rest of Spain, which has been investigated with equal vigor, can deliver little else. A couple of settlements here and a few fragments of pottery there, usually of doubtful date and often described as "presumably" ninth

---

2 The estimates provided for Islamic Cordoba's population have gone down bit by bit as archaeological investigation has progressed. Thus for example in the 1970s Angus MacKay could still claim that the tenth century city held 100,000 inhabitants, down 400,000 from Moss's 1930s estimate of half a million, but still about 60,000 more than recent estimates. See Angus MacKay, *Spain in the Middle Ages: From Frontier to Empire, 1000-1500* (Macmillan Books, 1977).

century or such like. Altogether, the *Oxford Guide* lists a total of no more than eleven sites and individual buildings in the whole country (three of which are those from Cordoba mentioned above) which are supposed to date from before the first quarter of the tenth century. These are, in addition to the above three: (a) Balaguer: A fortress whose northern wall, with its square tower, "is almost entirely attributable" to the late-9th century. (p. 73); (b) Fontanarejo: An early Berber settlement, whose ceramic finds date it to "no later than the 9th century." (p. 129); (c) Guardamar: A ribat or fortress mosque, which was completed, according to an inscription, in 944. However, "Elements in its construction have led to its being dated to the 9th cent." (pp. 143-4); (d) Huesca: An Arab fortress which "has been dated to the period around 875." (p. 145); (e) Madrid: Fortress foundations dating to around 870. (p. 172); (f) Merida: A fortress attributed to Abd' er-Rahman II (822-852). (p. 194); (g) Monte Marinet: A Berber settlement with ceramics within "a possible chronological range" from the 7th to the early 9th century. (p. 202); (h) Olmos: An Arab fortress with ceramics "dated to the 9th century" (pp. 216-7).

The above meager list contrasts sharply with the hundreds of sites and structures from the Visigothic epoch - a comparable time-span - mentioned in the same place. (It is impossible to be precise about the Visigothic period, since many sites, such as Reccopolis, contain literally hundreds of individual structures. If we were to enumerate the Visigoth structures by the same criteria as we did the Islamic remains above, then the Visigoth period would reveal not hundreds, but thousands of finds). And it needs to be stressed that most of the above Islamic finds suffer from a problem highlighted by Richard Hodges and David Whitehouse in regard to finds from other parts of Europe during the Dark Ages: an almost unconscious attempt to backdate material of the tenth century into the ninth and eighth in order to have something to assign to the latter epoch. Look for example at the fortress of Guardamar. Although an inscription dates the completion of the edifice to 944, we are told that "elements" in its construction have led to it being dated to the ninth century. What these elements are is not clear; yet we should note that such defended mosques, being essentially fortresses, must have been raised very quickly - certainly in no more than a decade. Why then are we told that this one took fifty or perhaps seventy-five years to complete? Bearing this in mind, we can say that there is scarcely a single undisputed archaeological site attributable to the first two centuries of Islamic rule; whilst there are, to date, hundreds of rich and undisputed sites linked to the Visigothic epoch! The first real Islamic archaeology in Spain occurs during the time of Abd' er Rahman III, in the third or fourth decade of the tenth century (when the Guardamar fortress was completed.

The same poverty of material remains and signs of occupation is found throughout Islamic North Africa between the mid-seventh and mid-tenth centuries, and Richard Hodges and David Whitehouse speak of an Arab-created "Dark Age" in the region during those years.[3]

What could all this mean? Whatever interpretation we might put on it - and there are several possibilities - one thing is very clear: The opulent and refined Islamic civilization which up till now has been placed alongside and contemporary with a dark, ignorant and impoverished Christian Europe of the seventh to tenth centuries, is a myth. When Islamic cities do appear, in the middle of the tenth century, they are very comparable, in terms of size and level of culture, to the contemporary cities of Christian Europe. Our entire understanding of European and Middle Eastern history during the seventh to tenth centuries needs a radical rethink.

So, irrespective of what the textbooks tell us, the real history of Islamic Spain seems to begin in the tenth century. In that epoch, it is true, there existed a powerful Muslim society, one that, in the words of Stephen Runciman, "represented a very real threat to Christendom."[4] Under Abd er-Rahman III (912-961) the followers of Islam found a leader who promised to repeat the successes of the eighth century. His forces battled the Christians to the north, and the boundary between the two religions was marked by the battles he fought. The most decisive of these were at Simancas (939), between Salamanca and Valladolid on the Duoro River, where he was stopped. These were areas that had been overrun by the Muslims two centuries earlier, though the Christians had apparently retaken them in the interim. And this new conquering impulse continued under Al-Mansur (980-1002), whose career was to see Muslim power once again enveloping all of Spain, including the far north. He burned Leon, Barcelona and Santiago de Compostela, and, copying his Muslim predecessors almost three centuries earlier, advanced over the Pyrenees. We are told that in Al-Mansur's time, "Never had the Christians found themselves in such a critical position."[5]

It was the attacks of Al-Mansur that finally roused Christian Europe into undertaking the Reconquista, which commenced with the campaigns of the Norman Baron Roger de Tony in the 1020s.

---

3 Hodges and Whitehouse, *op cit.*, p. 71.

4 Stephen Runciman, *The History of the Crusades Vol. 1* (Cambridge University Press, 1951), p. 89.

5 Bertrand, *op cit.*, p. 57.

It was indeed during this epoch that Islamic Spain experienced its real Golden Age. Never before and never again would the Iberian Caliphate enjoy such wealth, prosperity and splendor. Science and the arts were encouraged and a spirit of tolerance (so we have been told now for many decades), prevailed. It was of this epoch that Robert Briffault wrote: "Under absolute religious tolerance, Christians enjoyed complete freedom. … From all parts of Europe numerous students betook themselves to the great Arab seats of learning in search of the light which only there was to be found. … The famous Gerbert of Aurillac brought from Spain some rudiments of astronomy and mathematics, and taught his astonished students from terrestrial and celestial globes."[6] Furthermore, "The Jews shared under the complete tolerance of Moorish rule in the cultural evolution of the Khalifate; and as they scattered over Europe, especially after the Almohadean conquest, became carriers of that culture to the remotest barbaric lands."[7] The humane and luxurious culture that prevailed in Islamic Iberia began, we are told, to improve the manners of their Christian neighbors to the north:

"The lustre of Moorish elegance circulated unimpeded throughout the [Iberian] peninsula and the South of France. … Rude, illiterate robber-barons gave place to men who delighted in poetry and music, and foregathered in tournaments of song. Loose woolen gowns and leather jerkins were exchanged for close-fitting braided pourpoints, first known as *gipons* (Ar. *jubba*) and mantels of shimmering silk, the fashion for which gradually extended to Northern Europe. Women joined as equals, as in Moorish Spain, in the intellectual interests and artistic tastes of men."[8] Again, "An Arab author, Ibn Jabair, thus describes the appearance of the women of the period: 'They went forth clad in robes of silk the colour of gold, wrapped in elegant mantles, covered with many-coloured veils, shod with gilt shoes, laden with collars, adorned with kohl and perfumed with attar, exactly in the costume of our Muslim ladies.'"[9]

Music and poetry, says Briffault, flourished in the caliphate: "Song and music, which filled the rose-gardens of Andalusia, where every court rang with the sound of romances and quatrains, where poets and musicians formed part of the retinue of every Moorish prince and every Emir, where skill in versification was counted an indispensable accomplishment of every knight and every lady, spread to the adjacent lands of Castile,

6 Briffault, *op cit,*. p. 198.

7 *Ibid.*, p. 199.

8 *Ibid.*, p. 204.

9 *Ibid.*, p. 210.

Catalonia and Provence."[10]

The above lines were written in 1919 and were at the time considered rather controversial. Since then however such opinions have become mainstream and more or less the default mode of thinking.[11] Along with major works published by tenured professors, every year sees the publication of quite literally hundreds of papers in academic publications and the popular media on a similar vein, as well as the appearance of numerous like-minded television documentaries. These are supplemented by countless lectures and symposia expounding an identical viewpoint. As just one example among many we may mention the paper delivered in April, 2010, in London by Dr. Peter Adamson, professor of ancient and medieval philosophy in King's College, London. The title of the lecture, "How the Muslims Saved Civilization: the Reception of Greek Learning in Arabic," speaks for itself.

But a very different picture of the Spanish Caliphate has been painted by other writers. Consider for example the statement of Richard Fletcher, an author very well-disposed to Islam and its culture: "Moorish Spain was not a tolerant and enlightened society even in its most cultivated epoch."[12] Indeed! One would never suspect from the descriptions of Messrs Briffault, Lewis, and many others, that Islamic Spain was the center of a vast slave-trading empire whose rulers believed it was their religious duty to wage ruthless war against their Christian neighbors to the north on an annual or even twice-yearly basis.

There is no question of course that during the tenth and eleventh centuries Islamic Spain was a wealthier society than contemporary Christian states; it could scarcely have been otherwise, as it had inherited the most prosperous and most populous province of the western Roman Empire. This native wealth was further augmented by the plunder of Christian communities, their churches and their lands, from Egypt to France. There is no question either that Islamic Spain maintained a high level of learning at this time. Again, it could scarcely have been otherwise: when Islam first appeared, in the seventh century, Europe was a rural backwater, whereas the House of Islam came into possession of the very centers of high civilization

---

10 *Ibid.*

11 See for example David Levering Lewis, *God's Crucible: Islam and the Making of Europe, 570-1215* (W. W. Norton and Company, New York, 2008); Thomas F. Glick, *Islamic and Christian Spain in the Early Middle Ages* (originally published by Princeton University in 1979); and John Freely, *Light from the East: How the Science of Medieval Islam helped shape the Western World* (2010).

12 Richard Fletcher, Moorish Spain (Weidenfeld and Nicolson, London, 1992), p. 173.

in Persia, Syria, and Egypt, with their universities, academies and libraries. Contemporary Europe was almost devoid of such things. But does that mean that, at the dawn of the High Middle Ages, the attitudes of Islam in the Iberian Peninsula were enlightened and humane? In the above passages Briffault extols the tolerance displayed by the Moorish emirs to Christians; other writers however beg to differ. In an essay entitled "Andalusian Myth, Eurabian Reality," Bat Ye'or and Andrew G. Bostom note that, "Segregated in special quarters, they [Christians] had to wear discriminatory clothing. Subjected to heavy taxes, the Christian peasantry formed a servile class attached to the Arab domains; many abandoned their land and fled to the towns. Harsh reprisals with mutilations and crucifixions would sanction the *Mozarab* (Christian *dhimmis*) calls for help from the Christian kings. Moreover, if one *dhimmi* harmed a Muslim, the whole community would lose its status of protection, leaving it open to pillage, enslavement and arbitrary killing."[13]

But surely, the reader might plead, the Jews at least were well treated by Islam. That is certainly the idea conveyed by Briffault and like-minded writers. Briffault characterizes Islamic rule as one of "complete tolerance" and notes how the Jews "especially after the Almohadean conquest," became "carriers of that [enlightened] culture to the remotest barbaric lands [of Europe]." It is impossible however to read this sentence without the suspicion that its author is involved in deliberate deception. Briffault is well aware of the ferocious persecution of both Jews and Christians which occurred in Spain in the thirteenth century during the rule of the fanatical Almohads. Why else would the Jews leave Spain at this time? Yet he refrains from mentioning the word persecution at all. Furthermore, as an extremely learned man he cannot have been unaware of the fact that the Jews suffered persecution long before the time of either the Almohads or their equally fanatical predecessors, the Almoravids, who caused havoc in the late eleventh and early twelfth centuries. Elsewhere, Briffault mentions the fact that a number of Spanish Jews accompanied William the Conqueror to England in 1066, where they constructed the first stone burgher houses in London.[14] Again, the author cannot have been unaware of the fact that these Jews left Spain in the first place because of an appalling pogrom which had occurred earlier that year in the city of Granada, when about five thousand of them were slaughtered in an unprovoked attack.[15] At this time no pogroms against Jews had ever occurred in Christian Europe. But

13 Bat Ye'or and Andrew Bostom, *loc. cit.*
14 *Ibid.*
15 Bernard Lewis, *The Jews and Islam* (Princeton University Press, 1987), p. 54.

even the massacre of 1066 was not the first: in 1011 a similar slaughter had taken place in the city of Cordoba.[16]

The real story of tenth and eleventh century Cordoban Caliphate is one of wealth and prosperity enjoyed by a privileged few and squalor for the many. An army of slaves and eunuchs, mainly from northern Europe, known as the *Saqaliba*, propped up the administration. Behind the walls of his palace, the caliph might enjoy music and poetry and his numerous wives and concubines might live in some form of caged luxury, but to claim that women enjoyed equality with men is laughable. Equally absurd is the notion that Christians and Jews suffered no discrimination, or that young men from Christian Europe flocked to the Caliphate to partake of their learning. A few Christians such as Gerbert of Aurillac did indeed enter the House of Islam, but they generally did so in disguise and at considerable personal risk. Massacres of Christians, even those living under the caliph and therefore theoretically *dhimmi* or "protected" were frequent, and massacres of Jews, though less frequent, also occurred. The annual raids of the caliph into the Christian lands of the north invariably involved massacres and slave-raiding.

And if things were grim under the caliphs, they became even worse under the Almoravids and Almohads during the twelfth and thirteenth centuries.

The Almoravids were a fanatical dynasty, or more accurately warrior confraternity, of North African Berber origin, who crossed over to Iberia in 1086 at the request of the Muslim princes of Al-Andalus, to defend their territories from the encroachment of Alfonso VI, King of León and Castile. They were "puritans, ascetics, zealots. They saw their role as one of purifying religious observance by reimposition where necessary of the strictest canons of Islamic orthodoxy."[17] Under their leader Ibn Yusuf (Yusuf ibn Rashfin), the Berbers inflicted a crushing defeat upon the Christians at the Battle of az-Zallaqah (or Sagrajas). They were prevented from following this victory up by trouble in Africa, which Ibn Yusuf chose to settle in person. In 1090 he returned to Iberia and immediately attacked his Spanish Muslims allies, whom he accused of moral laxity and religious indifference. Some were killed, others sent as prisoners to North Africa. It should be noted that Ibn Yusuf's actions in this regard were fully supported by Muslim religious leaders in Spain and by others in the east, most notably, al-Ghazali in Persia and al-Tartushi in Egypt, who was himself an Iberian by birth. These clerics issued a fatwa declaring that Ibn Yusuf

16 *Ibid.*
17 Fletcher, *op cit.*, p. 108.

was of sound morals and had the right to dethrone the Spanish princes. By 1094, the Almoravids had annexed most of the major Muslim principalities (*taifas*), with the exception of the one at Saragossa. They did not however reconquer much territory from the Christian kingdoms, except that of Valencia (the Cid's domain), though they seem to have hindered the progress of the Spanish Reconquista by uniting al-Andalus.

It goes without saying that a man like Ibn Yusuf, who would attack his co-religionists for being lax in the faith, would be ruthless against those of other faiths. Historians of an earlier generation told this story quite unadorned by euphemism. As might be expected however modern academics have been somewhat less straightforward, choosing to disguise barbarities under the most prosaic understatement. Consider for example the words of Robert Fletcher: "We hear of the destruction of a church at Granada by the Almoravids in 1099. A stray surviving papal letter of 1117 addressed to the Christian community of Málaga reveals that its bishop, Julian, had been imprisoned by the Almoravid authorities for the previous seven years. In the winter of 1125-26 Alfonso el Batallador of Aragon led a train down the Levantine coastline to the region of Granada and persuaded large numbers of the Christian inhabitants to return with him to Aragon to escape Almoravid persecution – and to colonise the lands captured by the Aragonese in the Ebro valley. By way of reprisal the Almoravid amir Ali, the son of Yusuf, in 1126 forcibly removed many Andalusi Christians to Morocco."[18]

The impression conveyed by the above passage is that Almoravid persecution was not really so bad. The destruction of a single church, plus the imprisonment of a single bishop, doesn't seem so severe by the standards of the time (or of any time for that matter). Even the deportation of the Christians of Andalusia was only a "reprisal" for an earlier Christian raid. Observe however how the same series of events is reported by Louis Bertrand, writing in 1945, before the epoch of political correctness: "From the outset of the Almoravid invasion the destruction of Christian churches had begun. Among them was destroyed a very old and very curious basilica in the neighbourhood of Granada, the church of Gudila. The *faquis* commenced to persecute the Christian *Mozarabs* [Christians under Muslim rule] so intolerably that they begged the King of Aragón, Alfonso the Warrior, to come and deliver them. The Aragonese did not succeed in taking Granada. When they retreated, the *faquis* avenged themselves on the *Mozarabs* in the most merciless fashion.

"Already ten thousand of them had been compelled to emigrate into

18 *Ibid.*, p. 112.

the territory of Alfonso to escape their enemies' repression. The remainder were deprived of their property, imprisoned, or put to death. Many of them were deported to Africa. They were established in the neighbourhood of Salé and Meknes, where oppression of all kinds compelled them to embrace Islam. Ten years later there was a fresh expulsion. The Christians were again deported to Morocco *en masse*."[19]

In spite of their initial successes and their brutality the Almoravids failed to stop the progress of the Christian Reconquista. Christian Europe, and along with it Spain, was experiencing, from the early eleventh century, a great expansion in population, and therefore in wealth. The Islamic world, by contrast, seemed to be either stagnant or even declining demographically. The resources of the Christians were greater, and Al-Andalus soon found itself under renewed pressure from the north. For this reason, by the mid-twelfth century, the Spanish Muslims again called in the support of their co-religionists across the Straits of Gibraltar; and once again the call was answered by a dynasty of fanatical bigots who were to impose a reign of terror upon both their Spanish Muslim allies and, even moreso, the Christians and Jews of the region.

The Almohads, also from North Africa, arrived in Spain in several waves, beginning in 1146. By 1173 they had taken control of all Muslim territories in Spain and gained several victories over the Christian powers. From the very start of their operations in Iberia they began an intense persecution of the Christians still under Muslim rule. There were indeed far fewer of these than there had been, owing to the mass deportations carried out by the Almoravids, but there still existed a rather numerous population of infidels in the region whom they could target: the Jews. Reports from the period tell how, after an initial seven-month period of grace, the Almohads killed or forcefully converted entire Jewish communities in each new city they conquered until "there was no Jew left from Silves to Mahdia."[20] Cases of mass martyrdom of Jews who refused to convert to Islam are also reported. Abraham Ibn Ezra (1089–1164), who himself fled the persecutions of the Almohads, composed an elegy mourning the destruction of many Jewish communities throughout Spain and the Maghreb under the Almohads.[21] Many Jews fled from territories ruled by the Almohads

---

19 Bertrand, *op cit.*, pp. 126-7.

20 See Amira K. Bennison and Maria Angeles Gallego, "Jewish Trading in Fez on the Eve of the Almohad Conquest," (2008) at http://digital.csic.es/bitstream/10261/39129/1/Almohad.MEAH.pdf

21 Ross Brann, *Power in the Portrayal: Representations of Jews and Muslims in Eleventh- and Twelfth-Century Islamic Spain* (Princeton University Press, 2009), pp. 121-2.

to Christian lands, and others, like the family of Maimonides, fled east to more tolerant Muslim lands It was during this epoch, as Ibn Warraq notes, that the Jews of Spain seem to have invented the myth of a golden age of tolerance during the earlier Caliphate. "The Golden Age," he says, "also turns out to be a myth, invented, ironically, by the Jews themselves. The myth may well have originated as early as the twelfth century, when Abraham Ibn Daud in his *Sefer ha-Qabbalah* contrasted an idealised period of tolerance of the salons of Toledo in contrast to the contemporary barbarism of the Berber [Almohad] dynasty. But the myth took a firm grip on the imagination of the Jews in the nineteenth century thanks to the bibliographer Moritz Steinschneider and historian Heinrich Graetz, and perhaps the influence of Benjamin Disraeli's novel *Coningsby*, published in 1844. Here is a passage from the latter novel giving a romantic picture of Muslim Spain, '...that fair and unrivaled civilization in which the children of Ishmael [the Arabs] rewarded the children of Israel with equal rights and privileges with themselves. During these halcyon centuries, it is difficult to distinguish the followers of Moses from the votary of Mohammed. Both alike built palaces, gardens and fountains; filled equally the highest offices of state, competed in an extensive and enlightened commerce, rivaled each other in renowned universities.' Against a background of a rise in the pseudo-scientific racism of the nineteenth century, Jane Gerber has observed that Jewish historians looked to Islam '... for support, seeking real or imagined allies and models of tolerance in the East. The cult of a powerful, dazzling and brilliant Andalusia in the midst of an ignorant and intolerant Europe formed an important component in these contemporary intellectual currents.' But Gerber concludes her sober assessment of the Golden Age Myth with these reflections, 'The aristocratic bearing of a select class of courtiers and poets, however, should not blind us to the reality that this tightly knit circle of leaders and aspirants to power was neither the whole of Spanish Jewish history nor of Spanish Jewish society. Their gilded moments of the tenth and eleventh century are but a brief chapter in a longer saga. No doubt, Ibn Daud's polemic provided consolation and inspiration to a crisis-ridden twelfth century elite, just as the golden age imagery could comfort dejected exiles after 1492. It suited the needs of nineteenth century advocates of Jewish emancipation in Europe or the twentieth century contestants in the ongoing debate over Palestine....The history of the Jews in Muslim lands, especially Muslim Spain, needs to be studied on its own terms, without myth or countermyth.'"[22]

---

22 Ibn Warraq, "The Mythistory of the Crusades," *New English Review* (October, 2013) at www.newenglishreview.org

5

THE CRUSADES

The First Crusade commenced in 1096 when Byzantine Emperor Alexius Comnenus appealed to the Pope and princes of Europe for assistance against the Seljuk Turks who had recently overrun the whole of Asia Minor and now threatened Constantinople itself. The fall of Constantinople must have placed the safety of Europe in jeopardy.

These are the bare facts, but one would never guess it if guided by much of what currently passes for scholarly comment on the topic: for the Crusades loom large in the current "clash of civilizations" debate, and they are invariably held up as a reproach to Europe and to Christianity. In the view of the greater part of the media and, sadly, much of academia, the Crusades constituted little more than an unprovoked attack by a barbarous Europe against a quiescent and cultured Islamic world. According to one frequently encountered opinion, the campaigns directed against the east were a convenient outlet for the aggressive energies of Europe's warrior-class, who were now "freed up" from their earlier occupation of fighting Vikings and Magyars. Consider for example the following:

"At the beginning of the eleventh century the Moslems held the southern two thirds of Spain, the Balearic Islands, Corsica, Sardinia, Sicily, the entire coast of North Africa, Palestine, and part of Syria. Religious enthusiasm and political and economic ambition moved the men of Western Europe to attack these Moslem lands. The feudal class, especially its cadets, or younger sons, saw unlimited opportunities to acquire both spiritual and temporal rewards, salvation and rich fiefs, through engaging in their favorite occupation [war]. The papacy may have had more complicated motives. Certainly the popes desired to spread the Christian faith and their own authority, but it is quite possible that they thought it an excellent idea to turn the turbulent belligerency of the feudal class into worthy channels. Finally, the rising Italian towns, especially Genoa and Pisa, were anxious to free themselves from the continuous danger of Moslem naval raids and to conduct their trade peacefully along the shores of the western Mediterranean."[1]

The above passage, from an extremely influential twentieth century historian, refers to conflicts earlier than the (official) First Crusade, which were almost without exception defensive operations to check Muslim aggression; yet the author makes no mention of any such aggression save at the end, where he concedes that the Genoese and Pisans may have wished to navigate around the Mediterranean without being intercepted by slave-raiding pirates. The basic premise, however, is of a somewhat fanatical and without question violent Christendom seeking to extend its boundaries at the expense of its peace-loving Muslim neighbors.

Whilst agreeing that the Crusaders were barbarous in comparison with their opponents, other historians have tried to present the whole phenomenon of the Crusades as a kind of prototype European colonialism; the first manifestation of a phenomenon which would eventually lead to the colonization of the Americas and the Atlantic slave trade. All of these ideas, routinely encountered these days on television and in newspapers, as well as on occasion in textbooks, are suffused with the spirit of guilt which so characterizes modern western thinking. Even more recent authors who profess to see beyond this tend fall into the same trap – often disguising their blatantly anti-European bias as simple impartiality. Take for example the following comment of Thomas Asbridge, whose 2010 book, *The Crusades*, is widely regarded as an authoritative and even-handed study:

"In fact, the crusades were just one expression of a much wider drive to rejuvenate western Christendom, championed by Rome from the mid-eleventh century onwards in the so-called 'Reform movement'. As far as the papacy was concerned, any failings within the Church were just the symptoms of a deeper malaise: the corrupting influence of the secular world, long enshrined by the links between clergymen and lay rulers. And the only way to break the stranglehold enjoyed by emperors and kings over the Church was for the Pope finally to realise his God-given right to supreme authority. The most vocal and extreme proponent of these views was Pope Gregory VII (1073-85). Gregory ardently believed that he had been set on Earth to transform Christendom by seizing absolute control of Latin ecclesiastical affairs. In pursuit of this ambition, he was willing to embrace almost any available means – even the potential use of violence,

---

1 Painter, *op cit.*, p. 191.

enacted by papal servants whom he called 'soldiers of Christ'. Although Gregory went too far, too fast and ended his pontificate in ignominious exile in southern Italy, his bold strides did much to advance the twinned causes of reform and papal empowerment, establishing a platform from which his successor (and former adviser), Pope Urban II (1088-99), could instigate the First Crusade."[2]

So, for Asbridge, the Crusades were a means by which the popes could bolster their own spiritual and temporal authority. It is notable that Asbridge first mentions the request for assistance made by the Byzantine emperor on page 34. An even more egregious and sadly predictable take on the issue is expressed in David Levering Lewis' *God's Crucible: Islam and the making of Europe, 570-1215* (2006). Lewis' view of the Crusades and of the Crusaders is predicated upon the belief – still almost universally held – that for centuries Europe was a semi-literate and semi-savage backwater, a cultural graveyard mired in poverty, brutality and illiteracy. For Lewis, as for so many others, the "energies" of Europe's warrior-class were simply directed by the papacy away from internal destruction onto the convenient targets of the Islamic world. This is the line of reasoning taken too by Marcus Bull in his examination of the origins of the Crusades in *The Oxford History of the Crusades*. In an article of almost ten thousand words, Bull fails to consider the Muslim threat at all. Indeed he mentions it only to dismiss it:

"The perspective of a Mediterranean-wide struggle [between Islam and Christianity] was visible only to those institutions, in particular the papacy, which had the intelligence networks, grasp of geography, and sense of long historical tradition to take a broad overview of Christendom and its threatened predicament, real or supposed. This is a point which needs to be emphasized because the terminology of the crusades is often applied inaccurately to all the occasions in the decades before 1095 when Christians and Muslims found themselves coming to blows. An idea which underpins the imprecise usage is that the First Crusade was the last in, and the culmination of, a series of wars in the eleventh century which had been crusading in character, effectively 'trial runs' which had introduced Europeans to the essential features of the crusade. This is an untenable view."[3]

With what justification, we might ask, does Bull dissociate the earlier Christian-Muslim conflicts of the eleventh century in Spain, Sicily, and

---

2 Thomas Asbridge, *The Crusades: The War for the Holy Land* (Simon and Schuster, London, 2010), p. 10.

3 Marcus Bull, "Origins," in Jonathan Riley-Smith (ed.) *The Oxford History of the Crusades*, p. 19.

Anatolia from the First Crusade? The answer can hardly be described as convincing. "There is plenty of evidence," he says, "to suggest that people regarded Pope Urban II's crusade appeal of 1095-6 as something of a shock to the communal system: it was felt to be effective precisely because it was different from anything attempted before."[4] Of course it was different: the Pope had called a meeting of all the potentates and prelates of Europe to urge the assembly of a mighty force to march to the relief of Constantinople and perhaps eventually to retake the Holy Land. It was new because of its scale and its ambition. But to thus dismiss the connection with what went before in Spain and Sicily – and Anatolia – is ridiculous. Such a statement can only derive from a mindset which somehow has to see the crusaders as the aggressors and to thereby detach them from the legitimate defensive wars which Christians had been fighting in Spain and throughout the Mediterranean in the decades immediately preceding 1095.

As Ibn Warraq shows in his recently-published *Sir Walter Scott's Crusades and other Fantasies*, whilst it is possible to discern several strands of thought which ultimately arrived at this anti-crusader consensus, all of these are predicated upon a generally negative view of Christianity, particularly Catholic Christianity, which first appeared during the Enlightenment. Modern scholars, such as those quoted above, who may often be unaware of the "Christianophobic" origin of their own ideas, nonetheless usually concede that the idea of "holy war" was essentially alien to the Christian faith, and that a great deal of philosophical soul-searching was necessary to justify spilling blood in the name of Christ. Nonetheless, they tend to argue that primitive Christianity's pacifism was only apparent, and that well before the appearance of Islam the Christians had already become inured to the idea of religious war. They cite, for example, Saint Augustine's defense of the "just war" concept, and they point to the wars waged by Christian kings against pagan Vikings and Magyars as examples of Christian "Holy War" preceding the Crusades.

Yet these arguments are strained: There is plenty of evidence to suggest that prior to the clash with Islam Christians had no concept of divinely-sanctioned violence. There can be no doubt, however, that the centuries of warfare against barbarians to the north and east which followed the collapse of the Western Roman Empire in 476 had produced a more "muscular" Christianity than that which prevailed in the early Christian centuries. We know that the arrival in Western Europe of the Germanic peoples in the fifth and sixth centuries had seen the appearance of a new ruling class thoroughly steeped in warrior culture. This had, over the next two or

---

4 *Ibid.*

three centuries, been modified by the Christian ethos, though somewhat more than a trace of the Germanic warrior ideal survived in the medieval institution of the knight. The knight represented a mildly Christianized version of the Teutonic warrior-hero. It is true too that the martial ethos of Europe's ruling Germanic elite can only have been further reinforced by the desperate struggle which raged throughout the tenth century against Vikings in the north, Hungarians in the east and Muslims in the south. This unsettled period saw the beginning of castle-building: by the middle years of the tenth century fortified hilltop strongholds, built initially of wood and later of stone, began to spring up all over the continent.[5] It was an age of uncertainty and violence, and such conditions naturally give rise to a more warlike mindset. Huge numbers of men were at any given time in arms. The end of hostilities against Vikings and Magyars in the eleventh century would certainly not have immediately produced universal pacifism. Huge numbers of men remained in arms, and the energies of these warriors, it is claimed, were often misplaced fighting one another and terrorizing the local population. The Church tried to stem this violence with the so-called Peace and Truce of God movements. These were partially successful, but trained soldiers always sought an outlet for their skills, which were, with the end of the Magyar and Viking threats, becoming scarcer in northern Europe. Spain and southern Italy provided important exceptions, where the wars against the Muslims continued unabated and with increasing ferocity. All the major battles between Christians and Muslims in Spain during the eleventh century involved large numbers of knights and foot-soldiers from all over western Europe, but especially from France and Germany. At the taking of Toledo, for example, the Burgundians played a pivotal role.[6]

It cannot be emphasized too strongly however that, unlike the wars against the Vikings and Magyars, these battles against Muslims were specifically about religion. They had been thus defined by the Muslims themselves. Their conquests all over North Africa and Asia had been motivated specifically to spread the faith. It is perfectly understandable that in such circumstances Christians would begin to think in similar terms; and it is becoming increasingly widely accepted amongst professional historians that the Christians of this time actually derived the concept of "Holy War"

---

5 Strangely, however, castle-building began in southern Europe along the shores of the Mediterranean – evidently to protect against piratical Muslim raids – three centuries earlier, in the middle of the seventh century. See Hodges and Whitehouse, *op cit.*, pp. 44-8.

6 Trevor-Roper, *op cit.*, p. 119.

from Islam. Thus for example in 2007 Bernard Lewis made the following unusually frank comment:

"We are now expected to believe that the Crusades were an unwarranted act of aggression against a peaceful Muslim world. Hardly. The first call for a crusade occurred in 846 CE, when an Arab expedition to Sicily sailed up the Tiber and sacked St Peter's in Rome. A synod in France issued an appeal to Christian sovereigns to rally against 'the enemies of Christ,' and the pope, Leo IV, offered a heavenly reward to those who died fighting the Muslims. A century and a half and many battles later, in 1096, the Crusaders actually arrived in the Middle East. The Crusades were a late, limited, and unsuccessful imitation of the *jihad* – an attempt to recover by holy war what was lost by holy war. It failed, and it was not followed up."[7]

Whether or not we agree with Lewis, there is no question whatsoever that the Crusades were primarily defensive, and attempts to portray the Crusaders as the aggressors are completely unjustified. Recent works by Thomas F. Madden have taken politically correct historians to task over the issue in a spirited way, and he has pointed out that the prevailing view of the Crusaders as early European colonialists (barbarous colonialists) is one that owes far more to modern American and European anti-colonialist prejudices than to the facts of history. He too emphasizes the defensive nature of the Crusades and is extremely critical of those historians who fail to see this.[8]

War was regulated by the church, and Medieval conflicts, at least within Europe, were not nearly as violent as many imagine. As Sidney Painter notes; "Even when kings and feudal princes fought supposedly serious wars in the early Middle Ages, they were not bloody. At the great and decisive battle of Lincoln in 1217, where some 600 knights on one side fought 800 on the other, only one knight was killed, and everyone was horrified at the unfortunate accident."[9]

There is no question that the Medieval custom of ransoming important hostages provided an economic motive for this remarkable unwillingness to use lethal force; but it is equally clear that the idea of chivalry, with its strongly Christian overtones, exerted a powerful moderating influence. Nor should we forget that during the centuries which followed the First Crusade, when we might imagine Christians in Europe to have become

---

7 Bernard Lewis, "2007 Irving Kristol Lecture," delivered to the American Enterprise Institute, Washington, DC. (March 7, 2007).

8 See Madden's "Crusade Propaganda: The Abuse of Christianity's Holy Wars," and *A Concise History of the Crusades* (Rowman and Littlefield, Maryland, 1999).

9 *Ibid.*, p. 119.

thoroughly accustomed to the idea of fighting and killing for Christ, there is much evidence to show that this did not happen. The idea of violence in the name of Christ was, in the words of Jonathan Riley-Smith, "without precedent" when it was first promoted in the eleventh century.[10] "So radical was the notion of devotional war," says Riley-Smith, "that it is surprising that there seem to have been no protests from senior churchmen."[11] Be that as it may, Christians could never be fully at ease with the idea, and enthusiasm for crusading soon waned. Riley-Smith notes that, following the success of the First Crusade, the supply of new recruits immediately dried up, even among those groups and families who had been its strongest supporters. These reverted, instead, to the traditional military pilgrimage to the Holy Land.[12] We should note too that statements like that of the English Franciscan Roger Bacon in the 1260s, who criticized the very idea of crusading, arguing that such military activities impeded efforts to peacefully convert Muslims.[13] Contrast this with the attitude in Islam, where all warriors who died in the Jihad were "martyrs" and guaranteed a place in Paradise. And the contrast is seen very clearly in the words of Gregory Palamas, an Orthodox metropolitan, who was a captive of the Turks in 1354: " ... these infamous people, hated by God and infamous, boast of having got the better of the Romans [Byzantines] by their love of God. ... They live by the bow, the sword, debauchery, finding pleasure in taking slaves, devoting themselves to murder, pillage, spoil ... and not only do they commit these crimes, but even − what an aberration − they believe that God approves of them."[14]

It is beyond question too that the First Crusade came as the culmination of over a century of desperate struggle against Muslims in Spain, Sicily and Asia Minor. To argue that the First Crusade was a completely new departure and unrelated to these earlier events, as do Bull and Asbridge, is unjustified. Whilst the Reconquista which had raged in Spain since the 1020s was not called "holy war," it was clearly in direct line of descent to the Crusades. The official religious sanction for a Christian "holy war" came eventually in 1063, when Pope Alexander II gave his blessing to the

10 Jonathan Riley-Smith, "The State of Mind of Crusaders to the East: 1095-1300," in Jonathan Riley-Smith (ed.) *Oxford History of the Crusades*, p. 79.

11 *Ibid.*, p. 78.

12 *Ibid.*, pp. 80-2.

13 Alan Forey, "The Military Orders, 1120-1312," in Jonathan Riley-Smith (ed.) *op cit.*, p. 205.

14 Robert Irwin, "Islam and the Crusades: 1096-1699," in Jonathan Riley-Smith (ed.) *Oxford History of the Crusades*, pp. 251.

warriors of the Reconquista in their struggle with the Moors, granting both a papal standard (*vexillum sancti Petri*) and an indulgence to those who fell in battle.

Yet it cannot be stressed to often that there always remained a deep unease within Christendom about the idea. The concept of fighting – and killing – for Christ was something quite new. In Runciman's words, "The Christian citizen had a fundamental problem to face: is he entitled to fight for his country? His religion is a religion of peace; and war means slaughter and destruction. The earlier Christian Fathers had no doubts. To them war was wholesale murder."[15] Runciman goes on to note that the rise of the Germanic kingdoms brought with it the glamorization of the warrior-hero and the knight, against which "the church could do little." Nonetheless, there was still resistance, especially in the East. Saint Basil, for example, maintained that anyone guilty of killing in war should refrain for three years from taking communion as a sign of repentance.[16] In fact, as Runciman notes, the Byzantine soldier was not treated as a murderer; but his profession brought him no glamor. "Byzantine history was remarkably free of wars of aggression. ... Justinian's campaigns had been undertaken to liberate Romans from heretic barbarian governors, Basil II's against the Bulgars to recover imperial provinces and to remove a danger that menaced Constantinople. Peaceful methods were always preferable, even if they involved tortuous diplomacy or the payment of money. ... The princess Anna Comnena, one of the most typical of Byzantines, makes it clear in her history that, deep as was her interest in military questions and much as she appreciated her father's success in battle, she considered war a shameful thing, and a last resort when all else had failed, indeed in itself a confession of failure."[17]

The western point of view was less enlightened, and there is no question that Western Christendom, after having had to absorb the warrior ideals of the Goths, Franks and Vandals, and having then to fight a life-and-death struggle against Muslims, Vikings and Magyars, was more amenable to the idea of fighting for Christ. In Runciman's words, "the military society that had emerged in the West out of the barbarian invasions inevitably sought to justify its habitual pastime. The code of chivalry that was developing, supported by popular epics, gave prestige to the military hero; and the pacifist acquired a disrepute from which he has never recovered.

15 Runciman, *op cit.*, p. 83.

16 J. P. Migne, *Patrologiae Graeco-Latina, Part II of Patrologiae Cursus Completus,* (Paris, 1857-66), Letter no. 188, Vol. XXXII, col. 681.

17 Runciman, *op cit.*, pp. 83-4.

Against this sentiment the Church could do little."[18]

We might conclude then, regarding the question of the origins of the Christian Holy War idea, that it derived in part from the Muslims and in part from the martial culture which characterized western Europe during the tenth and eleventh centuries. But that is not to say that the Europeans were the aggressors, or that Crusading represented a violent outpouring of Christian fanaticism: on the contrary, irrespective of what theological justification was found for "Holy War," the fact is that the Crusades were entirely defensive in nature and scope. In the twenty years before the First Crusade, Christendom had lost the whole of Anatolia, an area greater than France, and a region right on the doorstep of Europe. These wars were characterized by appalling atrocities, as were almost all the wars involving Islamic armies; and they sent shock-waves throughout Europe. In 1050 the Seljuk leader Togrul Beg, in conformity with the precepts of Sunni Islam, undertook *jihad* against the Christians of Anatolia, who had thus far resisted the power of the Caliphs. We are told that 130,000 Christians died in the war, which resulted in the complete subjugation of Armenia, a country which at that time comprised a large portion of the land we now call Turkey. Togrul Beg's death in 1063 was viewed by the Christians of the region as a chance for freedom, and Armenia reasserted its independence. Yet Togrul Beg's successor, his nephew Alp Arslan, was to prove as aggressive and relentless as himself. Immediately upon being proclaimed sultan, Alp Arslan renewed hostilities with the infidels. In 1064 the old Armenian capital of Ani was destroyed; and the prince of Kars, the last independent Armenian ruler, "gladly handed over his lands to the [Byzantine] Emperor in return for estates in the Taurus mountains. Large numbers of Armenians accompanied him to his new home."[19] In the above sentence Steven Runciman describes a human catastrophe: the transplantation of virtually the entire Armenian nation hundreds of miles to the south and west.

But, in accordance with the holy duty of *jihad*, the Turkish attacks continued. From 1065 onwards the great frontier-fortress of Edessa was assaulted yearly. In 1066 the Seljuks occupied the pass of the Amanus Mountains, and next spring they sacked the Cappadocian metropolis of Caesarea. Next winter the Byzantine armies were defeated at Melitene and Sebastea. These victories gave Alp Arslan control of all Armenia, and a year later he raided far into the Empire, to Neocaesarea and Amorium in 1068, to Iconium in 1069, and in 1070 to Chonae, near the Aegean coast.

---

18 *Ibid.*, p. 84.
19 *Ibid.*, p. 61.

These events make it perfectly clear that the Turks now threatened all the of the Eastern Empire's Asiatic possessions, with the position of Constantinople herself increasingly insecure. The imperial government was forced to take action. Constantine X, whose neglect of the army was largely responsible for the catastrophes which now overwhelmed the Byzantine world, had died in 1067, leaving a young son, Michael VII under the regency of the Empress-mother Eudocia. Next year Eudocia married the commander-in-chief, Romanus Diogenes, who was raised to the throne. Romanus was a distinguished soldier and a sincere patriot, who saw that the safety of the Empire depended on the rebuilding of the army and ultimately the reconquest of Armenia.[20] Within four months of his accession, the new emperor had gathered together a large but unreliable force, with which he set out to meet the foe. "In three laborious campaigns," writes Gibbon, "the Turks were driven beyond the Euphrates; in the fourth, and last, Romanus undertook the deliverance of Armenia."[21] Here however, at the seminal battle of Manzikert (1071), he was defeated and captured and all of Anatolia was irretrievably lost.

Any honest reading of these events leaves us in no doubt whatsoever that the aggressor was Alp Arslan and his Turks, and that Romanus Diogenes' march into Armenia was a last-ditch counter-attack by the Byzantines aimed at protecting his Armenian allies and securing the Empire's Asiatic possessions. Yet observe how Manzikert is described in the recently-published *Chambers Dictionary of World History*: "The Byzantine Emperor, Romanus IV Diogenes (1068/71), tried to extend his empire into Armenia but was defeated at Manzikert near Lake Van by the Seljuk Turks under Alp Arslan (1063/72), who then launched a full-scale invasion of Anatolia."[22]

We see in the above a graphic example of the distortion (and, we might say, disinformation) produced by modern academia's now default political correctness, where the Christian or European must invariably be presented as the villain and aggressor.

Alp Arslan was killed a year later, and the conquest of western Asia Minor, along the Aegean coast, virtually all that was left of Byzantium's Asiatic possessions, was completed by his son Malek Shah (1074 – 1084). These conquests left the Turks in possession of the fortress of Nicaea, on the southern shore of the Sea of Marmara, and the survival of Constantinople in question.

---

20 *Ibid.*

21 Gibbon, Chapter 57.

22 Bruce Lenman (ed.) *Chambers Dictionary of World History* (London, 2000), p. 585.

These then are the major political events which prefigured the First Crusade. Within a space of thirty-five years the Turks had seized control of Christian territories larger than the entire area of France, and they now stood poised on the very doorstep of Europe. We are accustomed to think of the Crusades as first and foremost an attempt by Christians to retake the Holy Land and Jerusalem; but this is a mistake. The Emperor Alexius Comnenus now made his famous plea to the Pope, not to free Jerusalem, but to drive the Turks from his door, to liberate the huge Christian territories in Asia Minor that had so recently been devastated and annexed by the followers of the crescent. It is true, of course, that the Turks, who had also assumed control of Syria/Palestine, now imposed a barbarous regime in that region; and that the sufferings of Christian pilgrims as well as native Christian populations in the area, described so vividly by Peter the Hermit and others, provided a powerful emotional impetus to the Crusading movement among ordinary Europeans; but the relief of pilgrims was not – to begin with at least – the primary goal of the Crusaders. Nonetheless, the barbarous nature of the Turkish actions in Palestine was a microcosm of their behavior throughout the Christian regions which they conquered. The nature of their rule in the Near East is described thus by Gibbon in his usual vivid manner:

"The Oriental Christians and the Latin pilgrims deplored a revolution, which, instead of the regular government and old alliance of the caliphs, imposed on their necks the iron yoke of the strangers of the north. In his court and camp the great sultan had adopted in some degree the arts and manners of Persia; but the body of the Turkish nation, and more especially the pastoral tribes, still breathed the fierceness of the desert. From Nicaea to Jerusalem, the western countries of Asia were a scene of foreign and domestic hostility; and the shepherds of Palestine, who held a precarious sway on a doubtful frontier, had neither leisure nor capacity to await the slow profits of commercial and religious freedom. The pilgrims, who, through innumerable perils, had reached the gates of Jerusalem, were the victims of private rapine or public oppression, and often sunk under the pressure of famine and disease, before they were permitted to salute the holy sepulchre. A spirit of native barbarism, or recent zeal, prompted the Turkmans to insult the clergy of every sect; the patriarch was dragged by the hair along the pavement and cast into a dungeon, to extort a ransom from the sympathy of his flock; and the divine worship in the church of the Resurrection was often disturbed by the savage rudeness of its masters."[23]

---

23 Gibbon, Chapter 57.

The ordinary peasants of Europe may not have been fully cognizant of the danger from the east, but the ruling classes and the Church could not have been anything but alarmed. Yet even if the peasantry and artisans of Europe knew little about Anatolia, they would certainly have had some knowledge of the Muslim threat. It is Marcus Bull's suggestion that they did not which is untenable. The advances of Abd er-Rahman III and Al-Mansur through northern Spain in the latter years of the tenth century had sent a flood of Christian refugees into southern France; and the raids even into southern France which continued well into the eleventh century sent refugees from there fleeing into central and northern France. These people would certainly have spread knowledge of the danger throughout western Europe. Granted, peasants and manual laborers would have had a very imperfect understanding of Islam and what Muslims actually believed; but that is not the point: They knew enough to know that Muslims were enemies of Christ; that they waged war against non-combatants and enslaved women and children, and that they had conquered all of Spain and threatened France.

And this is a point that needs to be stressed repeatedly: The reality is that, far from being quiescent and peaceful, by the latter years of the tenth century and the early years of the eleventh Islam was once again on the march. Muslim armies waged wars of conquest against non-believers from one end of the Islamic world to the other; from Spain in the west to India in the east; and this new aggression was not confined to the eastern and western extremities, but proceeded along the entire length of Islam's borders. The Christian kingdoms of Armenia, Georgia and Byzantium were threatened with extinction, and Muslim armies fought with Christians in Sicily and other Mediterranean lands. Many aspects of this new Islamic thrust, particularly those which occurred around the beginning of the eleventh century in Spain and India, are reminiscent of the earlier Islamic expansion in the eighth century, when the armies of Islam swept all before them. We recall how, in Runciman's words, the Muslims of Spain represented a "very real threat to Christendom" at the time, and how the campaigns of Al-Mansur at the beginning of the eleventh century had placed Christendom in an unprecedentedly critical position.

The idea that the Muslim world had been stable and passive for three centuries before the arrival of the Crusaders is nonsense.

The Crusades which followed the First need not concern us here. All we need note is that they were defensive in nature: The Muslims of Egypt and Mesopotamia never accepted the existence of Christian kingdoms in Palestine and Syria, and these came under repeated attack in the three centuries after the Crusaders founded them. There were indeed short periods of peaceful coexistence, but these were of necessity brief: Islamic law forbade the forging of permanent peace with the infidel, and a ten-year truce was the maximum permitted.

During the crusading centuries however Islam made no further gains at the expense of Christendom, and in fact the Muslim presence in Spain was reduced eventually to Andalusia in the extreme south. Yet Islam still controlled the main trading-routes, including the Silk Road, to the Far East, and Muslim pirates still made large parts the Mediterranean off limits to European merchants. For a brief period during the reigns of Genghis Khan's successors this stranglehold was relaxed, and Europe enjoyed the luxury of free association with China and India. Significant new technologies and ideas arrived in Europe at this time.

6
PERSECUTION OF THE JEWS

I t is a fact that the first mass murder of Jews to be carried out in Europe occurred in Spain, in Cordoba in 1011 and in Granada in 1066.[1] But these pogroms were not the work of Christian fanatics: They were carried out by Muslim mobs. Thirty years after the Granada slaughter, at the start of the First Crusade, Christian mobs on the Rhineland carried out similar attacks. These were the first mass-murders of Jews ever carried out by Europeans.

From these two bare facts we may deduce the following: The peculiarly violent anti-Semitism which characterised medieval Europe seems to have had its origin in Spain; and the rise of this new and virulent anti-Semitism in other areas of Europe is intimately connected with the clash between Islam and Christianity.

Christianity was of course always anti-Semitic, or, more accurately, anti-Judaistic. Christians blamed Jews for the murder of Christ; and right from the beginning relations between the two religions were fraught. However, Christianity did not invent anti-Semitism; nor were Christians, for a long time, a threat to Jews.

Anti-Semitism, or hatred of the Jews, in fact predated both the rise of Christianity and Islam. Relations between Gentiles and Jews were volatile as far back as Hellenistic times, and the antagonism between Jews and Gentiles in Egypt, for example, during the second and first centuries BC led to a lively and polemical debate amongst authors such as Apion, Manetho and Josephus. In the early years of the Roman Empire, the attempts of the Jews to free themselves from Imperial rule led to a series of bloody uprisings which were suppressed with great ferocity. The Roman authori-

---

1 See Bat Ye'or, *The Dhimmi*, p. 61. Also, Bernard Lewis, *The Jews and Islam*, p. 54.

ties, as a rule, were exasperated by the Jews, but tolerated what they saw as their peculiar customs, and granted them certain unusual privileges, such as an exemption from the requirement of offering sacrifice to the Emperor.

Fig. 5. Burning of the Jews of Nuremberg, 1493.
Such violence against the Jews was unknown in Christian Europe before the First Crusade, but had become common earlier in the Muslim world, including Muslim Spain.

From the very beginning, of course, the Jews, or rather, the Jewish authorities, were deeply antagonistic towards Christianity; a faith they looked upon as little more than a dangerous heresy. There is evidence that they would, as Gibbon puts it "gladly have extinguished the dangerous heresy [Christianity] in the blood of its adherents." (*Decline and Fall*, Ch. 16) It is pointless to go through the various animosities that existed at this time between the two groups, yet there is clear evidence that, well into the third century, Jewish religious leaders agitated in favor of persecuting Christians, and harbored much hatred towards them. This needs to be said, for early Christian writers are frequently attacked for their animosity towards the Jews. There currently exists on the internet, for example, a website named *Religious Tolerance* which, in a page titled "Anti-Judaism: 70 to 1200 CE", lists a series of anti-Jewish pronouncements by early Christian writers such as Saint John Chrysostom, Saint Hilary of Poitiers, Saint

Augustine and Saint Jerome. Now, there is no question that these men, and many others beside, did make statements which nowadays would be regarded as straightforwardly anti-Semitic, in a religious sense. Yet these are theological opinions of individuals, not imperial policy. Furthermore, it should be stressed that John Chrysostom's attack, which he launched when he was a priest in Antioch (386), was designed to put an end to the practice among Christians of going to synagogues and participating in their services. As Robert Spencer rightly notes, "the fact that Christian attendance in synagogues was widespread in late fourth-century Antioch indicates that neither anti-Semitism nor anti-Judaism were dominant among Christians at the time, many of whom understood that there was a bond between Christianity and Judaism."[2] We note too that what John Chrysostom and the rest said about the Jews was mild in comparison with the attacks they made against heretics such as Manicheans and Donatists; and Jewish writers of the time were equally vociferous in their condemnation of Christians. Furthermore, whilst Christians had suffered death – often on a large scale – simply for being Christian, Jews had not.

In view of the fraught history of relationships between Jews and Christians, it is remarkable that, when the Empire became Christian, there was little retaliation against the Jews. It is true that several Emperors, most notably Justinian, did pass anti-Jewish edicts. None of these however were severe, and rarely went beyond restrictions placed on the building of new synagogues and (in the case of Justinian) refusing to allow the Jews to celebrate Passover before the Christian Easter. Hardly draconian. And it needs to be stated that these measures were elicited far more by political than religious considerations. Since the time of the pagan Emperors, the Jews of Palestine and the eastern Mediterranean had consistently sided with the Persians in their perennial wars with the Romans. It happened again during the time of Justinian, and he reciprocated with these legal measures.[3] Again, it should be noted that even Justinian, regarded as the most intolerant of the Christian Emperors, had numerous Jewish friends and advisers.

Proof that the Jews experienced no real persecution from the early Christians is seen in the great increase in the numbers and the prosperity of the Jewish people in the centuries that preceded the First Crusade. By the eleventh century both France and Germany were home to large and prosperous Jewish communities. Steven Runciman notes that, "Jewish colonies had been established for centuries past along the trade routes of western

---

2 Robert Spencer, *Religion of Peace? Why Chrisianity is and Islam isn't* (Regnery, 2000), p. 113.
3 See Cyril Mango, *Byzantium: the Empire of New Rome*, p. 92.

Europe."[4] These colonies "kept up connections with their co-religionists in Byzantium and in Arab lands, and were thus enabled to play a large part in international trade, more especially the trade between Moslem and Christian countries." Runciman notes that the Jews "had never undergone serious persecution in the West. ... The kings of France and Germany had always befriended them; and they were shown particular favour by the archbishops of the great cities of the Rhineland."

But if there was no prior serious persecution of the Jews, whence, we might ask, did that which characterized the Middle Ages arise?

Europe's largest Jewish community was located in Spain. Following the Islamic conquest of that land in 711, the Jews came under the domination of a faith that, so we are told, was from its inception virulently anti-Jewish. For Muslims the lead was given by none other than their founder, the Prophet Muhammad. It would be superfluous to enumerate the anti-Jewish pronouncements in the Qur'an and the Hadiths, where the Hebrews are portrayed as the craftiest, most persistent and most implacable enemies of Allah. In the Qur'an (2: 63-66) Allah transforms some Jews who profaned the Sabbath into apes: "Be as apes despicable!" In Qur'an 5: 59-60, He directs Muhammad to remind the "People of the Book" about "those who incurred the curse of Allah and His wrath, those whom some He transformed into apes and swine, those who worshipped evil." Again, in 7: 166, we hear of the Sabbath-breaking Jews that "when in their insolence they transgressed (all) prohibitions," Allah said to them, "Be ye apes, despised and rejected."

From the same sources we hear that Muhammad's first violent action against the Jews involved the Qaynuqa tribe, who dwelt at Medina, under the protection of the city. Muhammad "seized the occasion of an accidental tumult," and ordered the Qaynuqa (or Kainoka) to embrace his religion or fight. In the words of Gibbon, "The unequal conflict was terminated in fifteen days; and it was with extreme reluctance that Mahomet yielded to the importunity of his allies and consented to spare the lives of the captives." (*Decline and Fall*, Chapter 50) In later attacks on the Jews, the Hebrew captives were not so fortunate.

The most notorious of all Muhammad's attacks against the Jews was directed at the Banu Quraiza tribe. This community, which dwelt near Medina, was attacked without warning by the Prophet and his men, and, after its defeat, all the males over the age of puberty were beheaded. Some Islamic authorities claim that Muhammad personally participated in the executions. The doomed men and boys, whose numbers are estimated at

---

4 Runciman, *op cit.*, p. 134.

anything between 500 and 900, were ordered to dig the trench which was to be their communal grave. All of the women and children were enslaved, with Muhammad personally taking for himself one of the most beautiful of the prisoners. He also confiscated the property of the murdered Jews. These deeds are mentioned in the Qur'an as acts carried out by Allah himself and fully sanctioned by divine approval. Thus in Qur'an 33:26-27, we read:

> And he brought those of the People of the Book [Jewish people of Banu Qurayza] who supported them from their fortresses and cast terror into their hearts, some of them you slew (beheaded) and some you took prisoners (captive). And he made you heirs of their lands, their houses, and their goods, and of a land which ye had not frequented (before). And Allah has power over all things.

The killing of the Jewish prisoners is sanctioned in Qur'an 8:67:

> It is not fitting for an Apostle that he should have prisoners of war until He thoroughly subdued the land...

The Massacre of Banu Quraiza was followed soon after by the attack on the Khaybar tribe. On this occasion, the Prophet ordered the torture of a Jewish chieftain to extract information about where he had hidden his treasures. When the treasure was uncovered, the chieftain was beheaded. This chieftain was the husband of the most beautiful Jewish woman of Khaybar, the 17-year-old Safiyah. Safiyah's family members had been annihilated by Muhammad at the Banu Qurayza massacre. Now having beheaded her husband, the Prophet took Safiyah as his slave. The story is told thus by Sahih al-Bukhari, whose compilation of the acts and deeds attributed to Muhammad was written in the ninth century, and forms one of the two pillars of Islamic jurisprudence. (Volume 5, Book 59, Number 512):

> The Prophet offered the Fajr Prayer near Khaybar when it was still dark and then said, "Allahu-Akbar! Khaybar is destroyed, for whenever we approach a (hostile) nation (to fight), then evil will be the morning for those who have been warned." Then the inhabitants of Khaybar came out running on the roads. The Prophet had their warriors killed, their offspring and woman taken as captives. Safiya was amongst the captives,

She first came in the share of Dahya Alkali but later on she belonged to the Prophet. The Prophet made her manumission as her 'Mahr'. Muhammad was sixty (60) when he married Safiyyahh, a young girl of seventeen. She became his eighth wife.

The distribution of the booty is described thus in al-Bukhari Hadiths No.143, page-700:

> Sulaiman Ibne Harb…Aannas Ibne Malek (ra) narrated, "in the war of Khayber after the inhabitants of Banu Nadir were surrendered, Allah's apostle killed all the able/adult men, and he (prophet) took all women and children as captives (Ghani mateer maal).. Among the captives Safiyya Bint Huyy Akhtab was taken by Allah's Apostle as booty whom He married after freeing her and her freedom was her Mahr."

It is said that at first Dihyah al-Kalbi, one of Muhammad's followers, asked for Safiyah. But when Muhammad saw her exquisite beauty, he chose her for himself and gave her two cousins to Dihyah.

In the massacre of the Jewish Settlement of Bani Mustaliq, Muhammad is said to have captured their women and took twenty-year-old Jewish girl, Juwairiya as his personal slave. [Al-Bukhari 3.46.13.717, p. 431-432]. Sahih Muslim (2.2349, p. 520) says that Muhammad attacked the Banu Mustaliq tribe without any warning while they were heedlessly grazing their cattle. Juwairiya was a daughter of the chief. Sahih Muslim 3.4292, p. 942 and Abu Dawud 2.227, p. 728 and al-Tabari 39, p. 182-183 also say Juwairiya was captured in a raid on the Banu Mustaliq tribe. She had been married to Musafi' bin Safwan, who was killed in battle.

We need go no further into the horrific details of these events, as they have already been examined by numerous writers and their veracity denied by no Muslims, scholars or otherwise, since the middle of the eighth century. What needs to be emphasized is the attitude these reported atrocities betray, as well as the fact that they became the model for the behavior of all future followers of the Prophet.

What caused Muhammad's seemingly implacable hatred of the Jews? According to Gibbon, it was their refusal to recognize him as their long-awaited Messiah that "converted his friendship into an implacable hatred, with which he pursued that unfortunate people to the last moment of his life; and, in the double character of apostle and conqueror, his persecution was extended into both worlds." (*Decline and Fall*, Ch. 50)

As noted above, it is a widely-held fiction that, aside from the Prophet's persecution of the Jews of Arabia, Muslims in general and Islam as a rule was historically tolerant to this People of the Book, who were generally granted *dhimmi* ("protected") status in the Islamic Umma, or community. But *dhimmi* status, also accorded to Christians, did not, as Bat Ye'or has demonstrated at great length, imply equal rights with Muslims. On the contrary, *dhimmis* were subject, even at the best of times, to a whole series of discriminatory and humiliating laws and to relentless exploitation. At the worst of times, they could be slaughtered in the streets without any hope of legal redress. One of the most noxious measures directed against them was the requirement to wear an item or color of clothing by which they could be easily identified: identified for easy exploitation and abuse. The latter law was copied, significantly enough, by the Nazis. Bat Ye'or has shown that this law was enforced in Islam right from the beginning. The violence was not continuous, but the exploitation was, and the pattern of abuse initiated by Muhammad in Arabia in the seventh century was to be repeated throughout history. The first massacres of Jews in Europe, carried out by Muslim mobs in Spain, were preceded by other massacres carried out in North Africa, and clearly formed a continuum with Muhammad's massacres of that people in Arabia.

Nonetheless, there was, at times, a semblance of tolerance for both Jews and Christians. It could not have been otherwise. When the Arabs conquered the vast territories of Mesopotamia, Syria, and North Africa during the seventh century, they found themselves a small minority ruling over enormous populations comprising mainly Christians and, to a lesser degree, Jews. As such, they needed to proceed with caution. Like all conquerors, the Arab armies were quick to exploit any internal conflicts; and it was in their interests, above all, to divide the Christians from the Jews. This was particularly the case in Spain, where the Jewish population was very large. A united Jewish and Christian front could have proved extremely dangerous, and it was entirely in the interest of the conquerors to sow mistrust and suspicion between these communities. In the words of Bat Ye'or, "The [Arab] invaders knew how to take advantage of the dissensions between local groups in order to impose their own authority, favoring first one and then another, with the intention of weakening and ruining them all through a policy of 'divide and rule.'"[5]

Now, Jewish communities, both in Spain and elsewhere, tended to be both educated and prosperous. Jewish doctors, scientists and merchants could be usefully employed by any ruling group. And employed

5 Bat Ye'or, *The Dhimmi*, p. 87.

they were by the Arabs. Some, such as Ibn Naghrela, rose to positions of great prominence, whilst the international connections of the Jews and their mastery of languages proved invaluable to the new rulers. The Jews frequently found themselves in the role of intermediaries between Muslims and Christians. And we cannot pass over the role of Jewish merchants in supplying Muslim Spain with all its essentials – including slaves from northern and north-eastern Europe.[6]

Yet such favors as the Jews enjoyed was transitory and uncertain. There was never any real security, as the massacres of 1011 and 1066 illustrate only too well. On the other hand, it was entirely in the interests of the Muslims that the Christians believed the Jews were favored. And part of that narrative was the notion that the Jews had actually assisted the Muslims in their conquest of the country.

If what generations of Muslims have believed about Muhammad and his life is to be taken as real history, then it is extremely unlikely the Jews could have assisted the forces of Islam in their conquest of Spain. The massacres of Jews said to have been carried out by the Prophet in the early seventh century would scarcely have endeared him and his followers to Hebrews anywhere, especially when we consider the vibrant international links of that same people. Indeed, no people on earth was better placed to know of events at the other side of the Mediterranean than the Jews, and those of Spain would have been very much aware of Muhammad's behavior long before the first Muslim armies landed on Spanish soil. Thus, if the deeds of Muhammad as recounted in the Qur'an and the Hadiths are historical, the accounts of their co-operation with the Muslim invaders cannot possibly be true. Yet co-operate they did, as Muslim, Christian and Jewish records of the invasion all agree.[7]

What then is the solution?

The whole topic of Islam's origins is briefly examined in the Appendix to the present volume. Without going into details here, it should be sufficient to note that there is very good evidence to show that the entire narrative of Muhammad's life, as well as the story of Islam's early expansion beyond Arabia, is almost certainly an elaborate fiction. Muhammad himself almost certainly never existed, so his massacres of Jews in the Arabian Peninsula cannot have occurred. Furthermore, a religion or cult very similar to Islam – variously described as Arab Christianity or Ebionitism – flourished in Arabia between the fourth and sixth centuries and almost certainly was the first "Islam" encountered by archaeologists. This Arab

---

6 See *e.g.* Hugh Trevor-Roper, *op cit.*, p. 143.

7 See *e.g.* Fletcher, *op cit.*, p. 24.

"Christianity" was in most respects almost identical to Judaism and was quite different to the Trinitarian Christianity familiar to all. Circumcision, along with almost all the other rules delineated in the Code of Moses, was mandatory; and it seems that it was this version of "Christianity" which gained possession of the entire Middle East and North Africa from the middle of the seventh century. In *Mohammed and Charlemagne Revisited* I showed there were grounds for believing that the Arabs did not conquer Persia, as conventional history believes, but that the Sassanid monarch of Iran, Chosroes II, converted to "Arab Christianity," or what we might call proto-Islam, at the beginning of his great war against the Eastern Roman Empire in 602. One of the most important events of that war was the conquest of Jerusalem in 614, which was followed by a general massacre of the Christian inhabitants of the city. We are told that the Jewish inhabitants of Jerusalem, as well as Arab allies of Chosroes II, participated in the massacre.

If the Persian forces who captured Jerusalem at this time fought under a king who was a Muslim, or proto-Muslim, and if the anti-Semitic sections of the Qur'an and hadiths had yet to be written, it is conceivable that the Jews of Syria/Palestine, North Africa and Spain would have viewed the Muslim conquerors of these regions as allies, and have actively assisted them. By the middle of the eighth century however the Islamic canon of sacred scriptures was firmly established and the Jews, formerly allies of the Muslims – with whom they shared so much in common – were now viewed as enemies. From that time onwards their treatment differed little from that accorded to the *dhimmi* Christians, and indeed their lot may even have been more oppressive.

If we move forward to the tenth and eleventh centuries we arrive in an epoch during which the war for possession of the Iberian Peninsula raged as never before. This conflict was to grow into a real clash of civilizations, as Christians and Muslims called in the assistance of co-religionists from far and wide. The Shrine of Santiago de Compostela became a rallying symbol for the Christians of the north and for those of France and Germany, who crossed the Pyrenees to join the struggle against Islam. Their Christian allies in Spain already had the conviction that the Jews were inveterate allies of the Muslims – a belief, as we said, probably encouraged by the Muslims themselves. These Frankish and German warriors also came into contact with Muslim anti-Semitic attitudes – attitudes which they themselves began to imbibe.

Now, it is an acknowledged fact that it was in Spain that the warriors who later joined the First Crusade learnt to persecute the Jews. In Runciman's words, "Already in the Spanish wars there had been some inclination on the part of Christian armies to maltreat the Jews."[8] He notes that at the time of the expedition to Barbastro, in the mid-eleventh century, Pope Alexander II had written to the bishops of Spain to remind them that there was all the difference in the world between Muslims and Jews. The former were irreconcilable enemies of the Christians, but the latter were ready to work for them. However, in Spain "the Jews had enjoyed such favour from the hands of the Moslems that the Christian conquerors could not bring themselves to trust them."[9] This lack of trust is confirmed by more than one document of the period, several of which are listed by Runciman.

Just over a decade after the Christian knights of France and Germany had helped their co-religionists in Spain to retake the city of Toledo from the Muslims, some of them prepared to set out on the First (official) Crusade. Before they did so, a few of them took part in the mass murder of several thousand Jews in Germany and Bohemia – an atrocity unprecedented in European history.

In view of the fact that these pogroms were committed by warriors some of whom had learned their trade in Spain, and in view of the fact that such atrocities were hitherto unknown in Europe, we may state that there is strong circumstantial evidence to suggest that the Christians had been influenced by the Muslims. This is all the more probable in view of Islam's history (from the mid-eighth century) of virulent and violent anti-Semitism. And if the Europeans were influenced in this by the Muslims, this was by no means the only novelty learned by them from their Muslim foes. As we saw in the previous chapter, there are good grounds for believing that the very idea of "Holy War," previously unthinkable in Christian terms, was at least partly derived from the Islamic notion of *jihad*.

To conclude, I am not trying to argue that anti-Semitism did not exist among Christians before the rise of Islam. Obviously it did. Far less am I trying to excuse the appalling behavior of "Christians" toward the Jews in Europe from the eleventh century onwards. No one is to blame for the massacres and pogroms which disgraced the name of Europe for almost a thousand years but the Europeans themselves. Yet in tracing the origins of this sickening hatred we cannot turn a blind eye to the similarly appalling record amongst the Muslims, as well as to the undoubted influence of Islam upon Christendom. Furthermore, it is beyond question that the terrible struggle between the two intolerant ideologies of Christianity and

---

8 Runciman, *op cit.*, p. 135.

9 *Ibid.* Favor or not, however, the Jews had already suffered appalling mistreatment at the hands of the Spanish Muslims well before the Crusades, as we saw in Chapter 4.

Islam which began in the seventh century, had a profoundly detrimental effect upon the Jews; and it was then, and only then, that the virulent and murderous anti-Semitism so characteristic of the Middle Ages entered European life.

7
THE MEDIEVAL THEOCRACY

I t is a fact that all ancient societies were to some degree or other theocracies, where spiritual and temporal power was united in one figure or small group. Ancient Egypt, for example, was a theocracy of the most absolute kind, as was ancient Babylonia and ancient China. Even Greece and Rome, whilst much less theocratic than these earlier cultures, were nonetheless by modern standards theocratic. Some Greek states, it is true, such as classical Athens, had democracies, and these were generally not guided by religious authority, yet even here there was a strong theological input into governance – certainly by modern standards. Socrates, we must remember, right at the peak of Athens' democratic Golden Age, was put to death for blasphemy.

One of the main criticisms of course leveled against Europe in the Middle Ages was its theocracy, or reputed theocracy. The power of the church at this time tends to be viewed by modern Westerners as a dead weight which imposed a tyranny on men's minds. Religious dissension, it is held, was not tolerated and the free exploration of nature and her laws inhibited by the church's stranglehold.

The strange fact is that neither of these accusations are true to the degree that is generally believed. A few well-known cases, such as that of Giordano Bruno and Galileo, have cast an altogether unfair light on the epoch. Yes, there were some constraints and there was a degree of church influence on public life that would be unthinkable in modern times, but the fact is that Europe in the Middle Ages was one of the least theocratic societies of the time. And in an earlier age it was even less so.

When Christianity was made the official religion of the Roman Empire in the fourth century the bishops and prelates had little power. The emperors continued to be the real masters of the state, and churchmen could at best hope to gain the emperor's ear. The fall of the Western Empire in 476 changed little of this. Indeed, if anything the influence of the church diminished. The barbarian kings of the Goths, Vandals and Franks, who came to dominate the Western provinces, were invariably Arian heretics not well disposed to the Catholic prelates who represented the majority of the population. Their sane and just view of religious affairs is perhaps no better illustrated than by the fact that the Ostrogothic king Theodoric the Great compelled the citizens of Ravenna to rebuild several synagogues, at their own expense, after these had been damaged in a riot. The gradual conversion of the Frankish and then Gothic kings to Catholicism certainly did increase the influence of the bishops, but they were still very much subordinate to the temporal authority. Indeed, as Henri Pirenne stressed at great length, the late Roman culture which prevailed in the West until the early seventh century was heavily secular. Literacy was widespread and the state employed a secular rather than a clerical bureacracy. Secular literature flourished, as did the philosophical tradition of pagan Greece and Rome. Thus for example Boethius, perhaps the greatest thinker of the West during the sixth century, spent many years working on a synthesis of Aristotle and Plato. So suffused with the spirit of classical paganism is Boethius' thinking that not a few modern commentators have doubted whether he was a Christian at all and have suspected secret paganism. And yet this same Boethius was and is regarded as a Saint by the Catholic Church.

The church then, at this time, was certainly more open-minded than in later centuries and occupied a subordinate role to that of the king. Yet by the tenth century things had changed dramatically. Pirenne maintained that, following the closure of the Mediterranean to European trade by Muslim piracy in the seventh century, the Frankish and Gothic kings lost a great deal of their tax income and were thus weakened *vis à vis* the barons and minor aristocrats, who now gained in power and independence. The kings desperately needed a counterbalance, and the support of the church carried great weight. With the church on their side the kings could – just about – keep the barons under control. But there was necessarily a trade-off. The church might keep the king on his throne, but it gained in return an increasing influence over the king.

Pirenne also suggested that with the closure of the Mediterranean to normal trade the supply of papyrus from Egypt was terminated and this produced a dramatic decline in literacy throughout Europe, which in turn led to an increasing dependence upon the church to supply writing skills and education. Secular literacy all but disappeared, and it is a fact that by the middle of the ninth century the Imperial Chancellory was dependent upon clerics for all written work. These clerics, who were under the direction of a head chaplain, were referred to as the *Kapelle* ("chapel"). From 975 the office of chancellor to the emperor was always held by the Archbishop of Mainz. The clerics in the *Hofkapelle* ("court chapel") also undertook political and diplomatic missions and many attained important feudal positions.

In years to come, the empire itself (refounded, it is said, by Charlemagne in 800) would be renamed the Holy Roman Empire – an appropriate title; for the new Western Empire represented a symbiotic union, at the heart of Europe, of spiritual and temporal authorities. The crowning of the emperor – for which the inauguration of Charlemagne became the model – was an event loaded with religious significance and symbolism. The Ottonian emperors of the tenth century were rulers *Dei gratis*, and they made the church the main instrument of royal government. Their authority would henceforth not simply be derived from their own military and economic strength, as it had been under the Caesars and Germanic kings of the fifth and sixth centuries, but, to some degree at least, upon the sanction and approval of the church. Eventually the kings of Europe became subordinate to the pope, who could even, in extreme cases, dethrone them. Everything a medieval ruler did, or proposed to do, he had to do with the sanction of the church. Even powerful and independent warriors, such as William of Normandy, could only proceed with a project like the invasion of England after gaining papal approval.

The Ottonian emperors thus laid the foundations of a kind of theocracy; yet even now the church had to fight for her position, a struggle which commenced in the tenth century, and which ended in the eleventh, with papal victory. "They [Church reformers] fought to secure ultimate control of a self-contained, independent, dominant, monarchical Church. Such a contest was a frontal challenge to the old system of the Roman Empire. It was a frontal attack on the kings who presumed that they had inherited the rights of the Roman emperors. It was an indirect attack on the emperor of Constantinople who, in the East, continued to maintain the old system [of secular supremacy] and was now called schismatic for his pains."[1]

Yet this European theocracy was never comparable to that of Islam. Even at the peak of his power the pope had little temporal authority: he invariably had to appeal to the secular rulers for support. And by the thirteenth and fourteenth centuries the popes were frequently at the mercy of German emperors and French kings. By contrast, the caliphs, and later the

1 Trevor-Roper, *op cit.*, p. 137.

sultans, united absolute spiritual and temporal authority in themselves.

The high point of the medieval church's power came in the early thirteenth century and in the person of Innocent III (1198 – 1216). This man judged between rival emperors in Germany and had Otto IV deposed. He laid England under an interdict and excommunicated King John for refusing to recognize Stephen Langdon as Archbishop of Canterbury. His two most memorable actions however were the establishment of the Inquisition and the launching of the notorious Albigensian Crusade, which led to the elimination of the Cathar movement. Innocent III then, the most powerful of medieval theocrats, was a proponent of Holy War, and an enforcer of absolute doctrinal conformity. Apostasy under Innocent III became a capital offense. During his time too the other Crusades, against Islam in Spain and in the Middle East, continued to rage.

Fig. 6. Innocent III, founder of the Inquisition
In establishing a body to root out heretics, Innocent III seems to have been influenced by similar bodies established in Spain by the Muslim Almohads, fifty years earlier. The Inquisition employed torture, a novelty in Europe at that time, but common practise in the Islamic world.

Ironically, Innocent's attitude to apostasy and doctrinal conformity – as well as to "Holy War" – was completely in accord with Islamic notions, and we must consider to what extent these extreme positions of the European theocracy were influenced by the Islamic one. For Islam itself was, of course, from the very beginning, theocratic in a way that Europe never was – even in the time of Innocent III. In Islam, there was no "render unto Caesar the things that are Caesar's, and unto God the things that are God's." Right from the start, in the person of Muhammad, spiritual and temporal power was united. After Muhammad, under the caliphs, the same situation pertained. Every caliph was, first and foremost, a "commander of the faithful." And doctrinal conformity was enforced in Islam from the beginning in a way that it never was in Europe: here apostasy and heresy were always seen as capital offenses.[2] The most notorious, though by no means the only, example of this is found in the fate of Mansur Al-Hallaj (858 – 922), the Persian mystic, whose death mimicked that of Christ – though before being crucified Al-Hallaj was first, it is said, blinded and otherwise tortured. And the killing of political and religious opponents, or those who deviated in any way from orthodox Islam, continued throughout Muslim history. So it was with infidels such as Christians and Jews who, though theoretically *dhimmi*, or "protected," were in fact always the subject of violent attack. We know, for example, that in 704 or 705 the Caliph Walid (705-715) "assembled the nobles of Armenia in the church of St Gregory in Naxcawan and the church of Xrain on the Araxis, and burned them to death. Others were crucified and decapitated and their wives and children taken into captivity. A violent persecution of Christians in Armenia is recorded from 852 to 855."[3] There even existed, as we have seen, in Spain and North Africa, at least from the time of the Almohads (early twelfth century), a commission of inquiry, a veritable "inquisition," for rooting out apostates. We are told that the Jews, who had at this time been forced to accept Islam, formed a mass of "new converts" who nevertheless continued to practice their own religion in secret. But the "Almohad inquisitors, doubting their sincerity, took away their children and raised them as Muslims."[4]

Medieval Christianity, beginning in the late twelfth/early thirteenth century, adopted the same attitude. Christians now had their own Inquisition for rooting out heretics, and the death penalty was now prescribed for

2 Muhammad said, "If anyone changes his religion, kill him." (Bukhari, Vol. 9, book 84, no. 57).

3 Bat Ye'or, *op cit.*, pp. 60-1.

4 *Ibid.*, p. 61.

such miscreants. The judicial use of torture too, "a novelty in Europe" at the time, became accepted practice.[5] All of these practices were in fact novel in Europe: There is no evidence of the lethal intolerance which marked the foundation of the Inquisition before Innocent III's time. It is true, of course, that in the early centuries, the church was involved in a series of prolonged and bitter disputes over the correct interpretation of Christ's words. Those who disagreed with the mainstream dogmas, as laid down by various councils, were decreed to be heretics, and fairly severe condemnation of these people and groups was common: indeed, it was almost endemic. Yet it has to be repeated that, intemperate as was the language used in these disputes, they rarely turned violent; and even when they did, the violence was on a comparatively small scale and invariably perpetrated by those with no official sanction or approval. Actually, the use of force to enforce orthodoxy was condemned by all the Church Fathers. Thus Lactantius declared that "religion cannot be imposed by force; the matter must be carried on by words rather than by blows, that the will may be affected." He wrote,

> Oh with what an honorable inclination the wretched men go astray! For they are aware that there is nothing among men more excellent than religion, and that this ought to be defended with the whole of our power; but as they are deceived in the matter of religion itself, so also are they in the manner of its defense. For religion is to be defended, not by putting to death, but by dying; not by cruelty, but by patient endurance; not by guilt, but by good faith. ... For if you wish to defend religion by bloodshed, and by tortures, and by guilt, it will no longer be defended, but will be polluted and profaned. For nothing is so much a matter of free will as religion; in which, if the mind of the worshipper is disinclined to it, religion is at once taken away, and ceases to exist.[6]

Later, St. John Chrysostom wrote that "it is not right to put a heretic to death, since an implacable war would be brought into the world."[7]

---

5 Trevor-Roper, *op cit.*, p. 159.

6 Lactantius, "The Divine Institutes," in "Fathers of the Third and Fourth Centuries," in *The Ante-Nicene Fathers*, 156-7.

7 John Chrysostom, Homily XLVI, in George Prevost, trans. "The Homilies of St. John Chrysostom" in Philip Schaff, ed. *A Select Library of the Nicene and Post-Nicene Fathers of the Christian Church*, Vol. X (Eedermans, Grand Rapids, MI, 1986) p. 288.

Likewise, St. Augustine was to write of heretics that "it is not their death, but their deliverance from error, that we seek."[8] In spite of these and many other such admonitions, incidents of violence against heretics did occur; but they were isolated and it was never sanctioned by Church authorities. Such, for example, was the case with the suppression of the so-called Priscillian Heresy in Spain in the latter years of the fourth and early years of the fifth century. Several followers of Priscillian were put to death, and the sect was persecuted in other ways. Yet the killing of Priscillian and his immediate associates (six in all) had no church sanction, and was thoroughly condemned by the ecclesiastical authorities.

The same was true of another, and more famous, case – the murder of Hypatia. This incident, in the early fifth century, has achieved, in some quarters, almost legendary status, and is seen as the example *par excellence* of Christian bigotry and obscurantism. From what little we know of this incident, it is clear that, like the killing of the Priscillians, the murder had no official sanction, and was carried out by a group of lawless fanatics. From the few sources we have, it is evident that Hypatia, daughter of the philosopher Theon, was a major figure in Alexandria during the latter years of the fourth and early years of the fifth centuries. She famously refused to embrace Christianity and remained a pagan, a Neoplatonist. She freely discussed her ideas with many, including not a few Christian theologians, with whom she was on friendly terms.

But being such a prominent figure, she attracted enemies. Rumor spread that she was a factor in the strained relationship between Bishop Cyril and the Prefect Orestes, and this attracted the ire of some elements in the Christian population, eager to see the two reconciled. One day in March 415, during the season of Lent, her chariot was waylaid on her route home by a Christian mob, possibly Nitrian monks led by a man identified only as "Peter." She was stripped naked and dragged through the streets to the newly christianised Caesareum church and killed. Some reports suggest she was flayed with *ostrakois* (literally, "oyster shells," though also used to refer to roof tiles or broken pottery) and set ablaze while still alive, though other accounts suggest those actions happened after her death.

In view of the differing and contradictory accounts of this incident, we should perhaps quote the earliest, that closest to the event, which stands the best chance of accuracy. In the words of Socrates Scholasticus (5th century):

---

8 St Augustine, Letter C, in "Letters of St. Augustine," in J. G. Cunningham, trans. in *A Select Library of the Nicene* (etc as above).

Yet even she [Hypatia] fell a victim to the political jealousy which at that time prevailed. For as she had frequent interviews with Orestes, it was calumniously reported among the Christian populace, that it was she who prevented Orestes from being reconciled to the bishop. Some of them therefore, hurried away by a fierce and bigoted zeal, whose ringleader was a reader named Peter, waylaid her returning home, and dragging her from her carriage, they took her to the church called Caesareum, where they completely stripped her, and then murdered her by scraping her skin off with tiles and bits of shell. After tearing her body in pieces, they took her mangled limbs to a place called Cinaron, and there burnt them.

Although this was a horrific manifestation of religious bigotry, it was not sanctioned by church leaders. Furthermore, it occurred in Egypt, a land with a long tradition of religious fanaticism. During the time of Julius Caesar, for example, an Egyptian mob lynched a Roman centurion (an act which could have brought upon them a terrible retribution) for having the temerity to kill a cat. Such isolated acts of fanaticism have occurred in all faiths at all periods of history. Even that most pacifist and tolerant of religious ideologies, Buddhism, is not entirely free of it. So, in itself, the murder of Hypatia cannot tell us much. That the Christian writer Socrates Scholasticus, in the fifth century, regarded it as a deplorable act of bigoted zeal, is very significant. Remember however what John of Nikiu, another Christian commentator, this time of the eighth century (about a century after the Muslim conquest), says. He described Hypatia as "a pagan" who was "devoted to magic" and who had "beguiled many people through Satanic wiles." And whilst Socrates Scholasticus condemned her killing, John of Nikiu approved it, speaking of "A multitude of believers in God" who, "under the guidance of Peter the magistrate … proceeded to seek for the pagan woman who had beguiled the people of the city and the prefect through her enchantments."[9]

John of Nikiu's attitude is clearly that of a medieval bigot and obscurantist, who regards all dissension from orthodox Christianity as the work of Satan. His thinking would not have been far removed from that of Innocent III, yet it was a world away from that of Socrates Scholasticus, his fellow-countryman. And whilst we might plausibly blame the medieval outlook on the general poverty and illiteracy of Europe after the termina-

9 John of Nikiu, *Chronicle*, 84.87-103, http://cosmopolis.com/alexandria/hypatia-bio-john.html

tion of the Mediterranean trade in the late seventh and eighth centuries, we cannot attribute John of Nikiu's attitudes to the same cause. He, after all, lived in a land that was not cut off from the great centers of learning of the Orient. He came from a land which, supposedly, remained wealthy and prosperous, and which was moreover ruled by caliphs friendly towards science and learning. The supply of papyrus was never cut off from Egypt! Whence, then, came John of Nikiu's dark and unenlightened view? And if his attitude had been confined to him alone, it would hardly be significant. Yet, the fact is, by the beginning of the eighth century, shortly after the Muslim conquest, all writers in Egypt and throughout the Near East, both Christian and Muslim, took the same view. This is a crucial point: If the medieval outlook were simply the product of the illiteracy and poverty that prevailed in Europe after the closing of the Mediterranean (as one interpretation of Pirenne's ideas might have it), then we should not expect to find it in Muslim-controlled lands. Yet find it we do – and it occurs here even before it appears in Europe.

The view of the world we call "medieval" was one in which the reason and humanism of the classical world are said to have all but disappeared. Dark fantasies and superstitions took its place. Belief in the power of magicians and sorcerers, a belief associated with the most primitive type of mind-set, made a comeback. In the most backward of modern societies we still find perfectly innocent people accused of "witchcraft" and brutally put to death for a crime which they never committed and which does not even exist. By the end of the Middle Ages this mentality had returned to Europe; and in 1487 a papal Bull named *malleus maleficarum* ("hammer of the witches") pronounced the death of witches and Satanists.

Yet Europe, as she emerged from the so-called Dark Age in the tenth century, was still bathed in the light of reason and humanitarianism. Thus a tenth century canon of Church Law criticized and condemned the belief among country folk that "certain women" were in the habit of riding out on beasts in the dead of night and crossing great distances before daybreak. According to the canon, anyone who believed this was "beyond doubt an infidel and a pagan." Somewhat earlier, Saint Agobard, Bishop of Lyons, declared it was not true that witches could call up storms and destroy harvests. Nor could they devour people from within nor kill them with the "evil eye."[10] "In reality, the church vigorously opposed belief in witchcraft and sorecery throughout the whole of the Middle Ages, such beliefs being rightly identified as a surviving relic of paganism; and it was only with the

10 Colin Wilson and Christopher Evans, eds. *Strange but True* (Parragon Books, 1995), p. 285.

decline of the Middle Ages, in the fifteenth century, that church authorities began the persecution of supposed witches and sorcerers. In short, the witch-hunting mania was a manifestation not of medieval Christendom but of the weakening of medieval Christendom."[11] What happened in the intervening years to change the church's attitude?

In answer to that question, let us recall the comments of Louis Bertrand, who noted how, in the eleventh and twelfth centuries inquisitive young men from northern Europe flocked to Islamic Spain to study their knowledge and learning. But it was not so much the "science" of the Moors that attracted them as the pseudo-science: the alchemy, the astrology and the sorcery. Largely deprived of books and the urban society which fostered them, Islamic Spain and Islamic North Africa became the teachers of Medieval Europe. But what these regions taught was a far cry from the learning now so widely praised in the politically-correct textbooks that fill our libraries and bookshops.

Sorcery and alchemy were not the only things learned by the Europeans from the Muslims. We know, and this is admitted by all, that European theology was profoundly influenced at this time by Islamic. But it was not just Avicenna and Averroes that the Christians took from their Muslim teachers. They took also ideas directly from the Qur'an and the Hadith; ideas about how heretics, apostates and sorcerers should be treated. And it is by no means impossible that in establishing his own Inquisition Innocent III was directly imitating the example of the Almohads in Spain, who had set up their own commission for investigating heretics and apostates fifty years earlier.

Innocent III is viewed by the enemies of Christianity as the *bête noir*, the living embodiment of everything that was and is wrong with Christianity. Yet the fact that his attitudes were fairly identical to those found in Islam at an earlier date is never mentioned. Furthermore, whilst we do not seek to minimize the enormity of Innocent's actions, we must remember that his crusade against the Cathars was only launched after they had become a widespread movement, with their own bishops, churches and cathedrals, throughout southern France and into Italy and Spain. Until the time of Innocent III tolerance had been the order of the day – for centuries. Such a situation would of course never have arisen in the Islamic world, at any time in its history. There religious dissent and apostasy was crushed immediately as it occurred in the individual: such persons were (and sometimes still are) put to death without mercy. The few heresies

---

11 David Bentley Hart, *Atheist Delusions: The Christian Revolution and its Fashionable Enemies* (Yale University Press, 2010).

which arose and survived in Islam did so only with the most powerful political support. The Druze sect, for example, arose under the patronage of the Caliph Al-Hakim, who actively fostered it. It survived after his time largely under the protection of the Crusaders.

And whilst we consider Innocent's war against freedom of conscience we must never forget that in the twelfth and thirteenth centuries the Muslim threat had by no means disappeared: it remained as potent and dangerous as ever. In such circumstances – indeed, in any war situation – internal dissent (such as the Cathars represented) is liable to be viewed as representing a fifth column working for the enemy. And it is well-known fact that all wartime dissent is suppressed with a thoroughness and ruthlessness much more severe than would normally be the case. The later Spanish Inquisition, which implemented draconian measures against dissenters in the Iberian Peninsula, must be seen in the same light. The threat of Islam was ever present, and we can be reasonably certain that the severe repression of Muslims at this time was directly attributable to the fear of a renewed Muslim invasion of the Peninsula (by the Ottomans) and the possibility that the native Muslims would form a fifth column in support of the invaders.

*   *   *

So much for religious freedom. The other accusation thrown against the church during the Middle Ages is that it stifled the free exploration of the natural world and generally inhibited scientific progress. This is now such a widespread belief that it is accepted unquestioningly in the popular media and even in academia. Consider for example the comments of Sidney Painter just over sixty years ago:

"The early Middle Ages was inevitably a dark age in respect to the physical and natural sciences. As they were only remotely related to salvation, they aroused little interest. When they were discussed, the primary motive was to draw from them religious inspiration."[12] It should be almost superfluous to note here that some of the greatest scientists of the Renaissance and the Enlightenment, such as Galileo and Isaac Newton, also explored the physical universe with a view to draw from it religious inspiration. Apart from its obsession with theology, the main problem with medieval science, according to Painter, was that it embraced the theological concept known as "Realism." This idea, based ultimately upon Plato's work, "taught that reality was a world of ideal models. The real man was

12 Painter, *op cit.*, p. 433.

an ideal man; reality lay in the species rather than in the individual. The Patristic Fathers, especially St. Augustine, fully accepted this point of view. Our senses supply us with knowledge about individuals, and our minds comprehend the ideal. The ideal is reality, and the characteristics of individuals are but 'accidents.' To the extreme Realist only the ideal, the species, was of importance and the individual was of no significance."[13] Devotees of extreme realism, says Painter, "were unlikely to carry observation [of nature] very far. What was observed by the senses was the accidents that marked individuals and hence was of little importance."[14] Having said all that, Painter concedes that,

"... by the middle of the thirteenth century the scientific works of the Greeks and Arabs had been thoroughly absorbed, and the knowledge they contained had become an integral port of the culture of Western Europe. Scholars began to take an interest in the possibilities of observation and experiment. Aristotle had realized the importance of these methods of obtaining knowledge, and they were emphasized by the great commentator on Aristotle, Albertus Magnus. Although science as such was of little interest to Thomas Aquinas, he too pointed out the value of observation and experiment. But the chief figure of thirteenth-century scientific thought was the English Franciscan, Roger Bacon, who was a contemporary of St. Thomas. Bacon's basic point of view was thoroughly traditional. He accepted without question the divine inspiration of the Bible and the works of the Church Fathers. He insisted that knowledge was of value only in so far as it contributed to man's struggle for salvation. At the same time he had an eager, inquiring mind that was completely devoted to the enlargement of his knowledge. He attempted to extend the fields in which reason should have full play by limiting that of theology. He argued that many subjects covered by the great summa of the theologians were properly the concern of philosophy rather than theology. He also believed that new techniques, especially the study of languages, would be of great aid to both philosophy and theology. ... Finally, he advocated the confirmation of knowledge by means of observation and experiment."[15]

None of this sounds like a man or a society under the yoke of a stifling theocratic dictatorship. However, Painter qualifies his statement about Bacon with the following:

"Bacon's independence of mind endeared him neither to other schol-

---

13 *Ibid.*, p. 431.
14 *Ibid.*, p. 433.
15 *Ibid.*, p. 434.

ars nor to his superiors in the Franciscan order. If he had not received the special protection of the pope, he might never have been able to write his learned works. ... He did little toward making use of the methods of inquiry that he advocated so vigorously, and even if he had done so his conventional basic point of view would have seriously limited the usefulness of his observations and experiments."

Fig. 7. Roger Bacon
Roger Bacon was one of many natural philosophers involved in scientific research during the Middle Ages. The work of such men transformed Europe from a rural backwater in the tenth century to the most advanced society in the world by the fifteenth.

In spite of this negative conclusion, the writer has to admit that the use of observation of nature did become important in Europe in the fourteenth century. As an example of this, says Painter, "one can take a subject of primary significance for the physical sciences – the nature and cause of motion. Aristotle believed that all material bodies had a natural motion toward the center of the universe. Motion in any other direction required a violent impetus. Observation soon raised doubts about this theory. If it were correct, an arrow should fall to the ground as soon as it left the bow. And how account for the increasing speed of falling bodies? Soon a theory was developed that once a body was put in motion the commotion caused by it in the air kept it moving. This same force increased the speed of falling bodies. Unfortunately the view was open to a serious objection; if it were correct, an arrow would never fall. Then, in the fourteenth century a group of scholars at the university of Paris arrived at a more satisfactory explanation: once started, the impetus of the motion itself kept the body moving. The problem of the perpetual motion of celestial bodies was neatly solved in true medieval fashion; they received their impetus from God. Thus observation was used to refute accepted hypothesis, and reason was called upon to provide more satisfactory ones."[16]

On the whole however Painter has a decidedly negative view of medieval science and philosophy:

"The men of the Middle Ages accepted the classical theory that the earth was composed of four elements: earth, water, air, and fire. The scholars of the early Middle Ages believed that the earth was flat, with the land mass occupying the center and the water flowing around the edge. Although this crude idea probably continued throughout the period in the minds of the uneducated, it did not survive among scholars after the absorption of Greek and Arab learning. Later scholars thought of the earth as a sphere. The basest matter, earth, formed the center, then there was a layer of water, then one of air, and finally came the finest element, fire. In the northern hemisphere, the force of the stars drew the earth above the water in some places. Beyond the earth, the universe consisted of spheres. All these spheres except the outermost revolved about the earth under the impulsion of spirits. The topmost sphere, Heaven, remained still. As time went on, observation obliged scholars to make some modifications in this scheme. Thus the eight sphere carried the stars, but it was clear that not all the stars moved in the same direction. Hence they produced the hypothesis that subsidiary spheres revolving independently were attached to the eighth sphere."[17]

The above cosmogony does sound primitive and naïve to a modern, yet it has to be stated that it was no more primitive, and a good deal less so, than other contemporary civilizations. Incidentally, the claim that scholars in the early Middle Ages believed the earth was flat is without foundation,

16 *Ibid.*, p. 435.
17 *Ibid.*

and part of the general "flat earth" myth invented by Washington Irving in the early nineteenth century, and now thoroughly debunked.[18] In spite of his generally negative view of medieval science, Painter does however concede that real progress was made in the practical fields of technology and medicine:

"In assaying the progress made in the development of human knowledge during the Middle Ages, it is important to distinguish between the theoretical and purely pragmatic. Thus in medicine little or no progress was made in theory over the classical and Arab physicians. Hippocrates and Galen remained the accepted authorities. But decided progress was made in the use of herbs and other practical remedies, and physicians were continually concocting new and ingenious therapeutic devices. Some of these brought them into difficulty with the ecclesiastical authorities. Thus, in the twelfth century there was a general belief that a man could be cured of certain ills by having intercourse with a virgin; but the church could not be expected to approve this remedy. Nevertheless, in the course of their experiments the medieval physicians invented some methods of treatment that have found support in modern medical theory. Increase of knowledge by observation and experience was particularly great in agriculture and industrial techniques. The invention of the horse collar was a development of enormous importance. By the thirteenth century the best agriculturalists had discovered that crops were improved if the seed came from other land. In building, working metals, making colored glass, and many other fields, mediaeval technologists made important discoveries. Finally, the alchemists who devoted their efforts to attempts to turn base metals into gold observed many chemical reactions and were the ancestors of the chemists of today. In short, experience guided men with considerable accuracy in many things that we consider to lie within the domain of science. Workmen with no exact knowledge of the laws of physics, of comparative stresses and strains and of strength of materials, built magnificent Gothic cathedrals, which only occasionally fell down."[19]

In fact, the advances made by the doctors, alchemists, architects, metallurgists, and agriculturalists during the Middle Ages were much more dramatic than Painter admits and he fails, as do almost all historians, to recognize that Europe was virtually unique in this regard during these centuries. From the early eleventh century universities began to appear throughout the continent, and by the twelfth century Christendom

18 See Jeffrey Burton Russell, *Inventing the Flat Earth: Columbus and Modern Historians* (Praeger Publication, 1991).

19 Painter, *op cit.*, pp. 435-6.

had caught up with the House of Islam – and then began to overtake it. Towns grew dramatically in wealth and population and from the early thirteenth century a spate of cathedral-building, in the new "Gothic" style, would bequeath to future generations some of Europe's most magnificent monuments. No one who has viewed these structures, with their complex geometry and stunning artwork, can be under the illusion that the society which produced them was in any way "primitive." Nothing to compare with these houses of worship ever appeared in the Islamic world. As the cathedrals were being built, new technologies were developed wholesale. The thirteenth century saw the appearance of gunpowder, magnifying glasses and spectacles, as well as elaborate mechanical clocks and a host of other things. These were followed by further revolutionary innovations during the fourteenth century. Firearms evolved rapidly during the fourteenth century and revolutionized warfare; giving Europe the advantage in future conflicts with the Islamic world and with other civilizations. During the fifteenth century the Turks who besieged Constantinople were compelled to rely on the services of a renegade Transylvanian armorer to build them cannons with which to assault the city walls.

It is not true that the Renaissance began in the fifteenth century. Rather it began in the late tenth and simply moved up a gear during the fifteenth. The whole period in between was dynamic and progressive. Populations grew and so did towns. Literacy became more and more widespread as trade increased and business life expanded. New technologies appeared regularly, and all this process simply reached a crescendo in the fifteenth and sixteenth centuries. So much for Europe's repressive theocracy!

Yet a truly repressive theocracy did indeed exist in the Middle Ages. The Islamic world, which impressed itself so strongly on Europe during the tenth and eleventh centuries with its wealth, splendor and cruelty, was, by the fifteenth century immersed in squalor and poverty. It is futile to blame this development on outside enemies, as Bernard Lewis has noted. The fact is, Europe was a largely rural backwater in the tenth century, when the House of Islam incorporated the great cities and population centers of the Middle East and North Africa. During this period it seems that the Arabs did permit and even encourage new research. That most of this research was not carried out by real Arabs is almost beside the point. At this stage, Islam did at least permit learning and research. But then again what kind of learning was it, and what was its purpose? Even Islamophilic writers such as Briffault admit that the early Arabs, those supposedly imbued with an almost unquenchable thirst for knowledge, had little or no interest in the histories and cultures of the great civilizations they conquered.[20] The truth of this is demonstrated in the fact that by the eighth century Arab writers had no idea who constructed the Great Pyramid or indeed any of the monuments of Egypt. Yet this knowledge had been widely available in the writings of such classical authors as Herodotus and Diodorus, whose works were preserved in the great libraries of Egypt and Babylonia. Take for example the comments of Ibn Jubayr, who worked as a secretary to the Moorish governor of Granada, and who visited Cairo in 1182. He commented on "the ancient pyramids, of miraculous construction and wonderful to look upon, [which looked] like huge pavilions rearing to the skies; two in particular shock the firmament …" He wondered whether they might be the tombs of early prophets mention in the Qur'an, or whether they were granaries of the biblical patriarch Joseph, but in the end came to the conclusion, "To be short, none but the Great and Glorious God can know their story."[21] The complete ignorance of the Arabs in this regard strongly suggests that they did indeed (as Christian polemicists for centuries argued) destroy much Classical literature – at least that literature not of any practical or utilitarian import. In Persia too, the newly-converted Muslims quickly lost track of their own inheritance. By the time of poet and mathematician Omar Khayyam (eleventh-twelfth century), the natives of the country had forgotten almost everything about their illustrious history. Thus the ancient city of Persepolis, capital of the Achaemenid kings Darius I and Xerxes, was believed by the poet to have been built by the genie king Jamshid; and the same daemon was credited by him with raising the pyramids of Egypt. Islamic chroniclers in Egypt itself had their own mythical figures and genie-kings to whom they attributed the erection of the pyramids. Such was their regard for the literature of the classical age and for the critical method!

Within a short time worse was to follow. Muslim rulers began to systematically plunder the ancient monuments of Egypt, and an official department existed whose purpose was the location and despoliation of pharaohnic tombs. The larger monuments were plundered for their cut-stone, and Saladin, the Muslim hero lionized in so much politically-correct literature and art, began the process by the exploitation of the smaller Giza monuments. From these, he constructed the citadel at Cairo (between 1193 and 1198). His son and successor, Al-Aziz Uthman, went further,

---

20 Briffault writes, "Of the poets and historians of Greece, beyond satisfying their curiosity by a few samples, they [the Arabs] took little account." *op. cit.*, p. 192.
21 Beattie, *op cit.*, p. 50.

and made a determined effort to demolish the Great Pyramid itself.[22] He succeeded in stripping the outer casing of smooth limestone blocks from the structure (covered with historically invaluable inscriptions), but eventually canceled the project owing to its cost.

And that attitude to learning was displayed in the treatment meted out to two of the biggest luminaries of Muslim Spain, Averroes and Maimonides. Despite being an Islamic judge, Averroes was banished, his books burnt, and he was forced to emigrate to Morocco (in 1195) where he died in 1198. Maimonides in his turn had to flee in order to escape Almohad persecution.

Louis Bertrand issued this cautionary note to those who extol Islamic learning: "When we are told about Musulman tolerance and about the cult of literature, science, and art at the court of the Caliphs, when the praises of the universities of Cordova, Seville, and Toledo are sung to us, it would be very naïve to judge them by our standards, and to see in these universities something like the Sorbonne, even that of the Middle Ages."[23] Illustrating his point, Bertrand looks at the work of the Arab historians. "The Arab 'histories,' as they are generously called, can only be regarded from our point of view as dry annalists or, in general, compilers without any critical faculty. As Gobineau has already remarked, in connection with the Persian writers, they do not possess the sense of what we understand by truth, or, more exactly, the sense of Yes and No. They have a hazy idea of the boundaries of history and poetry, properly so-called.

"Thus their histories are strewn with long fragments of poetry, to which they attribute the value of historical evidence; they accept the most fabulous legends and traditions without interpreting them; they fall into all kinds of Oriental exaggeration; and, when they quote figures, they let themselves go to astronomical valuations. As for marshalling of narrative and methodical exposition, nothing could be further from their habits of mind. Everything is put on the same plane – trivial incidents and important events which led to changes of regime or the fall of empires."

Bertrand complains too of the chopping of narrative into annual sections, a feature that "produces extraordinary complexity and intricacy, something like the inextricable labyrinth of lines in an arabesque." In the end; "These histories – if one dare give them that name – only too often leave us with the impression of an absurd and unintelligible chaos."[24]

---

22 *Ibid.*
23 Bertrand, *op cit.*, p. 22.
24 *Ibid.*

Schools certainly existed in the Spanish Caliphate; yet they were not schools as we imagine them: "These schools ... were strictly sectarian, and the teaching was purely religious. Those which Hakam [II] subsidized were intended to 'teach the Koran' to poor children of the capital. That did not even mean that the children were taught to read and write in Arabic. Teaching the Koran means teaching recitation of the suras of the Holy Book by heart."[25] As for the "universities," Bertrand notes: "Learning, as we understand it, had only the most restricted place in them. It was regarded with suspicion by the religious intolerance of the faquis, which was often translated into very drastic prohibitions and persecutions. During periods of extreme rigour, all that was permitted to students of mathematics was to acquire the knowledge necessary to orientate the mosques in the direction of Mecca and determine the seasons, the phases of the moon, and the exact hour of prayer. Everything else was regarded as dangerous."[26]

Some areas of research were more acceptable to the religious sensibilities of the imams: "Medicine and botany, by reason of their practical utility, escaped the severity of religious censorship. There were famous Spanish doctors and surgeons ... who were mostly of Christian or Jewish origin." Yet the medicine practiced "makes us smile to-day." And, "All this so-called science had nothing in common with ours. It was the liquidation of the old Greco-Latin empiricism plus an Alexandrine and Oriental endowment. It was a farrago which the modern age had to abandon." Bertrand concludes that, "The bulk of this teaching – terrible in its verbalism and almost entirely theological – reduced itself to some ideas of medicine, mathematics, and astronomy, but especially of astrology, alchemy, and demonology. The occult part of the Judeo-Arab learning was what most attracted the Christians, not only of Spain, but also of the whole of medieval Europe."[27]

The rejection of reason is said by some apologists for Islam to have been the fault of philosopher/theologian Al-Ghazali (1058-1111). Yet, as Catholic priest and physicist Stanley Jaki has explained, the rejection of reason is implicit in the Qur'an. There is no question that Al-Ghazali, one of the pillars of Islamic jurisprudence, "denounced natural laws, the very objective of science, as a blasphemous constraint upon the free will of Allah."[28] Yet from the very beginning, "Muslim mystics decried the notion of scientific law (as formulated by Aristotle) as blasphemous and irrational,

---

25 *Ibid.*, p. 75.
26 *Ibid.*, p. 76.
27 *Ibid.*, p. 157.
28 Jaki, *op cit.*, p. 242.

depriving as it does the Creator of his freedom."[29] Robert Spencer quotes social scientist Rodney Stark who notes that Islam does not have "a conception of God appropriate to underwrite the rise of science. ... Allah is not presented as a lawful creator but is conceived of as an extremely active God who intrudes in the world as he deems it appropriate. This prompted the formation of a major theological bloc within Islam that condemns all efforts to formulate natural laws as blasphemy in that they deny Allah's freedom to act."[30]

Allah's freedom to act is seen all too clearly in the outlandish events of Muhammad's life, where sacred moral laws are broken by the Prophet and his followers, only to be vindicated – afterward – by new "revelations" from Allah.

We have already seen, in Chapter 1, what Maimonides thought of Islamic "science," and indeed the antipathy of the Islamic world to all forms of scientific research and even technical innovation since at least the twelfth century – and probably earlier – is well known and denied by no one, not even Bernard Lewis. Thus for example in *What Went Wrong?* Lewis mentions the thirteenth century Syrian physician Ibn al-Nafis, who theorized on the circulation of blood, but whose ideas remained ignored and forgotten until the modern age.[31] Again, Lewis notes the case of the Egyptian (or perhaps Syrian) astronomer Taqi al-Din, who in the sixteenth century constructed a great observatory, "comparable in its technical equipment and its specialist personnel with that of his celebrated contemporary, the Danish astronomer Tycho Brahe." But it was there, as Lewis concedes, that the comparison ends; for whereas Tycho Brahe's observatory "opened the way to a vast new development of astronomical science," Taqi al-Din's observatory "was razed to the ground by a squad of Janissaries, by the order of the sultan, on the recommendation of the Chief Mufti."[32] Lewis might also have mentioned the Ottoman refusal, on religious grounds, to allow the opening of a printing press until the late eighteenth century, and the resistance to the development of new technologies of all kinds on the same grounds.

In summary, whilst Europeans may not have been perfectly free in terms of thinking and beliefs during the Middle Ages, they were a lot freer than most of the contemporary world's peoples; and this is particularly so when compared with those of the Islamic world. Furthermore, we cannot

---

29 *Ibid.*, p. 43.

30 Robert Spencer, *Religion of Peace?* p. 154, citing Rodney Stark, *op cit.*, pp. 20-1.

31 Lewis, *What Went Wrong?* pp. 79-80.

32 *Ibid.*, p. 80.

finish without remarking upon the astonishing dynamism of medieval Europe and the incredible progress it made in five centuries. At the dawn of the tenth century most of Europe was a rural backwater. All of the lands east of the Elbe (and almost all east of the Rhine) were barbarian-infested wastelands without a trace of literate civilization. Those to the west, in Gaul and Britain, and even in Italy, were not much better. In this region there prevailed an almost universal illiteracy and a subsistence barter economy of the most primitive kind. There existed only a handful of towns with more than 30,000 people, and even these were nothing like the towns of the Roman period. England had none, with the possible exception of London. Even Rome had little more than the same figure. Yet by 1492, when Columbus set out on his great voyage of discovery, Europe stood on the verge of world domination. The continent, from the Atlantic to the Urals, was full of towns and cities built partly of stone and brick, with dozens of universities and a thriving economy. The whole of Europe was crisscrossed with roads which conveyed an astonishing array of wealth and produce from one region to another. Printed books were everywhere, and literacy was extremely common, even among the relatively poor.

However, even this understates the transformative power of Christian civilization. By 1100 many of the above developments had already taken place. In the short space of time between around 950 and 1050 Christian civilization advanced from the borders of the Rhine and the Elbe to the Urals, raising towns, cathedrals, universities, schools and hospitals in every region. Indeed, the continent of Europe was civilized and transformed in this century even more quickly than the continent of North America was transformed in the years after 1700. It took two centuries for literate and urban civilization to spread in America from the Atlantic to the Pacific. The vast space between Rhine and Urals was civilized in little more than a century.

Islam, by contrast, began the tenth century as possibly the most splendid civilization on the earth. It possessed great cities like Baghdad, Samarra, Damascus and Alexandria, some of which had about 500,000 souls.[33] Its civilization at the time was suffused with the spirit of Sassanid Persia and Byzantine Syria and Egypt, whose wealth, learning and population it had inherited. Yet five centuries later the whole region was a declin-

---

33 It should be noted however that this is precisely the same situation as that which had existed before the appearance of Islam: In the early seventh century the cities of the Byzantine Empire and Sassanid Persia were enormous compared to the small towns of contemporary Europe. Islam therefore inherited the population, as well as the wealth, of these regions. It actually created neither.

ing relic, in some places a wasteland. What a contrast with Europe in the same five centuries, and what a rebuke to those who argue that Islam was free and progressive during the Middle Ages.

8
THE OTTOMANS AND EUROPE

The immediate cause of the First Crusade was the threat posed to Constantinople by the Seljuk Turks. The danger from the Seljuks having been removed, another Turkish clan, named Ottoman after its founder Osman, or Othman, renewed the attack on Byzantium in the late thirteenth century. Portion by portion the whole of Anatolia was overrun. Devastation followed in the wake of the Turkish warriors. From the moment the forces of Orhan, son of Osman, crossed into Europe in 1345, the history of the Balkans was a long litany of war, massacre, enslavement and deportation. As good Muslims the Turks religiously adhered to the principle of permanent war against the infidel; for them any permanent peace with Christians was unacceptable, and they renewed the conflict with their Christian neighbours on an annual basis. As the sphere of Turkish control moved inexorably westwards and northwards, so did the attendant devastation and destruction on the frontier.

Yet even those Christians living under the direct rule of the sultan were never again to know peace and security. The intolerable burdens placed on them – including, as we shall see, a human tax of one male child per family – elicited frequent rebellions amongst the subdued Greeks, Bulgarians, Serbians, and Albanians; and these uprisings were quelled with the utmost ferocity.

It is impossible in these pages to catalogue in detail the endless oppressions endured by the peoples of south-eastern Europe during the centuries which they lived under the heel of the Turks, though a few of the more atrocious examples shall be highlighted as we proceed. This is necessary, for the full horror of Turkish rule is not widely known outside the Balkan lands affected by it, even though the conquests of the Ottomans brought the scimitar of Islam as far as the borders of Poland and the gates of Vienna – the latter on two memorable occasions. Nor was their ambition confined to the conquest and exploitation of eastern and central Europe. The whole continent was within their sights, and they made several determined efforts to add Italy to their acquisitions. Spain too, with its own native Muslim population in the south, felt the effects of Ottoman ambitions, and the desire on the part of the Spaniards and Portuguese to find a way to China and the Indies which bypassed the Turkish domains was to have far-reaching consequences.

Fig. 8. The Fall of Constantinople, 1453

The arrival of the first Turkish forces in Europe in 1345 was not viewed with undue alarm by the Christian rulers of the continent. That they were actually invited in by a disgruntled Byzantine prince who sought to use them to bolster his own claim to the throne, should not surprise us. Invasions throughout history have commenced in precisely the same way. But the kings and potentates of Europe did not foresee a major threat. Almost three centuries had passed since the Seljuk Turks had first stood at the gates of Constantinople and thereby provoked the First Crusade. Since then Christendom had taken the fight into the heart of the House of Islam. It is true that by 1291 the last of the Christian kingdoms established by the Crusaders had fallen, and any Christians left in the region lived under the heel of Islam. Yet in the same thirteenth century the Dar al-Islam had suffered what must have seemed like a mortal blow at the hands of the Mongols, who smashed the power of the caliphs and shahs in central Asia and reduced to hills of ashes dozens of the great cities of the region, including Bukhara, Samarkand and Baghdad. That the Mongols did not completely destroy Islam was due entirely to the timely death of the Great Khan Möngke (or Mangu), whose demise ensured the withdrawal of his main forces, under the command of Hulagu, to Mongolia. The depleted army left in Palestine unwisely attempted the invasion of Egypt – the last independent Islamic power – and was defeated at the Battle of Ain Jalut ("Goliath's Well") in northern Palestine.

Yet Ain Jalut must have seemed like a temporary reprieve: the Mongols, it was felt, would surely return with a mighty force to wreak vengeance upon Egypt and her Mameluke rulers. The vengeance never came: The new Great Khan, Kublai, was less inimical to Islam than Möngke, and he concerned himself primarily with Chinese affairs. In the time of Kublai's successor Timur, the Mongol Empire was divided into several semi-independent kingdoms, which eventually became fully independent. The rulers of these states, reigning over predominantly Muslim populations, in time became Muslims themselves. Such was the case with the Persian-based Ilkhanate, whose ruler Ghazan embraced Islam in 1295, as well as with the Khanate of the Golden Horde (or Kipchak Khanate), which took in the whole of Central Asia and the Ukraine. It adopted Islam during the reign of Uzbag (1312-41).

For all that, the damage done to Islam by the earlier Mongol rulers was vast, and there remained a sense among Europeans that it was no longer a great threat. In addition, the Mongol conquests had brought stability to the heart of Asia, and peaceful intercourse was established for the first time between the West and the great civilizations of the Orient.

Across the Silk Road, which wound its way from China through Central Asia to the Middle East, there flowed great quantities of goods and ideas in both directions. In the words of Trevor-Roper, "The great, orderly, tolerant Mongol Empire, crossed and re-crossed by continual caravans, provided one of the most effective means for the diffusion of culture and technology. It was in those years that some of the great Chinese inventions came to Europe. Gunpowder was first mentioned in Europe by Roger Bacon, the friend of Guillaume de Rubrouck who had visited Karakorum [the Mongol capital]. It was first used in the West, by both Christians and Moslems, in the early fourteenth century. Printing also reached Europe from China during the period of the Mongol peace. The first printed document in Europe is perhaps the stamped signature of the reply of Kayuk Khan to the pope, written in Uighur script, which Giovanni da Piano Carpini brought from Karakorum and which, long unknown, was discovered in the Vatican archives in 1920."[1]

The feeling among Europeans during the Mongol epoch that Islam was no longer a threat was probably encouraged too by the steady progress of the Reconquista in Spain: By the early fourteenth century Muslim Spain had been reduced to little more than the Kingdom of Granada in the far south.

Taken all together then it must have seemed a matter of no great concern when a new Turkish dynasty began the conquest of Anatolia in the early years of the fourteenth century. The capture of Bursa in 1324 saw the Ottomans control almost all of Asia Minor and Turkish forces at the gates of Constantinople. A similar series of events in the latter eleventh century spurred the European powers to action; this time however there was to be no mobilization in the West. When Orhan brought his forces across the Dardanelles in 1345 in support of the Byzantine regent John VI Kantakouzenos, who was at war with the dowager queen, it was generally viewed as little more than an internal domestic struggle among the Greeks. A more incorrect assessment could hardly be imagined. The arrival of the Turks on European soil was to prove by far the greatest threat to Christendom's survival ever launched by Islam. With the arrival of the Ottomans in Thrace there appeared in Europe a power which was implacably opposed to Christian civilization in its entirety. Orhan quickly annexed the territories adjacent to Constantinople and spread his authority throughout the region. By the time of his successor, Murad I, the Turks were already clashing with other Christian states such as the Bulgarians and Serbians.

---

1 Trevor-Roper, *op cit.*, pp. 178-80.

Fig. 9. Janissaries
Janissaries were the elite fighting force of the Ottoman Empire. All of them
were forcibly conscripted from the Christian communities of the Balkans and
Anatolia.

The subjugation of the Balkans was facilitated by an elite body of
troops known as the Janissaries. These men, whose name derives from the
Turkish *yeniçeri* ("new soldiers"), were forcibly recruited from the Christian populations of Anatolia and south-east Europe. Tradition says that
it was Orhan himself who established the practice, though more recent
research indicates that its origin should be attributed to Murad I, in 1383.
Every five years or so the brightest and ablest Christian boys, normally between the ages of 10 to 12, were "gathered" as a human tax by the sultan's
troops, from the towns and villages of the Greeks (of Anatolia as well as

Europe), Serbs and Bulgarians, and later also from the Wallachians (Romanians), Croatians and Hungarians. The children would then be taken to Asia Minor, where they would be placed with Turkish families and instructed in the Muslim faith. They were subject to severe discipline, and abuse of all kinds was normal. They were trained as soldiers and forbidden to learn any other trade or to marry. In time, they would officially join the sultan's elite Janissary bodyguard. These boys would never see their families again and were entirely lost to them. This system of abduction, known as the *devshirme*, operated throughout the Ottoman Empire until the eighteenth century.

As with so much else when it comes to Islamic history, the *devshirme* system has been effectively sanitized in much current historical writing. The Wikipedia page on "Janissary" for example, which may be regarded as fairly accurately representing the opinion of current establishment "gatekeeper" thought, notes the following: "Greek Historian Dimitri Kitsikis in his book *Türk Yunan İmparatorluğu* ('Turco-Greek Empire') states that many Christian families were willing to comply with the *devşirme* because it offered a possibility of social advancement. Conscripts could one day become Janissary colonels, statesmen who might one day return to their home region as governors, or as Grand Viziers or Beylerbays (governor generals)."[2]

But this is a travesty: There is little or no evidence for such co-operation. (Note also the Turkish title and Turkish publisher of Wikipedia's supposed "Greek" author). *Devshirme* was nothing other than the kidnapping by a brutally oppressive state of children who were then forcibly converted to an alien and hostile faith. Rarely, if ever, did they return to their homelands; and if they did so it was as oppressors. The truth is that during the centuries of Turkish rule the Christian peoples of the Balkans suffered, what to modern Westerners, would seem an almost unimaginable oppression. Even before their entry into Europe the Turks wrought terrible destruction upon the Christians of Asia Minor. This, like so much of Ottoman history, is a tale almost unknown and rarely told in modern publications. Consider for example the following by Greek author Apostolos Vacaloupolis:

"… evidence as we have proves that the Hellenic population of Asia Minor, whose very vigor had so long sustained the Empire and might indeed be said to have constituted its greatest strength, succumbed so rapidly to Turkish pressure that by the fourteenth century, it was confined to a few

---

2 http://en.wikipedia.org/wiki/Janissary

limited areas. By that time, Asia Minor was already being called Turkey ... one after another, bishoprics and metropolitan sees which once throbbed with Christian vitality became vacant and ecclesiastical buildings fell into ruins. The metropolitan see of Chalcedon, for example, disappeared in the fourteenth century, and the sees of Laodicea, Kotyaeon (now Kutahya) and Synada in the fifteenth ... With the extermination of local populations or their precipitate flight, entire villages, cities, and sometimes whole provinces fell into decay. There were some fertile districts like the valley of the Maeander River, once stocked with thousands of sheep and cattle, which were laid waste and thereafter ceased to be in any way productive. Other districts were literally transformed into wildernesses. Impenetrable thickets sprang up in places where once there had been luxuriant fields and pastures. This is what happened to the district of Sangarius, for example, which Michael VIII Palaeologus had known formerly as a prosperous, cultivated land, but whose utter desolation he afterwards surveyed in utmost despair ... The mountainous region between Nicaea and Nicomedia, opposite Constantinople, once clustered with castles, cities, and villages, was depopulated. A few towns escaped total destruction — Laodicea, Iconium, Bursa (then Prusa), and Sinope, for example — but the extent of devastation elsewhere was such as to make a profound impression on visitors for many years to come. The fate of Antioch provides a graphic illustration of the kind of havoc wrought by the Turkish invaders: in 1432, only three hundred dwellings could be counted inside its walls, and its predominantly Turkish or Arab inhabitants subsisted by raising camels, goats, cattle, and sheep. Other cities in the southeastern part of Asia Minor fell into similar decay."[3]

The passage of the Turks into Europe brought more of the same to the latter region. The above-quoted writer continues;

"From the very beginning of the Turkish onslaught [in Thrace] under Suleiman [son of Orhan], the Turks tried to consolidate their position by the forcible imposition of Islam. If [the Ottoman historian] Sukrullah is to be believed, those who refused to accept the Moslem faith were slaughtered and their families enslaved. 'Where there were bells', writes the same author, 'Suleiman broke them up and cast them into fires. Where there were churches he destroyed them or converted them into mosques. Thus, in place of bells there were now muezzins. Wherever Christian infidels were still found, vassalage was imposed on their rulers. At least in public they could no longer say '*kyrie eleison*' but rather 'There is no God but Al-

---

3 Apostolos Vacalopoulos, *Origins of the Greek Nation – The Byzantine Period, 1204-1461* (Rutgers University Press, New Jersey, 1970), p. 73.

lah'; and where once their prayers had been addressed to Christ, they were now to 'Muhammad, the prophet of Allah'."[4]

Another author, again, generally unknown in the West, writes,

"... the conquest of the Balkan Peninsula accomplished by the Turks over the course of about two centuries caused the incalculable ruin of material goods, countless massacres, the enslavement and exile of a great part of the population — in a word, a general and protracted decline of productivity, as was the case with Asia Minor after it was occupied by the same invaders. This decline in productivity is all the more striking when one recalls that in the mid-fourteenth century, as the Ottomans were gaining a foothold on the peninsula, the States that existed there — Byzantium, Bulgaria and Serbia — had already reached a rather high level of economic and cultural development....The campaigns of Mourad II (1421-1451) and especially those of his successor, Mahomet II (1451-1481) in Serbia, Bosnia, Albania and in the Byzantine princedom of the Peloponnesus, were of a particularly devastating character. During the campaign that the Turks launched in Serbia in 1455-1456, Belgrade, Novo-Bardo and other towns were to a great extent destroyed. The invasion of the Turks in Albania during the summer of 1459 caused enormous havoc. According to the account of it written by Kritobulos, the invaders destroyed the entire harvest and leveled the fortified towns that they had captured. The country was afflicted with further devastation in 1466 when the Albanians, after putting up heroic resistance, had to withdraw into the most inaccessible regions, from which they continued the struggle. Many cities were likewise ruined during the course of the campaign led by Mahomet II in 1463 against Bosnia — among them Yaytz, the capital of the Kingdom of Bosnia...But it was the Peloponnesus that suffered most from the Turkish invasions. It was invaded in 1446 by the armies of Murad II, which destroyed a great number of places and took thousands of prisoners. Twelve years later, during the summer of 1458, the Balkan Peninsula was invaded by an enormous Turkish army under the command of Mahomet II and his first lieutenant Mahmoud Pasha. After a siege that lasted four months, Corinth fell into enemy hands. Its walls were razed, and many places that the sultan considered useless were destroyed. The work by Kritobulos contains an account of the Ottoman campaigns, which clearly shows us the vast destruction caused by the invaders in these regions. Two years later another Turkish army burst into the Peloponnesus. This time Gardiki and several other places were ruined. Finally, in 1464, for the third time, the destructive rage of the invaders was aimed at the Peloponnesus. That was

---

4 *Ibid.*

when the Ottomans battled the Venetians and leveled the city of Argos to its foundations."[5]

The wars of conquest were only the beginning of sorrows for the peoples of the region. From then on they must endure the hardships of life as *dhimmis*. In practice, their condition was little better than that of slaves. Indeed, in many respects it was considerably worse: For whereas a slave was property, and therefore of some value to someone (it was in the owner's interest to keep the slave reasonably well-fed and clothed), the *dhimmi* Christian might be exploited and ill-used by any Muslim he encountered. As in other Muslim-dominated lands, so it was in the Ottoman territories. Since a Christian's testimony carried no legal weight when opposed to that of a Muslim, even trivial disagreements between Christian and Muslim neighbours might rapidly escalate into an issue which could cost the Christian his property and his life. Furthermore, Christian women and girls, especially attractive ones, stood in perpetual danger of the unwanted and potentially catastrophic attention of Muslim neighbours and officials. And the kidnap and forcible marriage of Christian women and girls was an ongoing crucifixion endured by *dhimmi* communities and the Balkans for centuries.

The Ottoman view of the Christian peoples of Bulgaria, Greece, Serbia, Wallachia and Hungary was that of an endlessly exploitable resource. Their best sons were taken by force and trained as Muslim warriors and their most attractive women frequently torn from their families, and often their husbands, to be enjoyed by the sultan, as well as by minor officials and even by ordinary Muslims. And the rest of the population was crushed under an intolerable weight of taxation, one which kept the whole region in a state of perpetual economic stagnation and grinding poverty. Devastating famines were frequent occurrences.

In view of all this, the reader will not be surprised to learn that the Turks made little or no effort to convert their Christian subjects to Islam: indeed, they did not even want them to convert. For as soon as a household or village became Muslim it was cut-off as an exploitable resource: The *jizya* tax ceased, and the communities' sons and daughters were no longer available for use and abuse. Equally unsurprisingly, however, there were significant numbers of converts, and even more who went through a sham conversion: Whole families and communities in the Balkans, but especially in Albania and Bosnia, made public professions of conversion to Islam, often posing as Muslims for several generations, whilst keeping alive

---

5 Dimitar Angelov, "Certains aspects de la conquête des peuples balkaniques par les Turcs," *Byzantinoslavica*, 17 (1956), pp. 236, 238-9.

the family knowledge that they were not "real" Muslims. This of course carried its own dangers, since having been recognized as Muslims, any perceived "apostasy" to Christianity carried the death penalty. Yet it was a risk many Christian families were willing to take, if it could ease the burden of their lives under the Ottomans.

Fig. 10. Vlad Tepes, "The Impaler"
Vlad has become notorious for his impalement of victims, which is now widely viewed as an example of medieval European barbarism. However, the punishment was unknown in Europe before Vlad's time, and he learned it from the Turks, with whom he spent several years in his youth as a hostage.

For the Christians of the Balkans who refused to renounce their faith – the vast majority – life was a perpetual crucifixion. From various parts we hear of the desperate measures taken by villagers and peasants (and townsfolk) to prevent the kidnap of their sons and daughters. In Herzegovina and other areas, for example, boys would frequently have their fingers cut off by family members to make them useless as soldiers of the sultan.[6]

6 See for example John R. Schindler, *Unholy Terror: Bosnia, Al Qa'ida and the rise of global jihad* (Zenith Press, 2007), p. 23; Christos Yannaras, *Orthodoxy and the West: Hellenic self-identity in the modern age* (Holy Cross Orthodox Press, 2006), p. 112;

Girls, on the other hand, who could be taken into the sexual slavery of the harem, or raped before their marriage in a Turkish version of *droit de Signeur*, were frequently tattooed on their hands with a cross – a symbol anathema to the Muslims which often prevented their abduction.

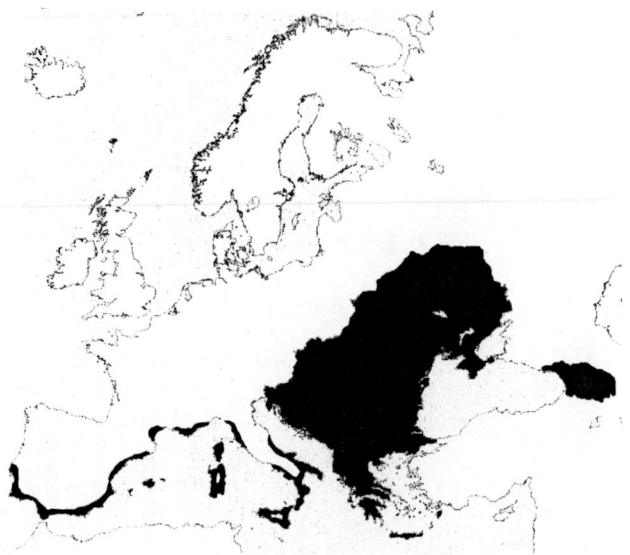

Fig. 11. Areas of Europe affected by Muslim slave-raiding between the 14th and 18th centuries

From Greece, accounts survive of the horrific tortures undergone by priests and monks at the hands of the Ottoman soldiery; even to the extent of mutilation involving the removal of jaws and cheek bones with a saw and skinning prisoners alive.[7]

The Turks conquered the Balkan lands piecemeal: one relatively small territory at a time was gobbled up in the endless annual campaigns of conquest waged by the sultans against the infidel. One feature of Turkish rule, particularly in the more outlying regions, was the complete destruc-

---

Andrew G. Bostom, "Jihad Conquests and the Imposition of Dhimmitude – A Survey" in Andrew G. Bostom (ed.) *The Legacy of Jihad: Islamic Holy War and the Fate of Non-Muslims* (Prometheus Book, New York, 2005), pp. 41-46; Serge Trifkovic, *The Sword of the Prophet: Islam; History, Theology, Impact on the World* (Regina Orthodox Press, Boston, 2002), p. 97.

7 The custom of impaling prisoners, for which Vlad Tepes (the "Impaler") became notorious, was learned by him from the Turks, when he was a hostage in Constantinople. This is not generally known, and, once again, is seen as a typical example of medieval European barbarism.

tion of all Christian places of worship. Thus in Hungary, in Croatia, in Bosnia-Herzegovina, in northern Serbia, hardly a single medieval Christian church survives.

Along with the destruction of churches came a vicious economic exploitation, and this pertained even to regions deep within Ottoman territory. It is a well-recognized fact that the centuries of Ottoman rule were ones of economic stagnation and depression. There was little or no investment by the sultans in Christian territories; no effort at all was made to encourage existing industries or to set up new ones. Even agriculture was neglected, and large tracts of formerly productive land frequently fell into disuse, to be overgrown with weeds and brush. Medieval towns and villages of the Balkans were in danger of going the same way as the Roman cities of the Middle East and North Africa. All this was an inevitable consequence of Islamic attitudes, which themselves grew from the idea that "the faithful" had a right to subsist off the wealth and work of the infidel. Such predatory and parasitic attitudes positively discouraged wealth creation and hard work. The more wealth one created, the more would be confiscated by the Ottoman state.

But there was one form of economic activity which did flourish under the Ottomans: the slave trade. Indeed, the growth of Ottoman power in the fourteenth century signaled a massive revival of the slave trade in Europe and elsewhere. The Ottomans themselves acquired European slaves from the territories under their control and more especially from border regions, which were raided incessantly. But Christian slaves were also now acquired from much further afield. Throughout North Africa Muslim rulers sent out fleets of raiders to scour the coasts of southern Europe for captives, whilst in eastern Europe Islamicized Tartars from the Crimea (the Khanate of Crimea) and from present-day Khazakhstan and eastern Russia (the Nogai Horde) launched incessant raids against Russian and Lithuanian/Polish peasant communities on a vast front.

The worst of the raiding in Russia occurred from 1441 onwards, when the Crimea, or Crimean Khanate (a kingdom much larger than the Crimean Peninsula), became independent. According to historian Alan Fisher, up to three million Slavic peasants were enslaved by Tartar raiders operating from the Crimea between 1441 and 1774, when the Russians conquered the territory.[8] Almost all of these were sold into the Ottoman Empire as eunuchs, harem women and galley slaves. These raids, virtually unknown amongst Westerners, are recognized by historians as playing an

---

8 Alan Fisher, "Muscovy and the Black Sea Slave Trade," *Canadian American Slavic Studies* Vol. 6 (1972), pp. 575-94.

enormous role in retarding Russia's economic and cultural development. They largely prevented the settlement and peopling of the Ukrainian steppe lands, a vast area which was eventually to become the bread basket of Russia and to support a large segment of the Russian population.

The slave-raids occurred on an annual basis, and reading contemporary accounts of them is harrowing. Consider for example the words of S. Herberstein, ambassador from Emperor Charles V to Muscovy in the 1520s, when he describes Mehmet Ghirey's slave-hunting expedition of 1521:

"He took with him from Muscovy so great a multitude of captives as would scarcely be considered credible; they say the number exceeded eight hundred thousand, part of whom he sold in Kaffa to the Turks, and part he slew. The old and infirmed men, who will not fetch much at a sale, are given up to the Tatar youths, either to be stoned, or to be thrown into the sea, or to be killed by any sort of death they might please."[9]

Mikhalon the Lithuanian wrote around 1550 in his book *De moribus Tatarorum Lituanorum et Moscorum*, "The Crimean Tatars have much more slaves than livestock. Therefore they supply them also to other lands. Many ships loaded with arms, clothes and horses came to them one after another from beyond the Pontus and from Asia, and left always from them with slaves. ... So these plunderers always are in possession not only of slaves for trade with other people but also have slaves for their own estates and to satisfy at home their cruelty and waywardness. In fact we often find among these unfortunate people very strong men, who, if not castrated, are branded on the forehead or on the cheek, and are tormented by day at work and by night in dungeons."[10]

In the words of Daniel Pipes, "The Crimean Khanate existed as a slave-hunting outpost of the Ottoman empire. Its whole economy was based on slave raids and slave trade. As one scholar points out in his work The Crimean Tatars and their Russian captive Slaves, 'From the beginning of the 16th century until the end of 17th century the Crimean Tatar raider bands made almost annual forays into agricultural Slavic lands searching for captives to sell as slaves ... the slave trade was the most important basis for the Crimean Tatar economy in the 16th and 17th centuries. During these centuries, the Crimean Khanate remained the main supplier of Slavic slaves, almost all of which were captured in southern Poland or Muscovite Russia, and brought back to the Crimea by their raiders. Most of their raids seemed neither to have had any military purpose, nor politico-terri-

---

9 Cited from Daniel Pipes, http://www.danielpipes.org/comments/193802
10 *Ibid.*

torial ambitions. The taking of captives and the selling them as slaves for the Crimean Tatars was purely an 'economic' activity. R. Hellie refers to the Crimean Tatar's raiding activities as their 'industry'.... "Slave raiding into Muscovy reached crisis proportions after 1475, when the Ottomans took over the Black Sea slave trade from the Genoese and the Crimean began slave raiding as a major industry, especially between 1514 and 1654.... The sale of slaves brought great profit to the Crimean raiders, because they were in great demand from the Ottoman Empire.'"[11]

The above-quoted writer continues: "The Crimean raiders have to hand over ten percent of their human booty to the government as a kind of custom tax at the frontier of the Crimean Khanate. Most captives were usually driven to Kaffa, the largest slave market of the Crimea under the direct administration of the Ottoman Empire, and were sold there to the slave merchants. ... Nearly seventy percent of the slaves sold in Kaffa were driven onto ships and dispatched to Istanbul. ... When they arrived, the Ottoman officials first examined the new 'cargos' and chose the best slaves: the most beautiful women for the sultan's harem, the most handsome and the strongest men for his palace service. The remaining ones were purchased either by the government for navy, or by the slave merchants of Istanbul..."

Pipes comments: "It is estimated that c.1,000,000 Poles were captured by the Tatar slave-hunters to be sold into Moslem slavery and a corresponding number of Russians. The problem of slave hunting was so acute and desperate for the Russian state that there existed a special 'Ministry of Ransom' and a special permanent tax was collected to redeem Slavic slaves from the Tatar/Turkish captivity whose horrors are hard to imagine today for a civilized person that is rarely confronted with contemporary historical sources and grim realities."[12]

Daniel Pipes, like Bat Ye'or and Andrew Bostom, is a critic of Islam; yet, as with them, none of the facts he cites is controversial or has been countered by politically-correct historians. These simply downplay the same material or decline to mention it altogether. As might be imagined, the activities of the Crimean and Nogai slave-raiders had a devastating effect on Russian society and its economic development. For one thing, it long prevented the exploitation of the immensely fertile grasslands of the Ukraine. These vast territories were known simply as the "Waste Lands" during this period. Even regions to the north of the Ukraine, in the for-

---

11 *Ibid.*
12 *Ibid.*

ested (and farmed) lands of Muscovy proper, had to be partially evacuated because of the slave-raids. Instead of utilizing their energies to improving agriculture, the Russians had to spend three centuries creating defensive works and training peasants in the use of arms. Normal economic activity only proceeded southwards in the wake of painfully slow military operations. It was the threat posed by the Muslim slavers which gave rise to the Cossacks, tribes of Slavic peasants trained in horsemanship, who formed a vanguard in the fight against the Tartars and Turks. As the Cossacks pushed southwards, so did farming and settlement.

The long struggle between the Slavs and the Islamic predators who preyed on them was to have a long-lasting effect on the character of the Russian people, a topic we shall examine presently.

Another vast new "theater" of the slave-trade with the Ottomans opened during the fourteenth century in the Mediterranean. In this region of course Muslim slave-raiding had never really ceased after its high-point in the tenth century, when fleets of Saracen pirates scoured the trade-routes in search of Christian victims. After the Genoese and Pisans had retaken several of the Mediterranean islands from the Arabs, including Sardinia in 1016 and Corsica shortly thereafter, Saracen piracy slackened. It was dealt a further blow by the Norman conquest of Sicily in 1091. Yet none of these things, even the possession of large and well-armed fleets by the Genoese and the Venetians, could entirely free the Mediterranean from Muslim pirates. Indeed, so serious had the problem again become in the fourteenth century that the Genoese were compelled to appeal to the French for assistance in clearing the seas of this pestilence. The "crusade" which the French launched in 1390 against the pirates of Mahdia in Tunisia was, as we have already mentioned, an abject failure, and their activities continued unabated in the years that followed.

Things in fact took a turn for the worse in the sixteenth century when the whole of North Africa came under the sovereignty of Ottoman Empire, either as directly administered provinces or as autonomous dependencies. Spurred by the demand for white-skinned slaves in the Ottoman provinces of the east, North African pirates intensified their activities, capturing thousands of ships and rendering, within a few decades, long stretches of coast in Spain and Italy almost completely uninhabited. From the sixteenth to the nineteenth centuries, it is estimated that the Barbary pirates captured and enslaved anything between 800,000 to 1.25 million Europeans.[13] Their predation extended throughout the Mediterranean south along West Africa and even, on one occasion at least, South Ameri-

---

13 See www.bbc.co.uk/history/british/empire_seapower/white_slaves_01.shtml#two

ca. They also on occasion raided far into the North Atlantic, taking slaves from the coasts of France, the Netherlands, Britain, Ireland, and even Iceland. But their main theater of operation was the western Mediterranean, where islands such as Sicily, Sardinia, Corsica and the Balearics suffered intensely. And their raids also inflicted severe damage upon coastal towns and villages in Italy, France, Spain, and Portugal. Most of the captives were sold in the slave markets of North Africa and the Ottoman heartlands in Constantinople and Anatolia.

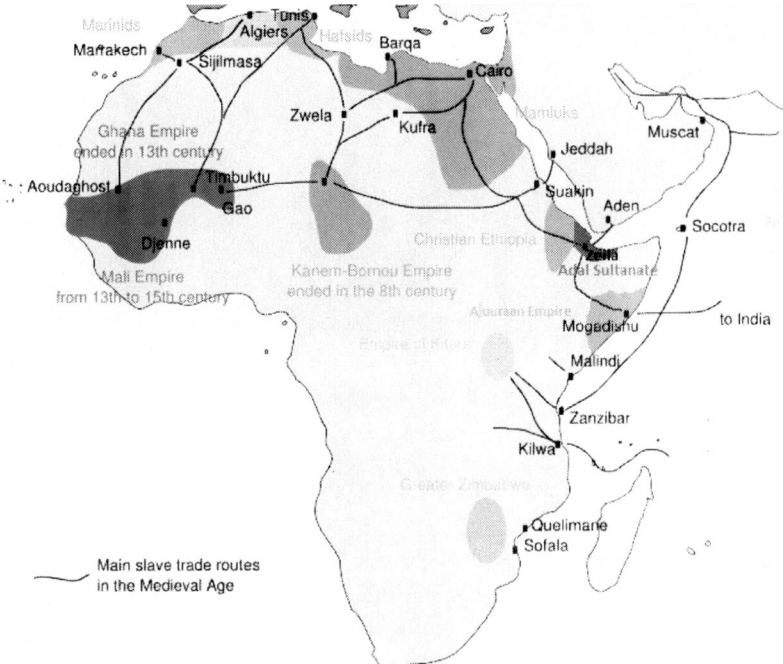

Fig. 12. The main slave routes in Africa during the Middle Ages

Whilst such depredations continued into the early nineteenth century, there was a little improvement towards the end of the seventeenth century, when European navies commenced regular patrols of the western Mediterranean and launched retaliatory actions against the pirates strongholds in North Africa. However, the ships and coasts of Christian states without such effective protection continued to suffer until the early years of the nineteenth century, and it was only after the Napoleonic Wars and the Congress of Vienna in 1814-5 that the European powers agreed upon the need to suppress the Barbary corsairs entirely. After this several punitive attacks against Algiers and Sale in Morocco were launched by the

British navy, which almost, but not entirely, destroyed their ability to raid. Nonetheless, so deeply ingrained was the tradition among the inhabitants of the region that even then there were occasional further incidents until the French invasion and conquest of Algiers in 1830.

At the height of their activities the Barbary States were so powerful that nations including the United States of America paid tribute in order to stave off their attacks.

IN THE SLAVE-MARKET AT KHARTOUM.

Fig. 13. A slave market in Sudan, 1876-79

In addition to slaves from Europe, the Ottomans also imported vast numbers of captives from black Africa. Again, the numbers involved are impossible to ascertain with any certainty, but it was without question several millions over a period of four to five centuries.[14] Most of these unfortunates were taken from east Africa, mainly modern Ethiopia, Kenya, Sudan, and Tanzania. Their fate mirrored that of Europeans similarly enslaved. Notwithstanding the millions of Africans imported into Constantinople and Anatolia during these centuries (roughly between the fifteenth and nineteenth), it is notable that they left barely a trace of their existence in the genetic makeup of modern Turks. This, a fact frequently noted by commentators, speaks of the appalling treatment suffered by these creatures before and after their arrival in Constantinople. It is also certain that large (perhaps vast) numbers of babies of mixed race born to black slave

14 The essential reading here is Ehud Toledano, *Slavery and Abolition in the Ottoman Middle East*, part of the series Publications on the Near East (University of Washington Press, 1997).

women were simply killed by their Turkish fathers.

If the women imported into the Ottoman domains were destined either for the sex slavery of the harems or as harem attendants, the fate of the men and boys was perhaps even worse. These were either castrated and made to perform the functions of eunuchs or sent to work as galley slaves – truly a fate worse than death. As regards the "operation" which rendered young men and boys as eunuchs, it is perhaps too obscene to describe in anything but a pornographic publication. Suffice to say that the death rate after the operation, either through infection or loss of blood and trauma, has been estimated at 90%. In short, for every thousand eunuchs in the Ottoman Empire, there were nine thousand youths and boys who died in agony; and at any given time there were many thousands of eunuchs.

An article published in the Journal of the Anthropological Society of London in 1871, shortly after the great emancipation of the slaves of America had occurred, looks in an unapologetic way at the Muslim tradition of slave-holding and comes to the conclusion that slavery was inherent to and an essential part of the Islamic faith. Needless to say, such an article could not possibly be published in our times in a similar "respectable" publication:

"... it must be taken into account that this great demand for Negro slaves is based upon reasons far above fashion or fancy, as slavery is inherent in the religious and social system of Mohammedanism, and is congenial to the ideas and customs of Mussulman nations. This assertion that slavery is inherent in the very system of Islamism will startle many who believe in the compatibility of that antiquated system with modern civilisation. The arguments, however, which I am going to bring forward cannot fail from establishing such a fact as an axiom, putting it thus beyond the pale of controversy. I will therefore prove that slavery is inherent in the religious system; inherent in the social system; and, also, congenial to the ideas and customs of Mohammedan nations.

"One of the earthly rewards which the Koran holds out to the victorious Moslem is that of reducing to bondage his foe, and of disposing of him as he chooses; his soul excepted, everything belongs to the conqueror, even his dead body. The religious and political system of Mussulmanism [Islam] being based on the principle of perpetual war, *Djehad [jihad]*, enticements for the present and for the future life constitute an essential part of the system, and the right of possessing slaves is one amongst them. This right is of course transferable, as any other title to property is; therefore the dealer who has made the acquisition of a slave from the original proprietor, the Negro conqueror, or the Arab kidnapper, commits, legally, his right to any customer (a Mussulman of course) who may bid the highest price. According to the Koranic law, such is the hold of the master over the slave that no earthly power is allowed to interfere between them; the master is answerable only to the Almighty for the manner in which he treats his slave. This un-limited power exerted over the slave is often the cause that masters take with impunity the lives of their slaves. The authorities, in such cases, either ignore or feign to ignore the event, because, legally, they have no right to interfere. According to the Koran, the only persons who may legally claim blood for blood in criminal cases are, either the nearest relations of the deceased, or (in case of a slave) his master. Now, in an instance of this sort, it is not likely that a master should present himself, asking from the tribunal justice for the blood of the slave he has himself slain. The Mussulmans, as a mass, are very tenacious of this right of holding slaves, and they will not allow that an infidel can indulge in such a luxury. As for European philanthropists, who try to put a stop to such a practice, they heartily wish them at the world's end.

"Having briefly explained the theory of slavery as it is established by the Koran and understood by its followers, I will now come to the second point, and show how slavery is a social necessity amongst Mussulmans; to be convinced of this, one must bear in mind that in Mohammed's system, religious tenets and social laws are twisted and impasted together, forming, of the whole concern, a thorough gordian knot. It is on account of these difficulties, of a technical as well as of a practical nature, that the action of modern ideas always meets in the Mussulman element with an inert mass which never yields to persuasion, but only recoils before pressure. And what other explanation can be given of the great obstacles Sir Samuel Baker avows to have met with in the execution of his scheme for the suppression of slavery? According to Lord Houghton's statement, made before the Royal Geographical Society, 'the Egyptians did not seem to be disposed to support any such undertaking of Sir Samuel Baker's as the suppression of slavery, for the very simple reason that it is through the slave trade that they obtain a constant supply of domestics for their households.' The discovery is a good one; but if this is so far true for the Egyptians, it is the same for the Turks, the Persians, and all other nations who live under the same system. Yes, this avowal of Sir Samuel Baker's discloses the secret of the demand for Negro slaves: a supply of domestics is required to keep up the harems of the high and middle classes of Mussulman society, and Negritia [black Africa] must pour forth a constant supply of slaves. And this, because slaves are as much an essential part of the harem system, as the harem itself is of the religious and social system of Islam. The seclusion of women is for the Mussulman what one of the ten commandments is for the Christian; but how can that seclusion be enforced, if all the members of the harem are not submitted to the pressure of the same bondage? One or two women cannot, evidently, be kept tightly under lock, while their maids and attendants are free. Slavery is the natural consequence of seclusion. The Mussulman religion once adopted, its system must be carried through; there is no alternative. If the Mussulman is to remain a Mussulman (I mean even of a medium standard, and not merely a bigoted one) he must protect the sacredness of the conjugal tie by shutting up his wife or wives in the best manner he can. Wives are, therefore, cut off from the outside world by all sorts of contrivances, amongst which is that of having slaves instead of free-born servants, who could serve as mediums to dangerous ideas and still more dangerous customs. It is evident that if the attendants of the harem were such, not only the hold of the master over them would be of little efficacy, but the outer world might become acquainted with scandals of all sorts. To employ slaves is by far more convenient. For this end, the prudent Turk takes good care that the slave he buys should have his eyes tied up, a phrase which means that the first quality which a slave must possess is to be blind to the tricks and disorders of his master. Once in the harem, the white or Negro slave is submitted to the same system of seclusion as her mistress or mistresses are. A circumstance which renders the use of slaves indispensable, and forms an obstacle to the employment of free-born female attendants, is the formal injunction of the Koran to the effect that, not only the face, but the hands also, of a free-born Mussulman woman are to be concealed from strangers. (The Sherihat [Sharia] orders that the upper part of the hand is to remain concealed. As for the inside, a woman can show it; otherwise she could not even beg alms for her relief.) Is it possible that a servant maid could serve about the harem, day and night, thus muffled up, fearing lest the master of the house should let his eyes fail upon her face or hands? Even if the maid happened to be not very particular on this point, custom, the fear of comments, and the disapprobation of her relatives, would prevent her from violating ostensibly the laws of Mussulman religion. It is easy to understand, then, how people should object to employing girls wrapped up like so many bogies in white veils and sheets. The employment of Christian women has been thought of, as their religion would remove the inconvenience above stated, but the Mussulmans strongly object to it on grounds of self-preservation against the encroachments of the Christian element. The few Pashas who have employed Christian servant girls, adopted this course from motives of policy with the object, I mean, of gaining in the eyes of Europeans.

"Having so far shown that slavery is inherent in the religion and social system of Islam, it remains to be seen how slavery is congenial to the ideas and customs of Mussulman nations. It is one of the characteristics of Orientals to lean towards despotism, whether it be actively or passively. The same annals which record the names of the despots who have crushed the East under their feet, testify to the servility of their subjects. Slavery has never had very repugnant features in the eyes of Orientals. The Turk is far from being an exception to the general rule: by instinct, in his own limited sphere, he must be either a despot, or the servant of a despot stronger than himself. Nothing can better satisfy the vanity of a Turk than to look upon himself as the master of some human being; as he contemplates two or three slaves standing silent and with folded arms before him, the Turk rises infinitely greater in his own estimation. This feature of the Turkish mind is tangible, and can be traced not only in the customs of the people but in their very idiom, common sayings, and proverbs. For instance, if, during the course of familiar conversation, a Turk wishes to say something in the shape of good omen, he will say, '*Kull kiolleh shaibih olah*' which means that the person in question may be lucky enough to become the master of numerous slaves. From the cradle, vaticinations of this sort are constantly made by mothers and nurses to their babies, while singing them to sleep; one of those verses ends in this way, '*Kull alaik hep bundah*,' the meaning of which is, 'Male slaves, female slaves, all will belong to him.' Another remarkable thing of this sort is, that the phrase, 'your servant,' *votre serviteur*, is never employed by the Turks, but 'your slave,' 'the most abject of your slaves,' etc. In all such phrases, the word slave is employed instead of servant. On the strength of such evidences, I do not hesitate to assert that the slave holding passion has its roots in the very heart of the Turks, and that it is congenial to them as well as to the other Mussulman nations."[15]

The above description of slavery in Islam stands in stark contrast to the utterly unfounded and frankly disingenuous assertion of Bernard Lewis that slaves in Islam had "rights."[16]

---

15 "On the Negro Slaves in Turkey," *Journal of the Anthropological Society of London,* Vol. 8 (1870-1871), pp. 85-96, quoted from www.americanthinker.com/2013/01/ sesquincentennial comparisons black slavery in america and ottoman turkey. html#ixzz2i5S3UTnQ

16 Lewis, *What went Wrong?* p. 85.

9
ISLAM AND THE AGE OF DISCOVERY

The years following the capture of Constantinople were character-ized by the inexorable expansion of Turkish rule in Europe. It is true that, for a while, Ottoman ambitions were checked by the dynamic leadership of the Hungarian warrior John Hunyadi. The latter inflicted a series of defeats on the Turks, culminating in the destruction of their army at the Siege of Belgrade in 1456; and though Hunyadi died of the plague in the immediate aftermath of the siege, he bequeathed a powerful and sta-ble Hungary to his son Matthias Corvinus, whose reign marked the end of Turkish expansion for a generation. But King Matthias' rule proved to be a temporary respite: his death signaled the renewal of Ottoman aggression, and their crushing defeat of Matthias' inexperienced successor Louis II at the Battle of Mohacs in 1526 marked the end of Hungary as a great power and the commencement of a centuries' long crucifixion of her people.

In the hundred years following Mohacs, the Turks renewed the at-tack again and again, striking into the heart of Europe, with repeated expeditions against Austria and even southern Poland. These enterprises brought Ottoman arms to the gates of Vienna for the first time in 1529. Simultaneous with the effort to overwhelm the Hapsburg lands, the Sul-tans also directed their attention westwards, to Italy and even to Spain. In-deed, a key aim of all Ottoman rulers, after the fall of Constantinople, was the subjugation of the capital of the Western Empire, Rome. And Turk-ish intentions in this regard were signaled within a year of the taking of Constantinople, when Mehmed II launched a full-scale invasion of Italy. As it transpired, the expedition floundered during the prolonged Siege of Otranto, in the extreme south of the Peninsula, where 900 of the citizens were slaughtered following their refusal to embrace Islam. The arrival of a massive Turkish force on Italian soil caused panic throughout Europe, and the Pope made preparations to flee north of the Alps. The Ottomans' failure to crush the power of the Empire in central Europe brought them back on the offensive in Europe's "soft underbelly" in the second half of the sixteenth century. Thus in 1571 the Sultan Selim II gathered together a gigantic naval force with the intention of subjugating Italy. To counter this Pope Pius V succeeded in bringing together the Holy League, an alliance comprising forces from Austria, Spain and the Italian states. Rather than await the arrival of the Ottoman fleet in Italy, the Christian navy advanced to meet it off the shore of Greece, and a great battle was fought near the isle of Lepanto.

Fig. 14. The Battle of Lepanto
The Battle of Lepanto temporarily halted Turkish plans for the conquest of Italy and Western Europe, but it by no means removed the threat completely. A year later the Turks had constructed another equally large fleet.

It is difficult to convey in a few sentences the sense of gloom which prevailed throughout Europe on the eve of Lepanto. Almost every year for two centuries the Ottoman sultan had renewed the assault upon Christendom with all the resources at his command. During the course of the sixteenth century alone Hungary and Croatia periodically witnessed the arrival on their soil of vast Turkish hosts bent on pushing the sultan's empire into the very heart of Europe. Again and again Austria and Poland found themselves in the utmost danger. Several smallish towns in Hungary and Croatia, such as Eger and Güns, could afterward boast of defenses no less astonishing than anything accomplished by the heroes of Hellas in the epic war against Xerxes. The sieges of Güns (Hungarian Kőszeg) in 1532, and Eger in 1552 deserve special mention. In Güns (modern Croatia), a force of 800 men, with no cannons and few guns, under Nicholas Jurisich, managed to hold off an enormous Ottoman army of something between 120,000 and 200,000 men. After a siege lasting 25 days the Turks abandoned the attack and moved on towards Vienna. The losses they sustained at Güns however eventually compelled them to abort the Vienna campaign.

In the same year however, Temesvar and Szolnok were taken by the Turks, a loss blamed on mercenary soldiers within the Hungarian ranks. When the Ottomans turned their attention shortly afterwards to the northern fortress town of Eger few expected the defenders to put up much resistance, particularly as the two great armies of the Ottoman lords Ahmed and Ali, which had crushed all opposition previously, united under Eger.

Eger was an important stronghold and key to the defense of the remainder of Hungary: North of the town lay the poorly reinforced city of Kassa (present day Košice), the centre of an important region of mines and associated mints, which provided the Hungarian Kingdom with large amounts of quality silver and gold coinage. Besides allowing a take-over of that revenue source, the fall of Eger would also have enabled the Ottomans to secure an alternative route for further westward military expansion, possibly opening a more direct route to Vienna.

A tiny force of Hungarian troops and foreign mercenaries, together with civilian townspeople (including women), numbering altogether no more than just over 2,000 souls, were all that stood against the mighty Turkish army of perhaps 40,000 men which now appeared before the fortress walls. The Ottoman forces were armed with 16 large siege guns and about 150 medium and smaller pieces, as against the defenders' 6 large cannons and around a dozen smaller ones. The attack began almost immediately with a massive bombardment, and this was followed on the second day by a major assault. There was desperate fighting on the walls and the women of the town proved themselves equal to the men in courage and resourcefulness. Assault after assault was repelled by the desperate courage of the townspeople, with even the wounded dragging themselves from their sickbeds and helping in various ways, some of them suicidal. The Turks tried mining under the walls, but these mines were met by counter mines from the defenders. Eventually, after an epic 39-day siege the Turks abandoned the attack and retreated south.[1]

---

1 Incredibly, very little in English has been written about these epic engagements. A reasonably good account is found in Peter F. Sugar (ed.) *A History of Hungary* (Indiana

Fig. 15. The Siege of Eger
The defense of Eger in Hungary is one of the most heroic actions in European military history, but is virtually unknown outside of Hungary.

The defense of Eger and Güns rank among the most heroic military actions in European history, on a par at least with the actions of the 300 Lacedaemonians who stood at the Pass of Thermopylae in 480 BC. They delayed the Turkish advance towards Vienna at a crucial period when the Ottomans might well have captured the Habsburg capital, from which vantage point they would have been well placed to press the attack into the rest of Germany and France. Yet these events are virtually unknown in Western Europe, where their importance is neither understood or appreciated. It is a good bet however that had these events been part of English history they would no doubt have already been the subject of dozens of popular novels, plays and Hollywood movies.

Yet in spite of the appalling losses the sultan's armies suffered in Hungary, he invariably returned the following year with equally colossal armies: The Ottoman's resources seemed inexhaustible and their determination adamantine.

Now, in 1571, it became clear that the Ottomans had decided once

University Press, 1990). Much has of course been written in Hungarian, *e.g.* Geza Gardonyi, *Egri Csillagok*, 2 Vols. (Europe Konyvkiado, Budapest, 1985).

again to turn their attention southward. The vast fleet which the sultan had gathered was aimed at Italy. Had it been permitted to sail unimpeded to the peninsula it is likely that the Turks would have swept all before them. The whole of Italy, including Rome, might swiftly have fallen, and these forces, pushing northward, would have joined others coming from Croatia in the east. A catastrophe was about to unfold, and preventative action was necessary. Yet the great fleet gathered by the Holy League was of inferior size to that of the Turks, and its commanders bickered amongst themselves. Victory was something they could hardly dare to hope for. In the end however superior tactics prevailed, and the battle was a clear victory for the Christians, who nonetheless lost ten galleys and 8,000 men. The Turks, by contrast, lost 200 ships and sustained 30,000 casualties. Although a decisive watershed in the Christian-Islamic conflict in the Mediterranean, the victory at Lepanto did not prevent the Ottomans from putting to sea with an equally large fleet the following year. Such were the resources and such was the determination of the Turkish holy warriors.

It is difficult for modern Europeans, particularly natives of northern Europe, to comprehend the impact of these events upon the psyche of Italians, Spaniards, Hungarians and Austrians of the time. We are used to seeing the fifteenth and sixteenth centuries in central and southern Europe as the dawning of the Renaissance, as the beginning of the great revival of European civilization, as the harbinger of the Age of Science and of Discovery. It is true of course that the fifteenth and sixteenth centuries did constitute an epoch of massive technical and economic progress. There was much ferment in art, music, literature, science, and technology. No doubt some of this – as has often been claimed – had been stimulated by the arrival in the West of Greek scholars fleeing Constantinople after its capture by the Turks. This was also an age of unprecedented discovery, as European caravels probed the southern reaches of the Atlantic, then reached across the ocean to the Americas. But, hard as it may be for us to imagine, the rosy picture of advancement and exuberant optimism which we now have of this epoch was not shared by the people of the time. Even as Cortes and Pizarro conquered the vastly wealthy lands of Mexico and Peru in his name, the Emperor Charles V gloomily awaited the dissolution of Christendom. "We set out to conquer worthless new empires beyond the seas," lamented Busbequius, the Belgian whom the king of the Romans sent as ambassador to the sultan of Turkey, "and we are losing the heart of Europe."[2] Christendom, he wrote, subsided precariously by the good will of the king of Persia, whose ambitions in the east continually called the

2 Trevor-Roper, *op cit.*, p. 17.

sultan of Turkey back from his European conquests.[3]

We know now, of course, that the Turks had reached the apex of their advancement in the time of Charles V, and that their history, from then onwards, would be one of continual retreat in the face of an increasingly powerful and confident Europe (though they were able to strike at the heart of the Empire one more time in the latter years of the seventeenth century). But this was not known by the contemporaries of Charles V, and a sense of gloom prevailed throughout his dominions. All seemed lost, or on the verge of being lost. The great fear that had haunted Christendom since the seventh century – that it would be overwhelmed by Islam – seemed on the verge of realization. Indeed, it was the very advance of Islam which had reorientated Europe westwards in the first place during the fourteenth and fifteenth centuries and eventually led to the epoch-making discovery of the Americas.

The fall of the Balkans and Constantinople to the Turks during the fifteenth century was viewed with alarm at the opposite end of the Mediterranean. For centuries the people of Spain had held a front line of the bloody clash with Islam. The war against the followers of Muhammad became the virtual *raison d'être* of Spanish kings. It was a perennial project: Not an obsession, more like a normal part of life. It was taken for granted that there could never be peace with the Islamic world. How could it be otherwise, when making war against the infidel world was a religious duty for every Muslim? The Spaniards, more than any other people of Europe, were aware that *jihad* was a state of permanent war which excluded the possibility of a true peace. In an earlier age the crusaders had come to understand this, and it was reiterated in the fourteenth century by the Islamic historian Ibn Khaldun, whom we quoted in Chapter 2. Ibn Khaldun was a native of Andalusia, but what he wrote about *jihad* would have been understood by every monarch of Spain, Christian and Moor. Thus for the kings of Castile the survival in the Iberian Peninsula of any region from which Islam could launch attacks was seen as a real and ever present threat, and the reduction of Islamic Spain to the southern strongholds of Andalusia did not make Christians feel any more secure. Now the threat was not from North Africa but from Turkey. And indeed the advancement of the Turks westwards towards Italy during the fifteenth century made such a possibility into a nightmarish probability. Thus Granada had to be reduced, no matter what the cost. And even after that, the Spaniards did not feel secure. The war against Islam would continue, as it always had. The Ottomans were threatening Italy and the entire western Mediterra-

---

3 *Ibid.*

nean, Spain herself could be next.

It was of course the rise of Ottoman power in the eastern Mediterranean which had during the fourteenth and fifteenth centuries first prompted Europeans to look towards the Atlantic, there to find a way to the Spice Lands of the east which bypassed the Islamic world altogether. These efforts were led initially by the Portuguese who, particularly under Henry the Navigator, sought to find a way to the Indies by circumnavigating Africa to the south. These voyages, which focused the attention of Europeans upon the Atlantic, were eventually to lead to the discovery of the Americas. Columbus believed the circumference of the earth to be much smaller than it is and imagined that across the Atlantic he would find – where in fact America is – eastern Asia and the Indies. Such a short route to China would facilitate a direct alliance between that country and Spain. The idea, according to Louis Bertrand, was to "take Islam in the rear," and "to effect an alliance with the Great Khan – a mythical personage who was believed to be the sovereign of all that region, and favourable to the Christian religion ..."[4] Bertrand was very insistent on this point, which he emphasized in half a dozen pages. The voyage of discovery was to begin a new phase, he says, in "the Crusade against the Moors which was to be continued by a new and surer route. It was by way of the Indies that Islam was to be dealt a mortal blow."[5]

So certain was Bertrand of the connection between the exploits of the conquistadors in the Americas and the war against Islam that he actually describes the conquest of America as the "last Crusade."

The record of the conquistadors in the New World needs no repetition here: It is one of cruelty and greed on a truly monumental scale. Yet the habits of the Spaniards here, habits which gave rise to the "Black Legend," were – at least in the opinion of Bertrand – learned at the school of the caliphs. In Bertrand's words: "Lust for gold, bloodthirsty rapacity, the feverish pursuit of hidden treasure, application of torture to the vanquished to wrest the secret of their hiding-places from them – all these barbarous proceedings and all these vices, which the conquistadores were to take to America, they learnt at the school of the caliphs, the emirs, and the Moorish kings."[6]

Indeed all of the traits associated with the Spaniards, for which they have been roundly criticized by Anglo-Saxon historians, can be traced, according to Bertrand, to the contact with Islam.

---

4 Bertrand, *op cit.*, p. 163.

5 *Ibid.*

6 *Ibid.*, p. 159.

Whether or not Bertrand is correct in this regard is a moot point, and it is a question we shall address again presently. For the moment, it is sufficient to note that the very discovery of the New World was connected with the conflict with Islam; with the need to bypass Muslim territory for trading purposes, and with the desire to establish contact, and alliance, with anti-Muslim powers in eastern Asia.

10
CONCLUSION

I n his book *What Went Wrong?* Bernard Lewis surveys a thousand years of Islamic backwardness, poverty, and oppression. Almost every page is packed with examples of how all of these things derived from attitudes which have their origins in Islam. Having done all that, he gets himself into a terrible muddle at the end: Looking at how modern Arabs and Muslims have sought to apportion blame for their predicament on outsiders, he then states that, "A more sophisticated form of the blame game finds its targets inside, rather than outside the society. One such target is religion, for some specifically Islam. But to blame Islam as such is hazardous and rarely attempted. Nor is it very plausible."[1] It's not plausible, he says, because, "For most of the Middle Ages, it was neither the older cultures of the Orient nor the newer cultures of the West that were the major centers of civilization and progress, but the world of Islam in the middle. It was there that old sciences were recovered and developed and new sciences created; there that new industries were born and manufacture and commerce expanded to a level previously without precedent. It was there, too, that governments and societies achieved a degree of freedom of thought and expression that led persecuted Jews and even dissident Christians to flee for refuge from Christendom to Islam."

The survey of medieval Islam undertaken in the present volume gives the lie to the above statements: Medieval Islam was never tolerant, and if persecuted Jews fled there, they fled even more frequently to Christendom. Nor was the House of Islam the major center of civilization and progress during "most of the Middle Ages." It was, for a very brief period (and just how brief that time may have been is one of the topics covered

---

1 Lewis, *op cit.*, p. 156.

in the Appendix to the present study) the wealthiest and perhaps the most technically advanced civilization on earth, but that wealth and technical knowledge was almost entirely derived from the great civilizations of the Middle East which Islam absorbed in the middle of the seventh century, namely Byzantine Egypt and Syria and Sassanid Persia. Other things, such as "Arabic" numerals, paper-making, etc., came from the great civilizations of the Orient, China and India. They may have reached Europe through the filter of the Islamic world; but they did not originate there, and they would undoubtedly have reached Europe whether Islam existed or not. And the suggestion that the arrival of this knowledge in the West at least suggests the existence of normal trading relations between Europe and the House of Islam during the tenth, eleventh and twelfth centuries is unfounded: A crucial technique may be transmitted from one society to another by a single knowledgeable individual. Indeed, there is evidence to suggest that much of the "Islamic" knowledge reaching Europe in the tenth and eleventh centuries arrived here with small groups of refugees from Islamic oppression. Such, for example, were the Spanish Jews who arrived in England with William the Conqueror in 1066: they were flee-ing the horrific violence launched against their coreligionists in Spain by Muslim mobs earlier in the same year. It was a Syrian refugee from Islam, Kallinikos (Callinicus), who had, in an earlier age, provided the Byzantines with the knowledge of "Greek Fire," with which they destroyed attacking Muslim fleets.

The truly Islamic thing which Muslims brought to Europe in the tenth century was a massive revival in the slave trade. The devastation wrought by Muslim slave-raiders over the centuries in Europe and else-where would need an extremely large volume in itself to catalog. As we saw in Chapter 2, large areas of southern Europe were turned into war-zones in the tenth century by this activity, whilst large areas of northern and eastern Europe were similarly blighted at the same time by the attentions of Scandinavian pirates – who were also motivated by Arab gold. The ar-rival of Arab piracy in the Mediterranean brought to a definitive end the peace of the region. From now on, the "Middle Sea" (or Mare Nostrum, as the Romans called it), would no longer be a highway, but a frontier, and a frontier of the most dangerous kind. War and piracy became the norm – in some areas for the best part of a thousand years. And this is something that has been almost completely overlooked by historians, especially those of northern European extraction. For the latter in particular, the Mediter-ranean is viewed through the prism of classical history. So bewitched have educated Europeans been by the civilizations of Greece and Rome, that they have treated the more recent part of Mediterranean history – over a thousand years of it – as if it never existed. The visitor to Mediterranean lands, perhaps on the Grand Tour, was shown the monuments of the classical world: here Caesar fought a battle; there Anthony brought his fleet, etc. The thirteen hundred years between modern times and the time of the Caesars tended to be completely ignored or even whitewashed.

This distorted and romanticized view of the Mediterranean and its past, which ignored the savagery and fear of the past millennium, was particularly characteristic of writers of Anglo-Saxon origin, with whom there was the added problem of religious antagonism. With the Reformation, English-speakers tended to take an increasingly negative view of medieval Europe and her civilization – and a correspondingly positive view of Europe's enemies and adversaries. This process was exacerbated by the Enlightenment, during which time the term "Dark Age" came to be widely applied to European history after the fall of Rome and before the fifteenth century Renaissance. Medieval Spain, which from the fourteenth century possessed its own and particularly egregious version of the Inquisition, became the focus of Enlightenment Europe's loathing. The Spaniards, who had fought a very long war against the Iberian Muslims, were increasingly seen as ignorant savages, whereas their Muslim opponents fared much better.

The reality however was that if some of the Catholics of medieval Spain were brutal, they had very good teachers in the Muslims of medieval Spain: For with the Muslim conquest of North Africa and Spain a reign of violence and terror was to commence that was to last for centuries. The myth of an idyllic and tolerant Caliphate of Cordoba, is just that – a myth, a myth popularized during the Enlightenment and propagated wholesale ever since.

Islamic Al-Andalus was reduced to little more than Granada by the middle of the thirteenth century and Islam looked to be a spent force. In the same century the Mongols came near to wiping Islam off the face of the earth. No doubt the princes and potentates of Europe became complacent; in any case they had their own internal quarrels and disputes to contend with. But by the late thirteenth century some of the Mongol princes in central Asia had converted to Islam, a development which would have long term consequences. At around the same time a group of Turks, nominally under the Ilkhanate of Persia, began expanding their power base into the Byzantine regions of Asia Minor. By the early fourteenth century these Ottoman Turks had extended their reach into south-east Europe, from which point they absorbed the nations of the region, Bulgarians, Serbs,

Croats, Greeks, and Wallachians, one by one.

The Ottomans were now to pose a threat to Europe's very existence more urgent than anything seen since the seventh century. In 1480 the Sultan Mehmed II launched an attempted invasion of Italy, and although this failed, the danger remained active and ever-present for the next two hundred years. Europe could not again breathe freely until the Turks were beaten at the gates of Vienna in 1683. In the interim, the pope was ready to flee from Rome on several occasions, as Ottoman fleets scoured the Adriatic and Ionian Seas. After the fall of Constantinople in 1453, it seemed that the whole of central Europe, including Hungary and Austria, was about to be overwhelmed; and though the imminent danger was averted by the victory of John Hunyadi at Belgrade (1456), it was renewed again in the sixteenth century, when an enormous Turkish invasion force was stopped by the Holy League at the naval battle of Lepanto (1571). And it is worth noting here that the Turkish losses at Lepanto, comprising 30,000 men and 200 out of 230 warships, did not prevent them returning the following year with another enormous fleet, which speaks volumes for their persistence and the perennial nature of the threat they posed. A short time before this, in the 1530s, the Turks had extended their rule westwards along the North African coast as far as Algeria, where they encouraged an intensification of slaving raids against Christian communities in southern Europe. Fleets of Muslim pirates brought devastation to the coastal regions of Italy, Spain, southern France, and Greece, repeating the depredations of the Arabs in the tenth and eleventh centuries. The Christians of the islands, in particular, Sicily, Sardinia, Corsica and the Balearics, had to get used to perennial and persistent surprise attack. There can be no doubt that these experiences left an indelible impression on the peoples of the region. The paranoid culture of feuding, assassination, and the stiletto, for which Sicily and Corsica in particular were to became famous, has to be viewed in the light of the persistent violence inflicted upon these lands by Muslim corsairs. Had the Viking raids in northern Europe lasted as long, we would no doubt have seen similar things there.

The coming of the Ottomans also prompted a vast renewal of the slave trade in central and eastern Europe. On an annual basis Turkish raiders penetrated the borders of Hungary, pillaging and enslaving. It is impossible to tell how many Europeans were taken into bondage in this way, but the figure was undoubtedly in the millions.

The Ottoman slave empire, it should be noted, appeared long before any European powers had commenced shipping captive Africans across the Atlantic; and it is scarcely to be doubted that the Turks provided an example to the Christian slavers of the sixteenth to nineteenth centuries. It is furthermore an absolute certainty that the Spaniards, the first European slavers, got the idea of taking captives from black Africa from the Muslims of Morocco and Algeria, who had been doing the same for centuries.[2] Again, it was unquestionably their intercourse with the Muslims of southern Spain which inured the Spanish Christians to the whole idea of slavery in the first place. As Louis Bertrand noted, slavery continued to exist in Christian Spain long after it had disappeared elsewhere in Europe. And this question leads us onto the wider issue: To what extent did Islamic ideas about war, religious tolerance (or intolerance) and the Jews influence European society during the Middle Ages and the early Modern period?

It is of course impossible to give a definite answer to such a question. Whatever opinion we might provide can only be advanced in terms of probability rather than provability. Nonetheless, there is clear evidence that Islamic cultural ideas had a profound influence upon Europeans, especially southern Europeans, throughout the medieval age. We noted above, for example, that slavery flourished as an institution in Christian Spain when it had ceased to exist further north. We should note too that Christian kings and princes in Spain copied their Muslim neighbors in other ways: It was not uncommon for a Spanish king to reign over a thoroughly Arabized court complete with a harem guarded by eunuchs. And the same tradition was found in another interface region, Sicily. The Emperor Frederick II, for example, was famous (or infamous) for this practice, in virtue of which he was popularly known as the "baptized Sultan of Sicily."[3]

The Spaniards of course became notorious for their behavior in the New World after 1500. Again, it is not beyond reason to suppose that their attitudes may have been influenced by their Muslim neighbors. That certainly was the opinion of Louis Bertrand:

"The worst characteristic which the Spaniards acquired was the parasitism of the Arabs and the nomad Africans: the custom of living off one's neighbour's territory, the raid raised to the level of an institution, marauding and brigandage recognized as the sole means of existence for the man-at-arms. In the same way they went to win their bread in Moorish territory, so the Spaniards later went to win gold and territory in Mexico and Peru.

---

2 According to Ralph A. Austen, around four million black Africans were taken across the Sahara into North Africa between the tenth century and the start of the twentieth. Another six million arrived in the Islamic world via the Red Sea and the Indian Ocean. See Austen, *Trans-Sharan Africa in World History* (Oxford University Press, 2010), p. 32.
3 Trevor-Roper, *op cit.*, p. 147.

"They were to introduce there, too, the barbarous, summary practices of the Arabs: putting everything to fire and sword, cutting down fruit-trees, razing crops, devastating whole districts to starve out the enemy and bring them to terms; making slaves everywhere, condemning the population of the conquered countries to forced labour. All these detestable ways the conquistadores learnt from the Arabs.

"For several centuries slavery maintained itself in Christian Spain, as in the Islamic lands. Very certainly, also, it was to the Arabs that the Spaniards owed the intransigence of their fanaticism, the pretension to be, if not the chosen of God, at least the most Catholic nation of Christendom. Philip II, like Abd er Rahman or Al-Mansour, was Defender of the Faith.

"Finally, it was not without contagion that the Spaniards lived for centuries in contact with a race of men who crucified their enemies and gloried in piling up thousands of severed heads by way of trophies. The cruelty of the Arabs and the Berbers also founded a school in the Peninsula. The ferocity of the emirs and the caliphs who killed their brothers or their sons with their own hands was to be handed on to Pedro the Cruel and Henry of Trastamare, those stranglers under canvas, no better than common assassins."[4]

Whilst I do not necessarily endorse Bertrand's opinion (I feel he has slightly overstated the case), it is nonetheless true to say that their long contact with Islam most certainly did not foster the development of humanitarianism in the Spanish character.

What then of "holy war," execution of religious dissidents, and violent anti-Semitism? As we have seen, all of these were found in Islam before they were found in Christianity – a fact almost never mentioned in mainstream textbooks. Bernard Lewis, for one, has certainly come round to believing that the Christian concept of holy war was derived from the Islamic one. Again, this is not a provable proposition; but then again it is safe to say that the Christians did not derive any pacifist tendencies from the Muslims. As regards religious intolerance, Christianity was never itself very tolerant, but it was almost invariably less violently intolerant than Islam. There was never any real persecution (and certainly no torture) of religious dissenters and heretics in the West before Innocent III launched his Inquisition in the final years of the twelfth century. Yet the Almohads had already established their own "inquisitions" in southern Spain fifty years earlier, and we cannot doubt that Innocent III was well aware of these tribunals. Did he copy them? Again, it is impossible to say; but he

---

4 Bertrand, *op cit.*, p. 160.

most certainly did not learn tolerance from the Spanish Muslims. And what about persecution of the Jews? Once more, it was Islam which led the way and Christendom which followed. The Jews were ultimately caught in the civilizational struggle between Islam and Christianity. They had found favor with the Muslims in an earlier age and had assisted them in some cases – especially in Spain. This seems to have sparked an almost paranoid suspicion in Europe which unscrupulous men periodically exploited in order to lay their hands on the wealth and property of Jewish communities.

No one denies that Europe copied many technologies and philosophical ideas from Islam; and in the eighth century the Byzantine practise of "iconoclasm," the destruction of sacred images, was unquestionably influenced by Islamic custom and belief. If the Byzantines could contemplate, under the influence of Islam, the overthrowing of icons – a central tenet of Orthodox Christian belief – it is surely not too difficult to believe that the Western Christians were also copying Islam when they launched their holy wars, inquisitions, and anti-Jewish pogroms.

Looking at the picture broadly, I feel it is reasonably safe to say that the cause of humanitarianism in Europe was most assuredly not advanced by the continent's contact with Islam. That Islam was at least partly responsible, as we saw in Chapter 9, for the discovery of the New World (by forcing Europe to focus to the West towards the Atlantic), is true. It is nonetheless fairly certain – given the dynamism of European society – that Europeans would eventually have found their way across the Atlantic whether Islam existed or not; but it seems equally evident that contact with the New World would have been considerably less violent and traumatic for its inhabitants had Europeans not been previously acquainted with Islam.

One may therefore argue endlessly about the extent to which Islam exercised a malign influence upon European civilization during the Middle Ages, but its devastating impact upon the nations and regions of the continent occupied by Muslim armies and raided by Muslim slavers is not to be doubted. The whole of eastern and central Europe, from the Volga to the outskirts of Vienna, was subject to perennial depredations at the hands of slave-raiders for several centuries, beginning in the fourteenth and continuing – in some areas – to the eighteenth. Interface areas, or regions on the border which the Muslims did not fully control, were reduced to uninhabited wastelands. So for example the Ukraine, as well as parts of southern Russia, was almost completely depopulated by the attentions of slavers operating from the Crimean Khanante between the fourteenth and seventeenth centuries. The same situation prevailed in Hungary. The great

Hungarian Plain, known as the Puszta, was a heavily-settled agricultural region, supporting numerous towns and cities, during the Middle Ages. By the sixteenth century it was a dreary prairie whose only inhabitants were feral horses and cattle; a prairie that was never again to see its former prosperity. The great central plain of Spain, known as La Mancha, is another case in point. During the Roman and Visigothic epochs this region supported an extremely large population inhabiting numerous towns and cities. After the Muslim conquest however it occupied the bloody border between Christendom and the House of Islam for several centuries. It never recovered, and remains to this day a bleak and barren semi-desert.

Russia, which suffered for centuries from the depredations of the Crimean slaver-raiders, remained a backwater of European civilization as a consequence. Centuries of tyranny and brutality at the hands of the Islamicized Mongols and their Turkish agents rendered Russia a land where despotism came to be seen as normal and where human life was cheap. It is perhaps no coincidence that these things insinuated themselves into the Russian character and that serfdom, for example, was only abolished in Russia in the latter half of the nineteenth century – hundreds of years after it had ceased to exist in most other parts of Europe. It is not to be doubted, I feel, that the particularly savage form of totalitarian tyranny which overwhelmed the Russian people from 1917 onwards, was part of the legacy of tyranny which ingrained itself into the land over the centuries. The main author of that savagery, a Georgian, came from a race of people who endured almost unimaginable brutality at the hands of Muslim masters for many centuries.

Perhaps the worst and most enduring damage was done to the regions of Europe which remained under Turkish control until the nineteenth and early twentieth centuries. Greece, for example, was exploited ruthlessly by the Ottomans for a period of five centuries: Once fertile and populous regions of the Hellenic Peninsula were systematically denuded by the Turks of their wealth and inhabitants. Whole regions of the Balkans were dragged back to a state of semi-barbarism, where there prevailed a primitive tribalism – a situation which persists, even to this day, in parts of Albania and Macedonia. Slavery, too, persisted in these regions long after it had disappeared in the rest of Europe. Thus for example, under the influence of Ottoman practice, Roma gypsies continued to be held as slaves in Wallachia until the middle of the nineteenth century.[5] And indeed slavery persisted as an institution in European Turkey even after its supposed suppression at the end of the nineteenth century. The last recorded slave

5 See www.roconsulboston.com/Pages/InfoPages/Culture/Roma150Yrs.html

auction took place in Constantinople in 1908, and it was not until 1930 that the (by now secular) Turkish state formally abolished the institution.[6]

Nor can we neglect to mention the atrocious massacres, often amounting to genocide – as in the case of the Armenians and Anatolian Greeks – which the Turks launched against the Christian peoples of the Balkans and Asia Minor throughout the nineteenth and into the early twentieth centuries.[7] These horrors, which claimed the lives of several millions, would disgrace the record of any nation; though they also stand as a rebuke to the governments of Western Europe (but most especially of Great Britain), who not only failed to prevent the Turkish attacks but actually defended the perpetrators against the repeated efforts of the Russians to put a stop to them.

But it was the territories which came under Islam during the seventh and eighth centuries which fared worst of all. Many once-thriving Roman and Byzantine cities of North Africa and the Middle East were reduced, within a short time of the Arab Conquests, to ghost towns – abandoned settlements whose skeletal remains still dot the landscape of those regions and have now become important tourist attractions. The coming of Islam into these regions saw a massive reduction in population. Exact figures are impossible to obtain, but it seems likely that by the eleventh century it had been reduced by around two-thirds of the figure under the Byzantines in the early seventh century. And what a burden, as Winston Churchill said, the Muslim faith placed on the shoulders of its own devotees. Women, who had formerly enjoyed great freedoms in the ancient Near East, were instantly reduced to chattels, every one of them the absolute property of some man, either father, brother, or husband: A chattel who must ask permission to leave the home and who could even then only do so draped in a shroud. The beating of these chattels is provided for in Islamic law, and the killing of them in Islamic tradition. How many women in the Muslim world have been mutilated and put to death by members of their own families over the centuries? It is impossible even to guess; but, given contemporary experience of such things the figure must surely run into the hundreds of thousands or even millions.

---

6 The Turks only acceded to the abolition of slavery under intense pressure from Europeans. There was never, at any time, an abolition movement within the Muslim world. Indeed slavery still persists in a more or less clandestine fashion in various parts of the Muslim world to this day.

7 Hitler, in planning the murder of Europe's Jews, is reputed to have quietened the fears of his fellow Nazis by asking "Who now remembers the Armenians [murdered by the Turks]?"

And Islam is scarcely less cruel to men. In a society where women are basically invisible and where in any case the rich and powerful fill their harems with those that are available, men's thoughts turn to what is available and visible: young boys. The House of Islam has been a house of rampant pederasty for centuries; a phenomenon so well accepted that it is scarcely remarked upon. Incredibly enough, Muslims have never regarded this as a moral issue and have at the same time ruthlessly executed adult men who indulged in such behavior with each other.[8]

The decline of the Islamic world, the subject of Bernard Lewis' *What Went Wrong?* is perhaps no better illustrated than in the wonder expressed by the fourteenth century Arab historian Ibn Khaldun, sitting amid the desolation and barbarism of Algeria, as he beheld the apparent wealth and prosperity displayed by visiting delegations of Italian merchants.[9] And indeed European travelers to the Middle East and North Africa throughout the centuries (from about the mid-twelfth onwards at least) consistently describe a region gripped in poverty, squalor and backwardness.[10] Lewis came very close to answering his own question about the decline of the Muslim world when he noted the curious fact that wheeled vehicles were virtually unknown, up until modern times, throughout the Islamic territories. This situation, so striking that it was remarked upon by visiting Europeans over the centuries, was all the more strange given the fact that the wheel was invented in the Middle East (in Babylonia) and had been commonly used in earlier ages. The conclusion Lewis comes to is startling: "A cart is large and, for a peasant, relatively costly. It is difficult to conceal and easy for requisition. At a time and place where neither law nor custom restricted the powers of even local authorities, visible and mobile assets were a poor investment. The same fear of predatory authority – or neighbors – may be seen in the structure of traditional houses and quarters: the high, windowless walls, the almost hidden entrances in narrow alleyways, the careful avoidance of any visible sign of wealth."[11] In the kleptocracy that was the caliphate, it seems, not even Muslims – far less Christians and Jews – were free to prosper. A society which cannot or will not guarantee

---

8 A BBC documentary of 2010 entitled "Afghanistan's Dancing Boys" describes the plight of young boys in that region who serve powerful men – usually warlords – as entertainers and catamites. Tank battles have on occasion been fought by Afghan warlords over the attentions some of these boys. See *e.g.* Polly Toynbee in *The Guardian*, 12 November 2002, "Was it worth it?"

9 Trevor-Roper, *op cit.*, p. 12.

10 There are very many of these, though perhaps that of Volney, C. F., *Travels through Syria and Egypt* 2 Vols. (London, 1787) is best known.

11 Lewis, *What Went Wrong?* p. 158.

the right to private property cannot thrive.

We should note also, before continuing, that the Muslim habit of concealing women behind all-encompassing veils probably had more to do, in its origins, with concealment of valuable assets than with modesty.

Finally, before finishing, there arrives the inevitable question: What if? What if Islam had been triumphant? What if Europe had become Muslim in the seventh and eighth, or even the tenth or eleventh, centuries? As I remarked *Mohammed and Charlemagne Revisited*, no less a person than Edward Gibbon mused on the likely outcome of an Islamic conquest of France in the eighth century, when he noted that, had such an event transpired, then the whole of western Europe must inevitably have fallen, and the Dean of Oxford would likely then have been expounding the truths of the Qur'an to a circumcised congregation. Against such "calamities," noted Gibbon, was Christendom rescued by the victory of Charles Martel at Tours in 732. Adolf Hitler also contemplated the outcome of a Muslim conquest at this time, and regretted the failure of Islam to dominate the continent. He reasoned that a Muslim Germany would have bred fierce warriors who might easily have dominated the world.[12]

However, neither the humorous prognostication of Gibbon nor the vicious one of Hitler are likely to have come anywhere near the truth. From what we have seen of Islam's record elsewhere, it is likely that the continent would have entered a Dark Age from which it would never have emerged. If we seek the model for Europe as a whole we might look to Albania or the Caucasus of the nineteenth century. These regions, inhabited by semi-Islamicized tribes, were the theaters of perpetual feuding. A Europe under Islam would have been no different: A backward and greatly under-populated wasteland fought over by Muslim tribal chiefs, conditions would have persisted right into the present century.

Europe of the seventh and eighth centuries was, after centuries of population decline under the Romans (from the second century at least) under-peopled and largely rural. Rome herself, by this time, had probably around 30,000 inhabitants or even less. No other town on the continent had any more. It is highly unlikely that the incoming Muslims would have altered that situation for the better. The whole region would certainly have been plundered for its human resources: white skinned slaves were always prized in the House of Islam. The few small urban centers, in Italy, France and Spain, would probably have survived and been transformed into local power bases of the caliphate. Rome may have emulated tenth century Cor-

---

12 Albert Speer, *Inside the Third Reich: Memoirs* (Simon and Schuster, London, 1997), p. 96.

doba and become temporarily prosperous on the plunder accrued from other regions of Europe. Throughout the continent there would probably have survived, for a while, an impoverished and sorely oppressed remnant population of Christians. In Rome the pope would have presided over a miserable and decaying Vatican, whose main monuments, such as the original Saint Peter's, founded by Constantine, would have been transformed into a mosque almost immediately after the Muslim takeover. All the artwork and statuary of imperial Rome would have been effaced and demolished. In such a Europe the entire heritage of classical civilization would have been forgotten. Of Caesar and his conquests, of Greece with her warriors and philosophers, the modern world would know nothing. The very names would have been lost. No child now would know of Troy or Mycenae, of Marathon or Thermopylae. The history of Egypt too, and all the great civilizations of the Near East, would lie buried in the drifting sands of those lands, forever lost and forgotten.

There would have been no High Middle Ages, with their Gothic cathedrals, no Renaissance, no Enlightenment, and no Age of Science.

The fall of Europe would have had consequences far beyond its shores; and the twenty-first century may have dawned with an Islamic (and under-populated and impoverished) India threatening the existence of China, which would then likely be the last significant non-Muslim civilization. The wars waged between the two would be pre-modern, and though the two sides might employ primitive firearms and cannons, the sword and the bow would remain the most important weaponry, and rules of engagement would be savage.

APPENDIX

THE MYSTERIOUS ORIGINS OF ISLAM

The story of Islam's origins is a familiar one and well-known even amongst non-Muslims. We are told how Muhammad, a youthful and pious member of the Hashem clan, who had earlier married a wealthy widow, regularly prayed in a cave outside Mecca. There he received a vision of the Archangel Gabriel, who instructed him to "recite" the words he spoke; which recitations became the book we now call the Qur'an.

Familiar too is the story of how Muhammad's revelations were rejected by the people of Mecca, compelling him to escape to Medina, where he found the people more ready to listen. Several years later he is said to have returned to Mecca at the head of a victorious army, overthrowing his most stubborn opponents. Following these events, the Prophet led his followers in numerous campaigns throughout the Arabian Peninsula, conquering and converting the entire country. We are told how, following his death, leadership of the new movement devolved upon a series of caliphs, who led the armies of Islam to victory over the mighty Byzantine and Persian empires.

That, in a nutshell, is the story that has been told of Islam's origins since the beginning of the eighth century. Unfortunately, there is not a single element of this narrative which can stand up to historical criticism. The past few years have seen a proliferation of studies into the faith's roots; studies which have begun to subject it to the same critical examination that Christianity has undergone now for a century and a half. And the results of these studies have revealed that almost everything traditionally accepted about Islam's origins is fictitious. It has been shown, for example, that the Qur'an could not possibly have been written when tradition says it was and that the very existence of a man called Muhammad is called into question.

Among the numerous titles which have appeared recently we may cite in particular *The Syro-Aramaic Reading of the Koran: A Contribution to the Decoding of the Language of the Koran* by Christoph Luxenberg (2007) and *The Hidden Origins of Islam: New Research into its Early History*, a series of essays edited by Karl-Heinz Ohlig and Gerd-R. Puin (2009). Upon the publication of Luxenberg's book, the popular media (perhaps typically) focused on his claim that the 72 virgins promised to Islamic martyrs was a mistranslation, and that what was actually on offer was 72 raisins, or grapes. Yet this was the very least of what Luxenberg was saying, the full import of which was ignored in the newspapers. In fact, he was claiming that the original language of the Qur'an was not Arabic (where the questionable word is read as "virgins") but Syriac or Aramaic, where the same word would translate as "grapes." He was furthermore claiming, sensationally enough, that the Qur'an was originally a Syriac Christian devotional text and had nothing to do with Muhammad or Islam.

Taking the lead from Luxenberg, several more recent studies have denied the existence of anyone called Muhammad in the first place. Amongst the better known of these are Norbert Pressburg's *Good Bye Mohammed* (2009) and Robert Spencer's *Did Muhammad Exist? An Enquiry into Islam's Obscure Origins* (2012). Though both Spencer and Pressburg are seen as critics of Islam, their books examine the evidence, both archaeological and textual, in a scholarly fashion, and the conclusions they reach are devastating to the accepted narrative of Islam's origins and early history.

Some of the earliest recognizably Muslim artefacts are coins, and the Spencer and Pressburg books consider the evidence of these in detail. There we find that the earliest Islamic coins minted in Syria show a figure holding a cross. Some of these, the earliest of which are from the time of Caliph Muawiya and traditionally dated between 647 and 658, have the name "Muhammad" beside the figure with the cross. Not surprisingly, these artefacts do not figure prominently in popularized accounts of the development of Islamic coinage: They are far too problematic. To begin with, they violate a number of principles which are now regarded as fundamental to the Islamic faith. They display an image – perhaps even that of the prophet Muhammad; and even worse, they have that image holding a cross. Among Muslims the cross is anathema; it is an anti-sign. Islamic tradition denies that Jesus (whom it admits was a prophet) died on the cross and dissociates Jesus entirely from what it considers a symbol of shame.

Evidently when these coins were minted, in the middle of the seventh century, the Islamic theology with which we are now familiar had not evolved. But there is even worse. It would appear that the figure holding the cross, beside which sometimes appears the name "Muhammad," may not represent the prophet of Islam at all, but Jesus. As Spencer emphasizes, the word "Muhammad" in Arabic and Syriac implies the "praised one" or "chosen one," and may be a title or epithet as much as a real name. As a personal name Muhammad is in fact unattested before the seventh century, and indeed, considering the word's meaning it is unlikely that anyone named Muhammad ever existed in Arabia before this time. Parents do not normally call their child by titles such as "chosen one." In short, even if an Arab prophet and war-leader called Muhammad existed, it is highly likely that this name was only given to him after his death, or at least late in life. But the fact that the figure on the coins is holding a cross would indicate very strongly that the "praised one" in question was not the prophet of Islam, but Jesus of Nazareth! And this is made all the more likely when we consider the strong links between Jesus and Muhammad in Islamic tradition. According to this, Jesus foretold the coming of Muhammad, who he named Ahmed. The "Muhammad prophecy" of Jesus is referred to by Ibn Ishaq, Muhammad's earliest biographer, who remarked that in the Gospel passage where Jesus refers to the coming of the Comforter [Aramaic Munahhemana], he is actually referring to the coming of Muhammad. Ibn Ishaq explains: "the Munahhemana (God bless and preserve him!) in Syriac is Muhammad; in Greek he is paraclete." However, Ibn Ishaq's English translator Alfred Guillaume notes that the word Munahhemana "in the Eastern patristic literature ... is applied to Our Lord Himself". The original bearer of the title "praised one," said Guillaume, was Jesus, and this title and the accompanying prophecy were "skillfully manipulated to provide the reading we have" in Ibn Ishaq's biography.[1]

What can all this possibly mean? Is it possible that the "prophet Muhammad" was invented several decades after Islam, or the faith we now call Islam, appeared on the world stage? This is a possibility considered by Spencer and he provides very good grounds for doing so.

As Spencer notes, none of the early texts or inscriptions of the seventh century which refer to Islam mention either Muhammad, the Qur'an or even the word Islam. Indeed, inscriptions – both on coins and elsewhere – of the early Islamic authorities use terms and expressions not found in the Qur'an. This, among other things, has prompted several historians to

---

1 Alfred Guillaume, "The Version of the Gospels Used in Medina Circa 700 AD." *Al-Andalus* 15 (1950), pp. 289-96.

suggest that the Qur'an did not then exist and would not exist until near the end of the seventh century – or even the early eighth century.

The evidence, taken together, would suggest that the "Islam" which conquered the Middle East and North Africa during the seventh century was substantially different from the Islam with which we are now familiar. Rules such as that prohibiting images and the cross apparently did not then exist. And there is good reason to believe that the Qur'an, as we now know it, had not yet appeared – and would not appear until the middle of the eighth century.

That Islam was deeply indebted to Christianity and Judaism has of course always been understood. The whole of the Qur'an is full of references to well-known biblical characters such as Adam, Noah, Abraham, Moses, and Jesus. Muslims accept all of the Old Testament as divinely revealed scripture and hold Jesus to be a great prophet. Islamic tradition speaks of the "Last Days" when the "Antichrist" will appear and when Jesus will return to judge mankind and destroy evildoers. But the more we investigate the faith the more thoroughly rooted in Judaism or Judeo-Christianity it appears. As Spencer notes, the earliest references to the followers of what we now call Islam by non-Muslims do not use the term "Muslim" or "Islam" at all, but instead speak of "Ishmaelites," "Hagarians," "Taiyaye," or "Saracens." The first two of these names are derived from the Book of Genesis, and indeed Islamic cultural vocabulary owes little to Arabia: There is scarcely a trace of native Arabian tradition in either the Qur'an or the hadiths. In the words of Arthur Jeffery, "the cultural vocabulary of the Koran is of non-Arabic origin."[2] He continues, "From the fact that Muhammad was an Arab, brought up in the midst of Arabian paganism and practising its rites himself until well on in manhood, one would naturally have expected to find that Islam had its roots deep down in this old Arabian paganism. It comes, therefore, as no little surprise, to find how little of the religious life of this Arabian paganism is reflected in the pages of the Koran."[3] Indeed, so little of Islam can be traced to Arabia that Luxenberg and several other commentators have suggested that we should seek its origins in the border regions of Israel and Syria.

Islam's cultural roots are in fact entirely biblical. The Torah, the first five books of the Bible, which are said to have been written by Moses, are accepted completely as divine revelation by Muslims. And the laws

---

2 Arthur Jeffery, *The Foreign Vocabulary of the Qur'an* (Oriental Institute Baroda, Vadodara, India, 1938), http://www.answering-islam.org/Books/Jeffrey/Vocabulary/intro.htm

3 *Ibid.*

outlined in the Torah, especially in Leviticus and Deuteronomy, find their precise equivalents in Islamic law. Indeed the Jewish origins of Islamic moral and temporal law are well known and obvious. The strict monotheism of the Torah is matched by that of the Qur'an. The divine injunction to conquer the Promised Land found in the Torah is matched by the divine injunction of the Qur'an to conquer the world for Islam. Laws concerning divorce and adultery are identical in both religions. Both have circumcision. Even laws governing food are the same, with the same foods proscribed and permitted, and the same method of slaughter recommended.

All of this leads to the suspicion that "Islam" was in origin a sect of Judaism, and this was the position adopted in the mid-twentieth century by Patricia Crone and Michael Cook. However, since Islam also honors Jesus, or Isha, then the purely Judaic origin of the faith seems doubtful. Much more likely is the proposition that it was originally a Jewish sect of Christianity – a line adopted by Gunter Luling and Christoph Luxenberg. We know in fact that several Judaizing sects of Christianity existed from the first century. These basically regarded Jesus as an orthodox Jew and demanded their followers accept the Law of Moses in its entirety. The best known of such groups was that of the Ebionites or Nazarites. The latter was declared heretical at the Council of Nicea in 325, and thereafter disappeared from history. It is presumed that its adherents moved to the Arabian interior, or at least to that part of Arabia bordering Syria. But this is more than a presumption: We know for a fact that by the fifth century there existed large Christian communities throughout the Arabian Peninsula. None of these held by the doctrines taught in Constantinople or in the other major centres of Christendom: they were all profoundly Judaizing in character – Ebionite in short. Jesus was accepted as the Messiah, but not the Son of God; he was the "messenger" of God, and was portrayed as an orthodox Jew. The Christians of Arabia were all circumcised and devout followers of the Law of Moses. The Gospels were not accepted as accurate accounts of the life of Jesus and other, alternative gospels were used instead.

In short, centuries before the supposed life of the prophet Muhammad there seems to have existed within Arabia a thriving religious movement which might be described as "proto-Islam."

The Ebionites were strongly Jewish, and Judaism in its origins, was a militant and even militaristic faith. Throughout the first centuries BC and AD leaders claiming to be the Messiah appeared regularly among the Jews, stirring up ruinous rebellions against the power of Rome. The idea that the Messiah would be a military commander was central to Jewish religious ideas of the time. A peaceful and suffering Messiah did not figure in their thinking. Even the disciples of Jesus, after his crucifixion, are said to have asked him when he would restore the kingdom of Israel to independence.

It is highly likely that these attitudes were shared by the Ebionites, who thus adhered to virtually all the beliefs and practices we now consider "Muslim." Islamic tradition itself admits that the Ebionite Christians of Arabia were among the first and most fervent followers of the new faith, and the Arab historians name an Ebionite monk, Waraqah ibn Nawfal, as one of the earliest converts to Islam.[4]

But even admitting the strongly Jewish tone of Ebionitism or proto-Islam, how are we to account for the transformation of the Christian Jesus – the "honored one" or "Muhammad" among the Ebionites – into the violent and warlike prophet of the Islamic Qur'an? The answer to this, I believe, is found in the identity of the names "Jesus" and "Joshua." In English, of course, these two look quite different; in Hebrew however they are one and the same – Yahoshua. "Jesus" is the English of the Greek transliteration of "Yahoshua" via Latin. Now Jesus of the New Testament may have been a complete pacifist, but Joshua of the Old Testament was anything but. He it was who became leader of the Israelite tribes after the death of Moses and subsequently led them across the River Jordan (from Arabia, no less) into the land of Canaan. In Canaan he prosecuted a war of extermination against the natives. In doing so, we are told, he was carrying out a divine injunction. The Arabs of the sixth and seventh centuries were almost entirely illiterate. In the minds of illiterates stories from one part of a book are easily conflated with stories from another. Since the Ebionite faith in any case stressed obedience to the Law of Moses, in its entirety (with such injunctions as "an eye for an eye and a tooth for a tooth" and the stoning of women to death for adultery), and since they also held that Jesus commanded obedience to these laws, it would have been the easiest thing in the world to confuse Jesus with Joshua, who also, remember, was an obedient follower of the Mosaic Code. And this surmise is startlingly confirmed by the fact that in the Qur'an Maryam, the mother of Isha (Jesus), is the sister of Moses and Aaron! In other words, it is beyond question that Islam has confused and conflated events of the Bible which are in fact separated from each other by many centuries.

What then of the origins of the Qur'an, the holy book supposed by Muslims to have been given to Muhammad by the Angel Gabriel?

Anyone who has read the Muslim holy book will recognize at once

---

4 Martin Lings, *Muhammad: his life based on the earliest sources* (Suhail Academy Co.)

that it is a puzzling document. It is not a story or a narrative in the normal sense, but a series of apparently unrelated incidents and statements. Muslims themselves only understand the Qur'an by allusion to the Hadiths, an enormous collection of "traditions" about the life of Muhammad which incidentally explain the obscure events and statements of the Qur'an. The hadiths however did not begin to appear until around a century after the supposed date of Muhammad's death, and it is well-known that there existed for several centuries a veritable industry of hadith composition. Muslim scholars themselves admit that the vast majority of these were fakes. It would appear that the Abbasid Caliphs sponsored the production of hadiths during the eighth and ninth centuries for political reasons. Numerous of these hadiths actually contradict each other in treating of one and the same statement of the Qur'an.

But even with the help of the hadiths, the Qur'an remains a strange and puzzling text. Whole sentences and paragraphs seem to make no sense at all. Philologist Ger-R. Puin expressed a typical opinion when he stated that "every fifth sentence or so [of the Qur'an] simple doesn't make sense." Why? Could it be that it was originally composed in a language other than Arabic and imperfectly transcribed into the latter tongue? That is increasingly the position adopted by the scholarly community; and the suspicion is greatly strengthened by the discovery that "the names in the Qur'an consistently show signs of having been derived from Syriac ..."[5] Syriac was the ancient language of large parts of the Middle East, a dialect of Aramaic, which had been the lingua franca of the region since the time of the Achaemenid Persian Empire. Syriac was closely related to Arabic, but sufficiently different to cause confusion if not properly understood. The deeper scholars have examined the Qur'an the more clear its Syriac roots have become. Whole passages and incidents which have defied the best efforts of scholars throughout the centuries to comprehend suddenly make perfect sense if read as Syriac. Thus for example in Qur'an 19:24 we read: "Then (one) cried unto her from below her, saying: Grieve not! Thy Lord hath placed a rivulet beneath thee." It is unclear from the text who is speaking, perhaps the newborn Jesus or someone else; and what the meaning of the "rivulet" is. However, read as a Syriac text we find that it refers to the Virgin Birth of Jesus. Thus the infant Jesus – who speaks elsewhere in the Qur'an – tells Mary: "Do not be sad, your Lord has made your delivery legitimate."

Indeed, read as a Syriac document, the Qur'an not only loses its obscurity, but is rapidly revealed as a Christian devotional text, or lection-

---

5 Spencer, *Did Muhammad Exist? op cit.*, p. 155.

ary. That, at least, is the opinion of two of the greatest philologists in the field, Gunter Lüling and Christoph Luxenberg. In the words of the latter, if Qur'an "really means lectionary, then one can assume that the Koran intended itself first of all to be understood as nothing more than a liturgical book with selected texts from the Scriptures (the Old and New Testament) and not at all as a substitute for the Scriptures themselves."[6] Even events which have traditionally been understood by Muslims as referring to crucial events of the life of Muhammad reveal themselves, upon transcription into Syriac, as events of the life of Jesus. In the words of Robert Spencer, "Many of the Qur'an's more obscure passages begin to make sense when read in the light of having a foundation in Christian theology. For example, there is an enigmatic sura on the Night of Power, *al-Qadr* ("Power") [the night when Muhammad supposedly received the Qur'an from the Angel Gabriel]: 'Behold, We sent it down on the Night of Power; and what shall teach thee what is the Night of Power? The Night of Power is better than a thousand months; in it the angles and the Spirit descend, by the leave of their Lord, upon every command. Peace it is, till the rising of dawn' (97:1-5). Muslims associate the Night of Power with the first appearance of Gabriel to Muhammad and the first revelation of the Qur'an; they commemorate this night during the fasting month of Ramadan. But the Qur'an makes no explicit connection between the Night of Power and the revelation of the Qur'an. The book doesn't explain what the Night of Power is, except to say it is the night on which the angels (not just one angel) and the Spirit descend and proclaim Peace.

> In the light of the Qur'an's Syriac Christian roots, there is another possible interpretation – that sura 97 refers to Christmas.

> The Qur'anic scholar Richard Bell saw in the night, angels, Spirit, and peace of the sura a hint of the Nativity even without a detailed philological examination: 'The origin of the idea of the Night of Power is unexplained. The only other passage in the Quran which has any bearing on it is XLIV, 2a, 3. In some ways what is here said of it suggests that some account of the Eve of the Nativity may have given rise to it.'

> Luxenberg points out that because the Night of Power is associated with the revelation of the Qur'an, Muslims undertook

---

6 *Ibid.*, p. 166.

vigils during Ramadan. 'However,' he notes, 'with regard to the history of religions this fact is all the more remarkable since Islam does not have a nocturnal liturgy (apart from the *tarawih*, prayers offered during the nights of Ramadan). There is thus every reason to think that these vigils corresponded originally to a Christian liturgical practice connected to the birth of Jesus Christ, and which was later adopted by Islam, but re-interpreted by Islamic theology to mean the descent of the Koran.'

A close textual analysis supports this argument. *Al-qadr*, the Arabic word for 'power,' also means 'fate' or 'destiny.' Luxenberg observes that the Syriac *qaaf-daal-raa* – the q-d-r root of the Arabic word *al-qadr* – has three meanings, designating 'i) the birth (meaning the moment of birth); ii) the star under which one is born and which determines the fate of the newly born; iii) The Nativity, or Christmas.' He continues: 'Thus defined, the term *al-qadr*, "destiny," is related to the star of birth, which the Koranic *al qadr* applies, in the context of this sure, to the Star of Christmas. As a result, a connection is found to be established with Matthew II.2, "Saying, Where is he that is born King of the Jews? For we have seen his star in the East and are come to worship him."' Then the verse 'the Night of Power is better than a thousand months' (97:4) would be rendered 'Christmas night is better than a thousand vigils.'

The Qur'an concludes the Night of Power passage with 'Peace it is, till the rising of dawn' (97:5). Luxenberg notes that this verse 'sends us back to the hymn of the Angels cited by Luke II.14: "Glory to God in the highest and on earth peace, good will toward men." This chant of the Angels has always constituted the principal theme of the Syriac vigils of the Nativity which lasts into Christmas night, with all sorts of hymns, more than all the other vigils.' Indeed, in the Syriac Orthodox Church, the Divine Liturgy of the Nativity was traditionally celebrated at dawn, after a nightlong vigil – 'Peace it is, till the rising of dawn.'[7]

If such crucial events of the Islamic faith as the Night of Power can

---

7 *Ibid.*, pp. 184-5.

so easily be interpreted in a Christian manner we will not then be surprised to find that even the Qur'an's five references to "Muhammad" (the "chosen one" or "praised one") could equally well refer to Jesus as to any supposed Arabian prophet.

The evidence then, taken together, would then suggest that no Arabian prophet named Muhammad existed, and that "Muhammad," was originally a title of Jesus. This means that what we now call Islam did not exist until near the end of the seventh century or even into the first half of the eighth. What existed before was proto-Islam, a branch of the Jewish Christian sect otherwise known as Ebionitism.

That a Judaizing form of Christianity, with little love for Rome or Byzantium, had already spread throughout Arabia by the fourth or at least fifth century is well enough known. From about the third century onwards we hear of "Saracens" raiding along the borders of the Roman Empire in Syria. It is true that these earlier Saracens cannot have been Ebionites or proto-Muslims, but it seems likely that the militaristic spirit of Judaism would have appealed to the nomad Arabs. Certainly by the fourth and fifth centuries there are reports of Saracen groups ranging as far east as Mesopotamia (modern Iraq) that were involved in battles on both the Persian and Roman sides.[8] They are described in the Roman administrative document Notitia dignitatum—dating from the time of Theodosius I in the 4th century—as comprising distinctive units in the composition of the Roman army and they are distinguished in the document from Arabs and Iiluturaens.[9]

*   *   *

Although Spencer does not go into the question of how the Arab empire came to exist in the first place, there are very good grounds for believing that it was not originally an Arab creation at all, and that the invention of an Arabian prophet as the spiritual fountain-head of this empire, was motivated by a desire to justify what was essentially the Arab takeover of an imperial machine that was not theirs.

The two greatest powers in the Middle East at the beginning of the seventh century were Byzantium and Sassanid Persia. In 602 the Persian king Chosroes (Khosrau) II went to war against the Byzantine usurper Phocas, who had earlier murdered Chosroes' friend and father-in-law the

8 Jan Retso, *The Arabs in Antiquity: Their History from the Assyrians to the Umayyads* (Rutledge and Kegan Paul, 2003), pp. 464-6.
9 *Ibid.*

Emperor Maurice. The war did not end with the death of Phocas (610), but continued into the reign of Heraclius, and was to prove ruinous to the Byzantines. Jerusalem was taken by the Persians in 614, a disaster which was quickly followed by the loss of most of Asia Minor between 616 and 618 and Egypt in 619/20. Chosroes II now equalled the achievements of his Persian predecessors in the sixth century BC, with his forces marching across North Africa to annex the Libyan province of Cyrenaea in 621. The story told by the Byzantines of how Heraclius, in the face of this overwhelming calamity, rallied his armies and reconquered all the lost territories – only to lose the same territories again to the Arabs from 632 onwards – has a ring of fantasy about it, and historians have long viewed it with scepticism. Certainly there is no doubting the power and influence of the Persians in this epoch.

The earliest Islam, as revealed by archaeology, is in fact profoundly Persian; and indeed the first trace of Islam recovered in excavation are coins of Sassanid Persian design bearing the image either of Chosroes II (d. 628) or of his grandson Yazdegerd III (d. 651). On one side we find the portrait of the king, on the reverse the picture of a Zoroastrian Fire Temple. The only thing that marks these out as Islamic is the legend *besm Allah* (in the name of God), written in the Syriac script, beside the Fire Temple. (The Arabic script did not then exist). According to the *Encyclopdaedia Iranica*:

> These coins usually have a portrait of a Sasanian emperor with an honorific inscription and various ornaments. To the right of the portrait is a ruler's or governor's name written in Pahlavi script. On the reverse there is a Zoroastrian fire altar with attendants on either side. At the far left is the year of issue expressed in words, and at the right is the place of minting. In all these features, the Arab-Sasanian coinages are similar to Sasanian silver drahms. The major difference between the two series is the presence of some additional Arabic inscription on most coins issued under Muslim authority, but some coins with no Arabic can still be attributed to the Islamic period. The Arab-Sasanian coinages are not imitations, since they were surely designed and manufactured by the same people as the late Sasanian issues, illustrating the continuity of administration and economic life in the early years of Muslim rule in Iran.[10]

Note the remark: "The Arab-Sasanian coinages are not imitations,"

---

10 "Arab-Sasanian Coins," *Encyclopdaedia Iranica*, at www.iranica.com/articles/arab-sasanian-coins

but were "designed and manufactured by the same people as the late Sa-sanian issues." We note also that the date provided on these artefacts is written in Persian script, and it would appear that those who minted the coins, native Persians, did not understand Arabic. We hear that under the Arabs the mints were "evidently allowed to go on as before," and that there are "a small number of coins indistinguishable from the drahms of the last emperor, Yazdegerd III, dated during his reign but after the Arab capture of the cities of issue. It was only when Yazdegerd died (A.D. 651) [in the time of the Ummayad Caliph Muawiya] that some mark of Arab authority was added to the coinage."[11] Even more puzzling is the fact that the most common coins during the first decades of Islamic rule were those of Yaz-degerd's predecessor Chosroes II, and many of these too bear the Arabic inscription (written however, as we saw, in the Syriac script) *besm Allah*. Now, it is just conceivable that invading Arabs might have issued slightly amended coins of the last Sassanid monarch, Yazdegerd III, but why con-tinue to issue money in the name of a previous Sassanid king (Chosroes II), one who, supposedly, had died ten years earlier? This surely stretches credulity.

The Persian-looking Islamic coins are of course believed to date from the time of Umar (d. 664), one of the "Rightly-guided Caliphs" who suc-ceeded Muhammad and supposedly conquered what became the Islamic Empire. Yet it has to be stated that there is no direct archaeological evi-dence for the existence either of Umar or any of the other "Rightly-guid-ed" caliphs – Abu Bakr, Uthman or Ali. None of these men left even a brick bearing his name.[12] Archaeologically, their existence is as unattested as Muhammad himself. The very first archaeological trace of the caliphs comes with Muawiya, who of course reigned after the death of the Persian Yazdegerd III.

Could it be then that these coins were minted not by conquering Arab caliphs but by the men whose names and images appear on them – the Sassanid emperors Chosroes II and Yazdegerd III? Could it be that Chosroes II converted to the Arab version of Christianity, Ebionitism, and

---

11 *Ibid.*

12 A single inscription, from north-west Arabia, mentions Umar, noting that he died the year (24) the writer, Zuhar, inscribed the message. It should be noted however that Umar is not described as a "commander of the faithful" as he should be if he were a caliph. Furthermore, the authenticity of the inscription is doubtful due to its very early use of diacritical marks, even though other evidence indicates that these were not employed in the Arabic script until much later. See http://www.nbcnews.com/id/27787506/ns/technology_and_science-science/t/-year-old-islamic-note-may-solve-mystery/#.Ui36K9IWL6Y

that it was he who built the "Islamic" empire?

The Persians, it should be noted, had a long history of religious antagonism towards Christianity and towards Byzantium. During the second half of the sixth century Chosroes II's grandfather Chosroes I had gone to the assistance of the southern Arabs whose country Yemen had been annexed by the Christian Abyssinians. And the Sassanids were extremely active during the fifth and sixth centuries building alliances with princes throughout the Arabian Peninsula. Amongst these were the Lakhmids, who occupied what would now be southern Iraq and north-east Arabia, and who converted to Christianity – presumably the Arab or Ebionite version – early in the seventh century. The war between Chosroes II and Heraclius which erupted in 602 had from the very beginning all the characteristics of a religious conflict – a veritable *jihad*, no less. The Persians, along with numerous contingents of Arab allies, who took Jerusalem in 614, carried out a general massacre of the Christian population;[13] after which they looted the churches and seized some of Christendom's most sacred relics – including the Holy Cross upon which Christ was crucified. As we saw, the story told by the Byzantines of how Heraclius, against all the odds, turned the tide of war and won back the sacred relics, strikes one as fictitious. Persian sources make no mention of Chosroes' supposed defeat at the hands of the Byzantines. On the contrary, he is known in Iranian tradition as Apervez, (later abbreviated to Pervez) "the undefeatable" or "ever-victorious." The most important Iranian source, Firdausi's Shahnameh, merely records how Chosroes was killed by his son Shirouyeh, who desired his father's beautiful wife Shirin.

It would appear then that the Byzantines may have been falsifying history with regard to Heraclius' later career. An earlier war between Romans and Persians, in the time of Alexander Severus (third century), was equally doctored by Roman chroniclers to make its outcome more palatible, as Gibbon dryly remarks: "If we credit what should seem the most authentic of all records, an oration, still extant, delivered by the emperor himself to the senate, we must allow that the victory of Alexander Severus was not inferior to any of those formerly obtained over the Persians by the son of Philip [Alexander the Great]." However, "far from being inclined to believe that the arms of Alexander [Severus] obtained any memorable advantage over the Persians, we are induced to suspect that all this blaze of imaginary glory was designed to conceal some real disgrace."[14]

If the Persians were the real architects of the Islamic Empire, this

---

13 See Gibbon, *Decline and Fall*, Chapter 46.
14 *Ibid.*, Chapter 8.

would explain why early Islam is so thoroughly Persian in character. The Islamic symbol par excellence, for example, the crescent moon enclosing a star, is Persian: the motif is encountered repeatedly on monumental Iranian art and Sassanid coins. And Persian influence is all-pervasive. The great Islamic cities of the time, including Baghdad and Samarra followed a typically Persian ground-plan, with Persian features such as "paradises," or ornamental gardens. The artwork found at the Mesopotamian city of Samarra, including pottery, painting, and architectural features, is all thoroughly Persian. It is well-known too that the early caliphs ruled largely, if not completely, through a Persian bureaucracy.[15] In addition, archaeologists have found that in Mesopotamia and Iran the transition from Sassanid to Islamic epochs has left no evident destruction layer – in marked contrast to the situation in the former Byzantine territories of Syria, Egypt and Anatolia. In the territories of the Sassanids all indications are of a peaceful transition from Zoroastrian to Islamic civilization. And we remind ourselves that the earliest Islamic coins are straightforwardly Persian, usually with the addition of an Arab or rather Syriac phrase such as *besm Allah*, and with the name of Chosroes II or his successor Yazdegerd III. But in all other particulars they are indistinguishable from Sassanid currency.

Did then Chosroes II convert to "Islam" or Arab Christianity at the start of his great war against Byzantium?

We know for a fact that Chosroes II did indeed embrace some form of Christianity. Shortly after ascending the throne he faced a rebellion from one of his generals, Bahram Chobin, who proclaimed himself King Bahram VI. In his hour of need Chosroes fled to the Byzantine Emperor Maurice, who put an army at his disposal with which he regained the crown. This fostered a liberal attitude to Christianity, as did his marriage to Maurice's daughter Maria and to the beautiful Shirin, another Christian, apparently from Syria. The Persian Emperor, we are told, adopted the religion of his favorite wife, though the sincerity of his faith was always suspect. Gibbon speaks of "the imaginary conversion of the king of Persia," which "was reduced to a local and superstitious veneration for Sergius, one of the saints of Antioch, who heard his prayers and appeared to him in dreams."[16] But if Chosroes' conversion to Christianity was suspect, his behavior at Jerusalem, where he plundered the most sacred relics of Christianity and ordered the massacre of the city's Christian population, marks him out as a fanatic, and a very violent one at that. The evidence indicates that Chosroes remained a Christian, of sorts, but of a very different kind to

15 See Trevor-Roper, *op cit.*, p. 142.
16 Gibbon, *Decline and Fall*, Chapter 46.

that which pertained at Constantinople. His "Christianity" was of a type violently opposed to the Nicean variety.

As historian Hugh Trevor-Roper so sagely noted, when one civilization converts to another's faith, it normally embraces a heresy of that faith:[17] thus the Roman Empire converted to a heresy of Judaism – Christianity – and thus it would appear that the Persian king and his people converted to a heresy of Christianity.

We are told that Chosroes' wife Shirin was a follower of the Nestorian branch of Christianity, though she later embraced the Syrian Miaphysite doctrine. Yet her exact beliefs are uncertain, and we may justifiably ask: Was it to the Syrian Miaphysite Church or the Syrian (or Arab) Ebionite Church which Shirin, Chosroes' favorite wife, adhered? If it was the Ebionite Church, then it was to a faith which was widespread in Arabia and which shared almost all its beliefs and customs with what we now call Islam. If this is the case, and if Chosroes II followed his wife into the Arab version of Christianity, then a host of hitherto intractable problems solve themselves.

To begin with, the astonishing narrative of the Arab conquests, which supposedly saw a few nomads on camels simultaneously attack and conquer the mighty Persian and Byzantine empires, is revealed as a fiction: it was the heavy cavalry of the Sassanid Persians which created the "Islamic" Empire, an empire which appeared quite suddenly in the middle of the seventh century and stretched from Libya to the borders of India. Secondly, the strange modesty of the "Rightly-guided" caliphs, Abu Bakr, Umar, and the others, in failing to leave a single coin or artifact bearing their names, is explained by the fact that they did not exist and were invented precisely to disguise the Arab usurpation of the Sassanid Empire. Thirdly, the "Islamic" coins of Chosroes II, a king who died supposedly over ten years before the Islamic conquest of Persia, are no longer a mystery and were minted not by a modest Arabian caliph, but by Chosroes II himself. And finally, the failure of the poet Firdausi to mention either a caliph named Umar or a prophet named Muhammad, is fully explained, and the war described in the Shahnameh during Yazdegerd's reign was a civil war pitting Islamicized (or Ebionitized) Persians against Arabs.

Huge numbers of Arab troops and irregular fighters had apparently accompanied the Persians on the march of conquest throughout Syria, Egypt and North Africa. The outcome of the Persian or rather "Islamic" civil war which broke out in the time of Yazdegerd III was an Arab *coup d'etat*: An Arab dynasty, under Mu'awyia (the Ummayads), seized con-

---

17 Trevor-Roper, *op cit.*, p. 57.

trol of the Sassanid proto-Islamic Empire. They were able to do this at least partly because of Yazdegerd's unpopularity and because a majority of the Persian king's subjects were already Arabs, or at least Semite-speakers closely related culturally to the Arabs. The Persian kings themselves were mostly born and raised in Mesopotamia, a land whose Semitic language was very close to Arabic. Furthermore, the regions of the Middle East which they conquered were predominantly Syriac in speech. Even North Africa around Carthage had large populations of Semitic peoples, whose Punic language was also very close to Syriac and Arabic. In addition, we must not forget that the victorious Persian armies contained numerous divisions of Arab allies and these were followed by hordes of nomadic Arabs from Arabia proper, whose privileged position in the new religious establishment gave them influence far beyond their numbers.

The Arab seizure of power led to a realignment and redefinition of the Ebionite or rather proto-Islamic faith. As we saw, even in the time of Muawiya and his immediate successors, there was no Islam in the present understanding of the word. Yet in the decades that followed there came a pressing need to justify the Arab seizure of power from the Persians. A new creation-myth, as it were, was needed. Hence, during the time of Abd al-Malik (d. 705) and of his son Al Walid, the last vestiges of Persian influence were removed from the coinage, and Arabic became the official language of the court at Damascus. Along with these measures, it became expedient to "Arabize" the faith, with the invention of an Arabian prophet quite different from the original muhammad (Jesus). It was then too that the story of an Arab conquest of Persia and the Middle East was invented, along with the conquering caliphs, Abu Bakr and Umar, who supposedly carried it out.

If the above reconstruction of events is correct, it means that Islam was created for political purposes and was therefore as much as political ideology as a religion – precisely as we argued in Chapter 2. The faith which Islam grew out of and replaced, Arab "Christianity" (or proto-Islam or Ebionitism), was without question not a peace-loving or a tolerant one; but at least it was not anti-Semitic. Whence then, we might ask, came the virulent anti-Semitism of Islam?

An ideology such as Islam, which aims ultimately at world domination, cannot easily coexist with other systems or ideologies. The ambitions of the Jewish people, it is true, was confined solely to the possession of Canaan, the Promised Land, the land from which they had been expelled by the Babylonians and then by the Romans. Yet they also claimed to be God's Chosen People and their faith had its own eschatology, which looked forward to a time (as the prophet Isaiah and others had said) when Jerusalem would be glorified among the nations. Islam of course claimed to be the fulfilment of this and other Old Testament prophecies: it was to the rise of Islam which the prophets had alluded and it was the conquests of Islam which would make Jerusalem the glorious city of all mankind. The refusal of the Jewish people to accept this would not have been well-received in Muslim circles; and it must have been this that led to the notorious antisemitic verses in the Qur'an, the Hadith and the Sira.

BIBLIOGRAPHY

Asbridge, Thomas. *The Crusades: The War for the Holy Land* (Simon and Schuster, London, 2010)

Atroshenko, V. I. and Judith Collins. *The Origins of the Romanesque* (Lund Humphries, London, 1985)

Austen, Ralph A. *Trans-Sharan Africa in World History* (Oxford University Press, 2010)

Bat Ye'or and Andrew Bostom, "Andalusian Myth, Eurabian Reality," retrieved from www.jihadwatch.org/dhimmiwatch/archives/001665.php

Bat Ye'or, *The Dhimmi: Jews and Christians Under Islam* (Fairleigh Dickinson University Press, 1985)

Beattie, Andrew. *Cairo: A Cultural History* (Oxford University Press, 2005)

Bennison, Amira K. and Maria Angeles Gallego, "Jewish Trading in Fez on the Eve of the Almohad Conquest," (2008) at http://digital.csic.es/bitstream/10261/39129/1/Almohad.MEAH.pdf

Bertrand, Louis and Sir Charles Petrie. *The History of Spain* (2nd ed., London, 1945)

Boyer, Carl B. *A History of Mathematics*, Second Edition (2nd ed. Wiley Books, 1991)

Brann, Ross. *Power in the Portrayal: Representations of Jews and Muslims in Eleventh- and Twelfth-Century Islamic Spain* (Princeton University Press, 2009)

Briffault, Robert, *The Making of Humanity* (London, 1919)

Bull, Marcus. "Origins," in Jonathan Riley-Smith (ed.) *The Oxford History of the Crusades* (Oxford University Press, 1995)

Bynum, Rebecca. *Allah is Dead: Why Islam is Not a Religion* (New English Review Press, 2011)

Churchill, Winston. *The River War*, Vol. 2 (Longmans, Green and Company, London, 1899)

Clarke, H. and B. Ambrosiani. *Towns in the Viking Age* (St. Martin's Press, New York, 1995)

Collins, Roger. *Spain: An Oxford Archaeological Guide to Spain* (Oxford University Press, 1998)

Crone, Patricia and Michael Cook. *Hagarism: The Making of the Islamic World* (Cambridge University Press, 1977)

Fisher, Alan. "Muscovy and the Black Sea Slave Trade," *Canadian American Slavic Studies* Vol. 6 (1972)

Fletcher, Richard. *Moorish Spain* (Weidenfeld and Nicolson, London, 1992)

Flick, Alexander Clarence. *The Rise of the Medieval Church* (New York, 1909)

Forey, Alan. "The Military Orders, 1120-1312," in Jonathan Riley-Smith (ed.) *Oxford History of the Crusades*, (Oxford University Press, 1995)

Freely, John. *Light from the East: How the Science of Medieval Islam helped shape the Western World* (I. B. Tauris and Co., 2010)

Gibbon, Edward. *Decline and Fall of the Roman Empire* (London, 1776-89)

Glick, Thomas F. *Islamic and Christian Spain in the Early Middle Ages* (Brill Publishers, New York, 2005)

Gorini, Rosanna. "Al-Haytham the Man of Experience. First Steps in the Science of Vision," *International Society for the History of Islamic Medicines* (Institute of Neurosciences, Laboratory and Psychobiology and Psychopharmacology, Rome, 2003)

Grégoire, Réginald, Léo Moulin, and Raymond Oursel. *The Monastic Realm* (Rizzoli Press, New York, 1985)

Guillaume, Alfred. "The Version of the Gospels Used in Medina Circa 700 AD." *Al-Andalus* 15 (1950)

Hart, David Bentley *Atheist Delusions: The Christian Revolution and its Fashionable Enemies* (Yale University Press, 2010)

Hodges, Richard and David Whitehouse. *Mohammed, Charlemagne and the Origins of Europe* (Cornell University Press, New York, 1983)

Huntington, Samuel P. "The Clash of Civilizations?" *Foreign Affairs*, (Summer, 1993)

Ibn Khaldun. *The Muqaddimah: An Introduction to History* Vol. 1 (Trans. Franz Rosenthal, Bollingen Series 43: Princeton University Press, 1958)

Ibn Warraq. "The Mythistory of the Crusades," *New English Review* (October, 2013) at www.newenglishreview.org

Ibn Warraq. *Sir Walter Scott's Crusades and other Fantasies* (New English Review Press, 2013)

Irwin, Robert. "Islam and the Crusades: 1096-1699," in Jonathan Riley-Smith (ed.) *The Oxford History of the Crusades* (Oxford University Press, 1995)

Irwin, Robert. "Islam and the Crusades: 1096-1699," in Jonathan Riley-

Smith (ed.) *Oxford History of the Crusades,* (Oxford University Press, 1995)

Jaki, Stanley. *The Savior of Science* (Regnery Gateway, Washington DC, 1988)

Korpås, Ola, Per Wideström and Jonas Ström. "The recently found hoards from Spillings farm on Gotland, Sweden," *Viking Heritage Magazine,* 4 (2000)

Lenman Bruce. (ed.) Chambers Dictionary of World History (London, 2000)

Lewis, Bernard. "2007 Irving Kristol Lecture," delivered to the American Enterprise Institute, Washington, DC. (March 7, 2007)

Lewis, Bernard. *The Jews and Islam* (Princeton University Press, 1987)

Lewis, David Levering. *God's Crucible: Islam and the Making of Europe, 570-1215* (W. W. Norton and Company, New York, 2008)

Livermore, Harold V. *The Origins of Spain and Portugal* (George Allen and Unwin, Ltd., London, 1971)

Luxenberg, Christoph. *The Syro-Aramaic Reading of the Koran: A Contribution to the Decoding of the Language of the Koran* (Verlag Hans Schiler, Berlin, 2000)

MacKay, Angus. *Spain in the Middle Ages: From Frontier to Empire, 1000-1500* (Macmillan Books, 1977)

Madden, Thomas F. *A Concise History of the Crusades* (Rowman and Littlefield, Maryland, 1999)

Mango, Cyril. *Byzantium: the Empire of New Rome* (Weidenfeld and Nicolson, London, 1980)

McCormick, Michael. *Origins of the European Economy: Communications and Commerce, AD 300-900* (Cambridge University Press, 2001)

Migne, J. P. *Patrologiae Graeco-Latina, Part II of Patrologiae Cursus Completus* (Paris, 1857-66)

Montalembert, Charles. *The Monks of the West: From St. Benedict to St. Bernard,* 5 Vols. (London, 1896)

Moss, H. St. L. B. *The Birth of the Middle Ages; 395-814* (Oxford University Press, 1935)

Newman, John Henry, in Charles Frederick Harrold, (ed.) *Essays and Sketches,* Vol. 3 (New York, 1948)

Ohlig, Karl-Heinz and Gerd-R Puin. (eds.) *The Hidden Origins of Islam: New Research into its Early History* (Prometheus Books, New York, 2010)

Pirenne, Henri. *Mohammed and Charlemagne* (London, 1939)

Pressburg, Norbert. *Good Bye Mohammed* (2009)

Prevost, George. (trans.) "The Homilies of St. John Chrysostom" in Philip Schaff, ed. *A Select Library of the Nicene and Post-Nicene Fathers of the Christian Church*, Vol. X (Eedermans, Grand Rapids, MI, 1986)

Riley-Smith, Jonathan. "The State of Mind of Crusaders to the East: 1095-1300," in Jonathan Riley-Smith (ed.) *Oxford History of the Crusades* (Oxford University Press, 1995)

Risse, Günter B. *Mending Bodies, Saving Souls: A History of Hospitals* (Oxford University Press, 1999)

Runciman, Stephen. *The History of the Crusades* 3 Vols. (Cambridge University Press, 1951)

Russell, Jeffrey Burton. *Inventing the Flat Earth: Columbus and Modern Historians* (Praeger Publication, 1991)

Schulz, Matthias. "Schwindel im Skriptorium. Reliquienkult, erfundene Märtyrer, gefälschte Kaiserurkunden - phantasievolle Kleriker haben im Mittelalter ein gigantisches Betrugswerk in Szene gesetzt. Neuester Forschungsstand: Über 60 Prozent aller Königsdokumente aus der Merowingerzeit wurden von Mönchen getürkt," *Der Spiegel*, 29 (1998)

Simmonds, Charles. *Alcohol: With Chapters on Methyl Alcohol, Fusel Oil, and Spirituous Beverages* (Macmillan, London, 1919)

Spencer, Robert. *Did Muhammad Exist? An Enquiry into Islam's Obscure Origins* (ISI Books, Wilmington, Delaware, 2012)

Spencer, Robert. *Religion of Peace? Why Christianity is and Islam isn't* (Regnery, Washington DC, 2007)

Stark, Rodney. *The Victory of Reason* (Random House, New York, 2005)

Stewart, H. F. "Thoughts and Ideas of the Period," in *The Cambridge Medieval History: The Christian Empire*, Vol. 1 (2nd ed. 1936)

Sugar, Peter F. (ed.) *A History of Hungary* (Indiana University Press, 1990)

Thompson, James W. and Edgar N. Johnson. *An Introduction to Medieval Europe, 300-1500* (New York, 1937)

Toledano, Ehud. *Slavery and Abolition in the Ottoman Middle East*, part of the series Publications on the Near East (University of Washington Press, 1997)

Tuchman, Barbara W. *A Distant Mirror: The Calamitous 14th Century* (Penguin Books, 1978)

Vita-Finzi, Claudio. *The Mediterranean Valleys* (Cambridge University Press, 1969)

Volney, C. F. *Travels through Syria and Egypt*, 2 Vols. (London, 1787)

Wolpert, Stanley. *A New History of India* (Oxford University Press, 1982)

INDEX

G

Galen 15, 34, 124
Galileo 110, 120
Genghis Khan 23, 98
Genoa 87
Genoese 73, 87, 145, 146
Gerbert 30, 38, 39, 79, 82
Gerbert of Aurillac 30, 38, 39, 79, 82
Germany 10, 16, 18, 22, 27, 37, 40, 75, 90, 101, 102, 107, 108, 113, 156, 171
Gibbon, Edward 43, 56, 95, 96, 100, 102, 104, 171, 185, 186
Giordano Bruno 110
Gospel(s) 51, 62, 175, 177
Granada 20, 53, 81, 83, 99, 126, 135, 158, 163
Greece 15, 16, 28, 29, 38, 69, 110, 111, 126, 140, 142, 154, 162, 164, 168, 172
Greek Fire 67, 162
Greeks 16, 22, 26, 121, 132, 135, 136, 164, 169
Gregory VII, pope 87
gunpowder 125

H

hadith(s) 12, 42, 43, 107, 119, 176, 179, 189
harem(s) 17, 49, 52, 58, 71, 142, 143, 145, 149-51, 165, 170
Henry the Navigator 159
Herzegovina 141, 143
Hindu(s) 44, 45
Hinduism 45, 50
Hippocrates 34, 124
Hitler, Adolf 169, 171
Holy Land 19, 88, 89, 92, 96
Holy League 154, 157, 164
Hungarian Plain 26, 168
Hungarians 26, 90, 137, 157
Hungary 22, 23, 27, 140, 143, 153-6, 164, 167

Hypatia 116, 117

I

Ibn al-Nafis 129
Ibn Daud 85
Ibn Ishaq 12, 42, 175
Ibn Khaldun 46, 158, 170
Ibn Naghrela 106
Ibn Warraq 85, 89
Ibn Yunis 28
Ibn Yusuf 82, 83
iconoclasm 167
India 9, 12, 15, 24, 29, 33-5, 44, 45, 97, 98, 162, 172, 173, 176, 187
Innocent III 21, 113-5, 117, 119, 166
Inquisition 21, 113-5, 119, 120, 163, 166
Iran 9, 107, 183, 186
Isha 51, 177, 178
Italy 15, 16, 23, 26, 28, 29, 38, 63, 68, 69, 73, 88, 90, 119, 130, 133, 146, 147, 153, 154, 157, 158, 164, 171

J

Jaki 128
Janissaries 129, 136
Jerusalem 96, 107, 183, 185, 186, 189
Jesus 51, 62, 174, 175-82, 188
Jew 52, 84, 177
Jews 10, 12-14, 18- 21, 34, 43, 50-5, 64, 71, 79, 81-5, 99, 100-09, 114, 161, 162, 165, 167, 169, 170, 177, 181
jihad(is) 11-13, 43, 52, 91, 94, 108, 141, 149, 158, 185
jizya 13, 46, 50, 51, 54, 140
John Hunyadi 153, 164
John of Nikiu 117, 118
Joshua 47, 51, 178
Judaism 44, 50, 51, 100, 101, 107, 176, 177, 182, 187
Justinian, emperor 63, 93, 101

Lightning Source UK Ltd.
Milton Keynes UK
UKOW05f1942271213

223625UK00001B/34/P